THE ART OF

Arranging Flowers

A Complete Guide to

JAPANESE IKEBANA

A COMPLETE GUIDE TO

JAPANESE IKEBANA

THE ART OF

Arranging Flowers

BY SHOZO SATO

HARRY N. ABRAMS, INC., *Publishers*

NEW YORK

Library of Congress Catalog Card Number: 65–20323
All rights reserved. No part of the contents of this book may be
reproduced without the written permission of the publishers,
HARRY N. ABRAMS, INCORPORATED, NEW YORK, N.Y.
Printed and Bound in Japan

CONTENTS

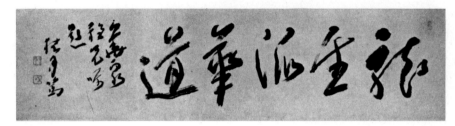

Plaque of the Ryūsei School

PREFACE

THE GROWING APPRECIATION OF JAPANESE ART and architecture in the West has extended to the Japanese way with flowers. This book is intended as a complete introduction to Ikebana, the Japanese art of flower arrangement.

Beginning with the history and development of the art, and its place in Japanese culture, we introduce the reader to the eleven basic styles. Next comes a large section devoted to vases, materials, tools, and methods. Text and pictures explain how to keep flowers fresh, how to select and prepare both fresh and dried materials, and how to make the most effective use of them.

Twelve lessons in creating arrangements in the Moribana style follow. I have tried to make this the most carefully detailed and profusely illustrated guide of its kind, enabling the reader to create many beautiful arrangements while learning all the necessary techniques of the art.

Finally, there is a section devoted to advanced techniques and designs, both classic and modern, and to the setting of mood. Appendixes suggest ways to keep cut flowers fresh, tell how to make effective arrangements from one's own garden flowers and what plant materials to combine, and describe the symbolism of plants and their enhancement. I hope the reader will find this book enjoyable to read, easy to understand, and fun to follow.

In conclusion, I wish to express my deep indebtedness to Mr. Kasen Yoshimura, head of the Ryūsei School of Ikebana and to Mrs. Ryōun Fuku and the other members of the faculty; also to Mrs. Margaret Fairbanks Marcus of the Cleveland Museum of Art. Last, but surely not least, I would like to express my appreciation to Mr. Harry N. Abrams for the opportunity to put my ideas and experience into a book; and to members of his staff—Mr. Milton S. Fox, Mr. Philip Grushkin, Mrs. Margaret L. Kaplan, Miss Kathleen Kazlau, Mrs. Rose Lewis, and Mr. Charles Terry—for their unfailing assistance and valuable suggestions.

Shōzō Satō

PART ONE

Ikebana in Japanese History

Flowers in Japanese Life

IT MAY WELL BE THAT TOO MUCH HAS ALREADY BEEN SAID about the contrast between the Western and the Japanese attitude toward flowers. Admirers of the Japanese art of flower arranging, Ikebana, are all too prone to comment disparagingly on the Western "insensitivity" to flowers and to suggest that some mysterious national trait is responsible for the celebrated Japanese skill at displaying flowers. Much of this talk is exaggerated, for many a Western housewife goes to as much trouble with her bouquets as does her Japanese counterpart and, after all, the suggestion that one segment of humankind is either more or less alive to the beauty of flowers is questionable at best. It may be that Eskimos of flowerless Arctic regions are unconscious of this beauty, or that the inhabitants of African jungles are too close to it to appreciate it, but the art and literature of the world testify to a universal love of flowers, as well as to a desire to possess them and have them near.

1. The sons of a samurai receive instruction in the art of flower arranging from a priest. From Nageire Hana Densho, *1684*

And yet no one can deny that Ikebana, the Japanese art of flower arrangement, is at once more subtle, more sensitive, and more sophisticated than the usual Western methods of arranging flowers. One reason is simply that Ikebana is an art, in the same sense that painting and sculpture are arts. It has a recorded history; it has undergone a coherent development; it has a technical discipline; it is backed up by articulate theories; and it is concerned with creativity. By comparison, the usual Western treatment is naïve, personal, and, on the whole, haphazard. In the Occidental world, flowers are used as decorations on a level with curtains, slip covers, and lamp shades, and in the past have followed the style prevailing in other arts of their time—whether Egyptian, Classical, Renaissance, Baroque, Rococo, Romantic, or Abstract. In Japan, flower arrangements are also used as decorations, but on a level with paintings and other art objects. It would be idle to argue that Mrs. Suzuki in Tokyo has any greater flair for flowers than Mrs. Smith in New York, but Mrs. Suzuki's flower arrangements are likely to be more artistic, because Mrs. Suzuki is accustomed to thinking of Ikebana as an established art rather than as a household chore. Moreover, if Mrs. Suzuki is like most Japanese ladies, she has been trained in the techniques of this art from childhood.

One indication of the status of floral art in Japan is that *Mr.* Suzuki may well be as accomplished in the field as his wife. Indeed, in the past Ikebana was considered an appropriate pastime for the toughest samurai (Figures 1, 2), and even today the leading flower arrangers are for the most part men. The Japanese Self-Defense Corps, which is, in effect, the nation's army, sees nothing incongruous in offering flower arrangement courses for soldiers who wish to attend, and one often

2. Early Edo period (1615–1868) wood-block print showing a samurai and his entourage formally admiring a flower arrangement

finds that the head of a flower school is also a seasoned businessman who dabbles in publishing and other enterprises on the side. In short, Ikebana is not only an art, but a legitimate occupation for men and women alike.

To say that Ikebana is a full-fledged art does not mean that it is esoteric. The greatest creations in the field, to be sure, are apt to be made by the most highly skilled experts, but, as in painting and sculpture, there is plenty of room for amateurs. Indeed, as this book will show, almost anyone with a little time and the inclination can acquire sufficient skill to make beautiful arrangements. Still, as in the other arts, it is necessary to master certain fundamental techniques before proceeding to free creation, and if these basics are not mastered, success is unlikely.

Several reasons can be mentioned for the remarkably high development of floral art in Japan. One of them is certainly the celebrated Japanese love of nature. People in all countries appreciate natural beauty, but in Japan this appreciation amounts almost to a religion. Perhaps one should not even say "almost," for the indigenous religion, Shinto, was based on the deification of natural objects and phenomena, and although Shinto has changed much under the influence of imported faiths, it still contains a strong element of nature worship. Indeed, there are many Shinto shrines in Japan today where the "deity" worshiped is not an anthropomorphic being, but the nebulous spirit residing in a particular mountain, tree, or rock, and few Japanese distinguish very clearly between the spirit and the tangible object in which it resides. Theoretically, the highest deity in Shinto is the Sun Goddess, Amaterasu O-mikami, who is considered to be the ancestress of the Imperial family, but to an objective observer the sight of an elderly Japanese bowing to the rising sun suggests that the object of this adoration is not so much the anthropomorphic goddess as the sun itself. In short, it seems likely that to most Shintoists, the god is the actual natural object rather than a disembodied spirit.

It is fruitless to speculate whether Shinto worship inspired a love of nature or vice versa. The fact remains that the Japanese in general have always felt a strong bond of intimacy with their natural surroundings, and even in the concrete-and-asphalt urban complexes of our times they display a remarkably strong desire to have a bit of nature near them. Foreign visitors to Tokyo are often surprised to notice, as they hold on for dear life in a careering taxi, that the driver has hung a little vase with a flower or two at the edge of the windshield, and the Japanese house that does not at all times contain some sort of floral arrangement is rare indeed.

Taxicabs and other unlikely places aside, it is important to understand that in principle the Ikebana arrangement aims not at bringing a finite piece of nature into the house, but at suggesting the whole of nature and at creating a link between indoors and outdoors. One consequence is that the arranger is likely to use several different types of plants in a single arrangement, and to give prominence not only to blossoms, but to leaves and flowerless branches as well. Even when a single type of flower is used, an attempt is made to bring out its full implications as a symbol of nature.

Another reason for the development of Ikebana in Japan must certainly be the age-old Japanese tendency to associate a wide range of human emotions with flowers. In classical Japanese poetry, the very mention of a flower's name is often enough to evoke a whole series of ideas, images, and meanings. A cherry blossom is not merely a beautiful flower, it is also a symbol of manliness and bravery: It blossoms briefly but gloriously, then falls quickly before it has withered. The grasses of autumn suggest the wanness of fading summer and the sadness of growing old. To the great majority of Japanese, each flower evokes a particular month of the year and the feelings appropriate to that month. Ikebana arrangements, accordingly, are expected not only to establish a link between man and nature, but to create a mood or atmosphere appropriate to the season and even to the occasion. Actually, the symbolism and imagery of flowers in Japanese literature and psychology are far more complicated than this would suggest, and a thorough discussion is properly the subject of another book. The Western student of Ikebana, however, should keep in mind that to

3. *The tokonoma in a Japanese house in modern Tokyo*

4. An early ninth-century Buddhist statue holds a vase containing a lotus blossom and leaf. From the Hakke-ji (Nunnery) in Nara, Japan

the Japanese viewer a flower or plant may have many connotations that would be alien to the Western mind.

These differences between the Japanese and the Western cultural heritage present some problems to the writer on Ikebana for a Western audience. Although the Western student can understand the symbolism intellectually, he will not feel it emotionally. Therefore we have attempted to indicate the Japanese attitudes and patterns of thought through concrete examples as they arise in the course of the book, but a listing of many flowers and their symbolic connotations to the Japanese is provided, in a special appendix, for the interested reader.

How Ikebana Came into the Japanese House

Still another factor in the course that flower arranging has taken in Japan is to be found in the architecture of the traditional Japanese house. Until very recently every Japanese dwelling with any claim to adequacy had at least one room with a special alcove known as a tokonoma, where the principal decorations of the house were displayed. It is not certain when or how the tokonoma first came into existence, but by the end of the fifteenth century it was in wide use, and a century later it had come to be considered indispensable in the better houses. As an architectural form, the tokonoma is considered a feature of the *shoin-zukuri* style, which reached maturity in the late sixteenth century and which, with the *shinden-zukuri* style of earlier times, are the two great styles of premodern Japanese residential architecture.

The size and design of the tokonoma varied, but in the typical dwelling of the past it was about six feet wide by three feet deep, and its upper space was hidden by a curtain wall that came down from the ceiling to a level of about six feet from the floor of the room. The floor within the recess was ordinarily several inches higher than in the room proper, so that it formed a kind of platform. For centuries it was the custom to decorate the tokonoma with a group of items: a hanging scroll painting or calligraphic inscription, a treasured art object of some sort, and a flower arrangement (Figure 3). These were, as a rule, the only ornaments in the room, save possibly paintings or

OPPOSITE: 5. *Detail of an early tenth-century embroidery showing a Buddhist deity holding a vase containing a lotus blossom and leaf. From the Kanshū-ji temple in Kyoto, Japan*

14

6. *Detail from the* Frolic of the Animals (Chōjū Giga), *a satiric scroll which portrays Buddhas and priests as animals. Most of the Buddhist offerings pictured in early Japanese scroll paintings are similar to the one seen here. From the Kōzan-ji temple in Kyoto, Japan*

designs on door or wall panels, and they constituted its focal point—all the more so since the room had few, if any, furnishings.

The very conspicuousness of the tokonoma decorations made it imperative that they be as interesting and of as high quality as possible. All three elements were changed periodically, and the painting and floral arrangement, at least, were made to accord with the season. When not in use, pictures, art objects, and vases were kept in a storeroom.

The interior space of Japanese rooms was and is dominated by straight lines, rectangular surfaces, and relatively neutral colors. The tokonoma decorations provided the only opportunity to depart from the severely plain geometric pattern, and of the three decorative objects, the floral arrangement, partly because of its relative impermanence, offered the greatest opportunity for experimenting with line and color. Small wonder, then, that the treatment of flowers came to be regarded as a serious art.

Japanese architecture may well have influenced the growth of Ikebana in other ways. One supposes, for example, that the general openness of the Japanese house and the intimacy of its interior space with the garden outside invited a naturalistic handling of the floral arrangement adorning the interior. It may also be that the overall asymmetry of Japanese houses, as well as the flowing quality of their interior spaces, are reflected in the asymmetrical linear patterns that prevail in traditional Ikebana. Asymmetry and emphasis on line are characteristics of Japanese art as a whole, however, and it could easily be argued that Ikebana and residential architectural design are simply two expressions of the same basic concept of aesthetics. Certainly, to be properly understood, Ikebana must be considered not only in relationship to architecture, but as one phase of an intricate aesthetic complex that includes all the arts of Japan, particularly painting and calligraphy.

Lavish Formality:
Buddhism and the Great Warlords

Ikebana as an art form was certainly practiced by the fifteenth century, as we shall see, but simple floral arrangements were made as early as the sixth century, when Buddhism was introduced to Japan from Korea and China. It was the custom at Buddhist monasteries to place flowers before images of the Buddha, and over the centuries these floral offerings acquired a fairly elaborate form.

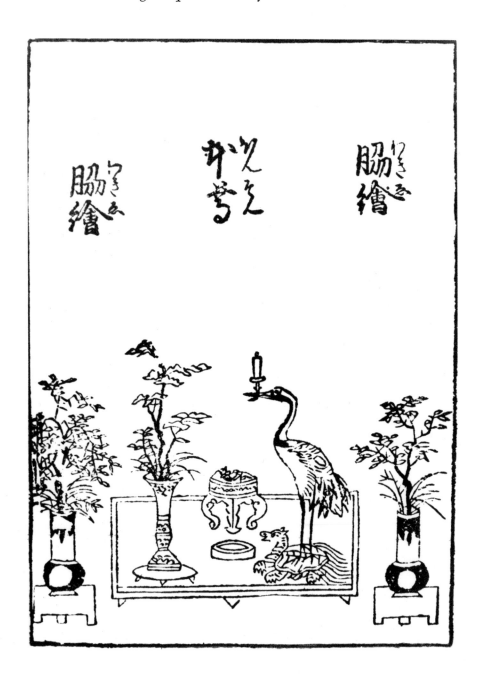

7. A modified three-article arrangement, probably intended for use in a house rather than in a temple. The central part consists of an incense burner and container, flanked by a candleholder and a flower arrangement. Additional vases of flowers have been added on either side. The calligraphy above the arrangement indicates that the flowers are to be placed before three hanging scrolls. The characters at the center mean "main Buddha," those on either side mean "attendant painting" or "side painting." The Buddhist orientation is obvious, although it may be that the term "main Buddha" merely refers to the main picture in the group. From the Sendenshō, *the earliest book on flower arrangement*

The coming of Buddhism is usually dated 538 or 552, with modern scholarship leaning toward the earlier date. The religion did not actually take root in Japan until the late years of the sixth century, however, when it was propagated far and wide by Prince Shotoku (578–622), regent to the Empress Suiko. In the succeeding two centuries it grew to be almost a state religion, eclipsing, although not completely displacing, the native Shinto. One of the most important national activities of the Nara period (710–794) was the construction in the capital at Nara of a huge Buddhist monastery called Tōdai-ji, which was intended as the center of a network of temples spreading out through every province of the nation. The main icon of the Tōdai-ji was a gilt-bronze statue of the Buddha fifty-three feet high. It is thought that when this colossus was dedicated in 752, the floral offerings were of immense size and scale. Actual records state that when the monastery was rededicated in the seventeenth century, the floral arrangements before the statue were forty feet high.

Exactly how flowers were arranged before Buddhist icons in early times is unknown, but it is assumed from later evidence that the typical arrangement consisted of a number of flowers or branches placed artlessly in a tall narrow-necked vase. Sometimes, it appears, stemless blossoms were floated on the surface of the water in a shallow bowl or basin. A ninth-century statue (Figure 4) and a tenth-century embroidery (Figure 5) show Buddhist deities holding similar vases, in which there are both a lotus blossom and a lotus leaf. The lotus being so intimately connected with Buddhist lore as a symbol of the universe, it seems likely that most early Buddhist floral offerings centered on this plant.

A number of scroll paintings from the Heian and Kamakura periods (794–1185 and 1185–1333) show floral arrangements placed before Buddhist images. One of the more amusing examples is in the scroll known as the *Frolic of the Animals* (*Chōjū Giga*), which dates from the eleventh, or possibly the twelfth century, and which irreverently portrays a frog sitting like a Buddha and monkeys as priests. As in many other examples, the arrangement consists of a tall lotus flower flanked by two shorter lotus buds (Figure 6). The general appearance is somewhat similar to the basic formula for the Seika style of later times, although far less studied and refined. The arrangement of the three parts, too, recalls the customary placement of Buddhist altar triads, with a Buddha in the middle and a smaller attendant on either side.

The picture scrolls show many floral offerings of the types known as *mitsu-gusoku* and *go-gusoku* (Figures 7, 8), or three-article arrangement and five-article arrangement. The three-article arrangement consisted of an incense burner with a candlestick on one side of it and a vase on the other; the five-article arrangement, of an incense

8. *A five-article arrangement placed before three hanging scrolls. The vase at the very center is not an intrinsic part of the group*

burner with a candlestick and a vase of flowers on either side. Although the individual floral arrangements are usually of the same general type as the three-flower group in the *Frolic of the Animals*, an interesting example in a fifteenth-century Buddhist print shows a three-vase offering in which each vase contains assorted flowers and plants (Figure 9). When the first type of secular Ikebana, known as Rikka, took form, it retained the three-vase arrangement (Figure 10) harking back to the Buddhist three-image group, and this is still considered orthodox, although the difficulty of preparing a Rikka arrangement is such that most modern arrangers confine themselves to a single vase.

There is no way of knowing just when flowers began to be used for nonreligious purposes. To judge from picture scrolls and documentary references, the typical *shinden-zukuri* mansion of the Heian period was singularly devoid of places where flowers might be put. It had no tokonoma, very few fixed walls or partitions, and almost no furniture. It did, however, have a place for a miniature Buddhist altar, where floral offerings were placed periodically, and it is not difficult to imagine that flowers spread quickly from the Buddha's room to other parts of the house. The lovers of this age were given to exchanging delicate poems, to which they often attached a spray of flowers, and it is likely that these flowers were then used as room decorations. Comparatively few purely decorative floral arrangements are to be found in the picture scrolls, however, despite the frequency with which flowers are depicted in altar decorations. When they do appear, they are less formal than the Buddhist flower offerings.

The Oldest Book

on Japanese Flower Arrangements

Later Japanese sources trace the origin of Ikebana to the time of the eighth Ashikaga shogun, Yoshimasa (1435–1490), a great patron of Zen Buddhism and the arts associated with it. By Yoshimasa's time, however, flower arranging must have been a fairly highly developed art, for the *Sendenshō*, the oldest book on the subject, dates from no later than 1445. This short treatise gives comparatively detailed instructions for arrangements to be used on various occasions, such as annual festivals and the celebrations held to commemorate a man's coming of age, entering the priesthood, or taking a wife. Already, it will be seen, the idea of suiting the arrangement to the season or event was firmly entrenched. The *Sendenshō* is not a sustained dis-

cussion but a series of brief rules and explanations, telling, among other things, what flowers should be used for various specific purposes, how the vase should be placed, what flowers and combinations of branches are to be avoided, and how to deal with flowers for a tea ceremony. It mentions only two technical words for the components of a flower arrangement: *shin*, or main branch, and *soe-mono*, or secondary branches. The book is of such a general nature that the lack of other terms does not necessarily mean that none existed, but it seems likely that the branches had not yet been given the more particularized names they were later to acquire.

At the end of the *Sendenshō* there is a notation to the effect that the book, having been transmitted to one Fuami in 1445, later passed through several hands and in 1536 was owned by a man named Senji. Senji is thought to be identical with the flower master Ikenobō Sennō, whose surname, Ikenobō, is the greatest name in the history of Japanese flower arranging.

The Ikenobō "family," which was in reality a succession of priests and flower artists, traces its origins back to the year 621, when Ono-no Imoko, famous as one of Prince Shōtoku's first Japanese envoys to China, assumed the priestly name Semmu and took up residence at a small temple by a pond in what was later to become Kyoto. The proper name of the temple was Rokkaku-dō, but Semmu's hermitage became known as Ikenobō, which means literally "priest's residence by a pond," and this word was used as a surname for the resident priests who succeeded Semmu. Since these men all chose names beginning with the same written character, *sen*, as Semmu (written *sen mu*), they tend to be confusing to the Western reader. One must be on guard, for example, to distinguish Ikenobō Sennō, the recipient of the *Sendenshō*, from Ikenobō Senkō, who was a prominent flower-arranging teacher of the late seventeenth century. Sometimes the names are even pronounced identically although the second characters are different. There was, for instance, an earlier Ikenobō Senkō who was summoned to the Imperial Palace to make flower arrangements in 1629. Often the confusion is avoided by adding a number indicating the order of succession; thus the Senkō summoned in 1629 was Senkō XXXII, while the late-seventeenth-century Senkō was Senkō XXXV. It is to be noted that Senkō XXXII and Senkō XXXV were not the thirty-second and thirty-fifth masters having the name Senkō, but the thirty-second and thirty-fifth masters of the Ikenobō School.

It is recorded that around 1470, Ikenobō Senkei (also called Sengyō) created a sensation in Kyoto with an arrangement in the Rikka style, and this date is often taken as the birth date of formal flower arrangement, although, as we have seen, the *Sendenshō* indicates an earlier beginning. While it would be as dangerous to assign a definite date to the beginning of flower arranging as it would be to say that painting or sculpture began in such-and-such a year, we may assume that the first great style of arrangement, the Rikka, was formulated during the fifteenth century.

During this century, as in the previous one, the influence of China was strong in both the arts and crafts. The great Japanese painters of the age worked, for the most part, in the styles of the Sung and Yüan periods (960–1279 and 1280–1368), and Chinese art objects of all sorts—including vases, tables, candleholders, tea vessels, and incense burners—were highly prized by the shogun and his entourage as household decorations. The vases and candlesticks shown in early pictures of five- and three-article flower arrangements have a distinctly Chinese look, and the flower arrangements were designed to accord with these exotic objects.

Ultimately, the early Buddhist floral decorations were intended to symbolize the gorgeous flowers of paradise, and as a result they were on the whole both ornate and idealistic. The same attributes were preserved in the Rikka style, which aimed not so much at revealing the beauty of flowers as at embodying with flowers an elevated concept of the cosmos. A Rikka arrangement can be interpreted on a number of different philosophical levels, but it invariably has within it a striving for something that transcends the natural world. Paradoxically, this means that it has a man-made look, for only man conceives of otherworldly beauties.

The Oriental tendency toward numerical classifications asserted itself in the Rikka style at an early stage. By 1542 Ikenobō Sennō had analyzed the Rikka arrangement into seven parts, or "branches," and the style became formalized into the combination of a number of fixed elements. Herein lay the danger of sterility, for excessive codification of an art form can only choke creativity. Herein also, however, lay a discipline which, if used with discretion and sensitivity, could form the basis for a genuine art. In a general way the development of the Rikka style resembles that of Oriental ink painting: Over the centuries so many technical rules were devised that there ceased to be much room for individual expression. On the other hand, the rules were valid to the extent that, by following them, even a person of little artistic ability could produce a work that was visually acceptable, if not inspiring or inspired. Although, as we shall see, later generations of flower arrangers have rebelled against excessive formalization, they have nonetheless accepted the principle of classifying the parts of the arrangement, and at least three of the seven branches in the Rikka form are still regarded as basic.

During much of the fifteenth and sixteenth centuries Japan was torn by internal warfare in which countless small landowners fought to attain a dominant position. After about 1550, however, a succession

10. *A classic three-vase Rikka arrangement attributed to Ikenobō Senmyō XLI, who was active in the early nineteenth century. If the central arrangement is considered to take the place of the Buddha, then the arrangement on the viewer's left is on the Buddha's right, thus creating the somewhat confusing tradition of calling an arrangement whose main branch curves to the left a right-hand arrangement, and one whose main emphasis seems to be on the right a left-hand arrangement*

of great generals gradually unified the realm, and in the late sixteenth century there was a period of general prosperity in which the members of the upper class, for the most part newly rich, outdid one another in quest of ostentation. The great warriors of the age constructed huge castles and palaces, whose interiors were decorated with lavishly colored wall and door paintings, many of them on gold or silver backgrounds (Figure 11). By this time the *shoin-zukuri* style was mature, and the tokonoma decorations—hanging scroll, art object, and flower arrangement—had become an accepted form (Figure 12). The formidable size and bold decor of the larger houses demanded large and opulent floral arrangements, and the flower arrangers of the time responded with Rikka that were not only big, but colorful and elaborate.

The Japanese upper class, and to some extent the common people as well, have always displayed a liking for elegant games, such as contests in which everyone tries to guess the name and provenance of several types of tea or incense, and poetry contests in which the participants vie to produce the most felicitous turn of phrase. As a matter of course, the upper class of the late sixteenth century began to hold flower-arrangement contests, which may be regarded as the origin of the flower exhibitions held all over Japan today.

Informality: Zen Buddhism and the Tea Ceremony

Even as the Rikka style was taking form, a very different movement was taking place under the influence of Zen Buddhism and the tea ceremony. Both Zen and the ritual drinking of tea are supposed to have been introduced in the late twelfth or early thirteenth century, and by the fifteenth century both had a large following among the upper classes. Today, both are noted for the strict simplicity of their aesthetic principles, but the tea ceremony at least was not always so austere as it later became. In the fifteenth century it seems to have been less a ritual than a large elaborate party. In the late sixteenth century there was a tea "ceremony" attended by hundreds of guests over a period of ten days. Still, the lovers of ceremonial tea generally favored quiet and refined tastes, and in the sixteenth century Sen-no Rikyū, the greatest tea master of all, carried austerity to an extreme. Rikyū believed that the ceremony should be held in tiny rooms of rustic character, in which the decor was at once severely limited and impeccably simple. Noted as a flower arranger, he favored small naturalistic arrangements, sometimes consisting of no more than one flower. Such arrangements were known as Chabana, or "tea flowers," and their austerity and simplicity represented the complete antithesis of the Rikka style.

Chabana belonged to a general class known as Nageire, which comprised all flower arrangements not in the Rikka style. The word Nageire means simply "thrown in," and at first it probably signified not a particular style, but rather the absence of style—merely a spontaneous way of putting together a floral decoration. The distinctive feature of the Nageire arrangement, from a technical viewpoint, was that the flowers in it were not made to stand erect by artificial means, but were allowed to rest in the vase naturally. Accordingly, the vase used had to be tall and narrow-mouthed. It was no doubt a result of the influence of Rikka that Nageire began to acquire certain vague rules, but in reaction to the elaborateness and artificiality of the Rikka style, the Nageire emphasized the natural beauty of flowers, and Nageire arrangers sought to achieve the effect of flowers growing wild in a wood or field.

It is by no means accidental that the Rikka style is associated with the more traditional forms of Buddhism while the Nageire style is associated with Zen, for Rikka arrangements grew ultimately from a philosophic attempt to conceive of an organized universe, whereas Nageire arrangements represent an antiphilosophic attempt to achieve immediate oneness with the universe. The Rikka arrangement is an appropriate offering to be placed before one of the many icons of traditional Buddhism, but the Nageire arrangement is a direct link between man and his natural surroundings. One style is conceptual and idealistic; the other, instinctive and naturalistic. The difference is similar to that between the arduous philosophic study associated with traditional Buddhism and the direct enlightenment of Zen Buddhism.

The Nageire style was especially popular in the seventeenth century, which was also the golden age of Rikka. The fact that these two contrasting styles came into their own almost simultaneously is not surprising when one considers that this was a period when the rich lived in the most lavish houses ever built in Japan, but retreated for spiritual comfort to diminutive and bucolic teahouses.

From a very practical point of view, the Nageire style was bound to gain wider currency than the Rikka because it could be put together from a limited number of materials in a very short time, whereas Rikka required many materials, highly developed techniques, and a good deal of time, not to speak of a fair amount of space for display. In a broad sense, Rikka was possible and appropriate only in large houses or monastic reception halls, but Nageire could be a thing of beauty in the smallest and most humble dwelling.

11. Detail of an elaborate sixteenth-century screen devoted to examples of the Rikka style. At this time the rules were not yet completely rigid—a little later it became mandatory for the tip of the main branch (shin) to stand vertically over its base. From the Tokyo National Museum

Simplicity and Formality:
A New Style

During the seventeenth century the two styles interacted on each other, and toward the beginning of the eighteenth century there emerged a compromise style in which some of the principles of Rikka remained, but in a much simplified form. This was the Seika style, also known by the name *shōka*. The two words, *seika* and *shōka*, are variant readings of the same two written characters (*sei* = fresh,

12. A tokonoma in the late fifteenth or early sixteenth century. The two wood-block prints are part of a single scene. Two Rikka arrangements flank an elaborate stand which holds an incense burner and under which there is a small third arrangement

ka = flowers). In general, present-day members of the Ikenobō School say Shōka, but members of other schools say Seika. The same word can also be, and today usually is, read Ikebana, but this reading did not become a part of the vernacular until the nineteenth century.

In the Seika style, three of the original seven branches of the Rikka arrangement, *shin*, *soe*, and *nagashi*, were retained, though *nagashi* came to be known as *tai-saki*. *Shin*, which was the central branch, was the tallest, followed by *soe*, which branched off to one side, and *tai*, which branched off to the other. Much of the simplicity of the Nageire style was retained, and only a limited variety of plants was used. The typical Seika arrangement was much smaller than the

13, 14. Two lively wood-block prints from the early Edo period (1615–1868) depicting a group of people preparing for a party, and a party in progress

15. A creation in the Abstract style made by melting lead over different gauges and styles of wire mesh and then hammering it into the desired pattern

Rikka, and so it was suitable for use in an ordinary tokonoma. At the same time, the Seika style was more formal than the Nageire, not only because the general position of the three principal branches was fixed, but because the arrangement was made to appear to rise from a single stalk. Whether the vase was tall and narrow-mouthed or low and wide-mouthed, the stems of the various parts were held together near the base in a wooden or metal device, so that the whole arrangement sprouted straight up from the center of the container.

The possibilities for variation were great, and many different types of Seika developed, becoming the focal points of a number of schools. In 1766 there appeared a book called *Seika Hyōban Tōsei Kakinozoki* (*A Look at Today's Popular Seika Styles*), which contained the following sentence: "Popular schools of this age include the Old Senke School, the Enshū School, the Yōken School, the Irie School, the Tan-no-sen School, the Genji School, the Shōfu School, the Senkega School, and the 'Only' Old School. The Ikenobō family heads the original school of Rikka, but there is also a split from this form known as the Seika."

In addition to the various schools named here there were minor subdivisions within each school, many of which in turn became entirely separate. One of these was the Ryūsei School, which originated within the Ikenobō School but separated from it in 1884. The Ryūsei School, whose tenets form the basis for the lessons in this book, and whose members prepared the arrangements reproduced here, has one distinctive feature in common with the parent Ikenobō School: it still maintains the ancient art of the Rikka style, which has always demanded the highest degree of technical skill. Other schools have, for the most part, dropped Rikka because of the time and trouble it involves.

A Century of Stagnation in Ikebana and the Arts

During the Edo period (1615–1868) Japan was almost entirely cut off from the rest of the world. The Tokugawa shogunate, which governed the country during this era, forbade all intercourse between Japan and other nations, except for a small amount of commerce with the Dutch and Chinese through the port of Nagasaki. The purpose of this policy of seclusion was ostensibly to protect the nation against foreign invasion, infiltration, or exploitation, but in fact the shogunate's principal aim seems to have been to stabilize its own rule by preventing changes that might result from foreign influences. All things considered, the Tokugawas succeeded to a remarkable extent, for they managed to stay in power for two and a half centuries, during which time the social structure remained intact, and there was little or no internal warfare. No one can stop time, of course, and little by little Japan was changing from a rice economy to a money economy, with corresponding social adjustments taking place beneath the seemingly unruffled surface. Nevertheless, in the arts the seclusion policy appears to have caused a general stagnation, particularly in the latter part of the eighteenth and in the nineteenth centuries. A number of minor arts, of which the most significant was the wood-block print (Figures 13, 14), continued to flourish, but in painting and architecture there was a pronounced trend toward formalism and academicism. Broadly speaking, there was more and more attention to technical detail and less and less creative inspiration. Someone has remarked, in speaking of the architecture of the age, that this was a period of carpentry rather than of architecture. A similar comment could be made with regard to painting and several of the crafts, and sculpture had virtually ceased to exist even before the Edo period began.

The West has often marveled at the speed with which Japan adopted Occidental ways after the opening of the country in the second half of the nineteenth century. Not only the political system, but the economy and the social organization changed in a matter of two or three decades, and this change was amply reflected in the arts, which almost immediately began to show the influence of nineteenth-century Europe. The rapidity of Japan's transformation was largely owing to the fact that the system so long maintained by the shogunate no longer had any real vitality or meaning. Technically, the Tokugawa government was overthrown by a coalition of clans favoring the restoration of power to the Emperor, but in reality the shogunate collapsed of its own dead weight and weakness. In the same fashion, Japanese art virtually collapsed before the onslaught of Western culture because it had ceased to be much more than an empty form.

It would be difficult to prove that flower arrangement became as formalistic and superficial as, say, painting in this period, for the actual arrangements no longer exist. The proliferation of schools emphasizing one or another variation on the Seika style, however, suggests to the student of Japanese art history not that a wide range of new ideas was being introduced, but rather that flower arrangers were dividing up and taking sides over relatively minor points.

The orthodox, and by far the largest, school of painting in Tokugawa times was the Kanō School, which traced its origins back to masters of the fifteenth and sixteenth centuries. By the latter part of the eighteenth century the Kanō style had grown so arid that a number of independently minded painter-scholars rebelled against it and developed very free and personal styles of their own. Their works came to be known as *bunjin-ga* (paintings by men of letters). During the late eighteenth and early nineteenth centuries men from the same group of literati created a similar movement in the field of flower arrangement, developing a number of free styles known collectively as *bunjin-ike* (arrangements by men of letters). The *bunjin-ike*, like the *bunjin-ga*, were a revolt against orthodoxy.

Rebirth and Revival: Modern Ikebana

The introduction of Western culture was bound to affect flower arranging, if only because it meant the introduction of new flowers to work with and the appearance of Western-style rooms to be decorated. In some ways the traditional art of flowers was more resistant than traditional painting or architecture to Occidental encroachments, because it was not confronted with an organized Western system as were the other arts. Ikebana at its dullest was a more highly developed art than anything similar in the West, and even the West was fairly quick to recognize this, so that in this case the principal "influence" was that of Japan on the Occident. In one respect the Westernization of Japan contributed to the strengthening of traditional Ikebana, for after 1888 flower arrangement was adopted as a part of the standard curriculum for girls in the Western-inspired school system.

Nevertheless, the impact of the Occident began to show up in floral arrangements. By 1907 the flower master Unshin Ohara was exhibiting Ikebana in which he used Western flowers. Ohara was a member of the Ikenobō School at the time, but he subsequently broke away and set up a new school of his own, which is still one of the largest and most prominent schools in Japan. The style that Ohara created, which featured shallow containers and free placement of branches, came to be known as Moribana, literally "piled flowers." Much freer in approach than the Seika style, Moribana rapidly became the most popular style of all.

A major innovation of the late nineteenth century was the appearance of the kenzan, a flat heavy metal holder with vertical needles on which branches and stems can be impaled. The kenzan is used in somewhat the same fashion as the Western frog, but it permits freer placement and positioning of flowers, since the stems can be firmly affixed to it at almost any angle. The kenzan is also more easily concealed than the usual frog. In a sense, the kenzan is the technical basis without which the Moribana style could not exist, for without it free and varied arrangements of plants in shallow containers would be almost impossible. Although the word kenzan can be translated in a number of ways, none of the translations is entirely satisfactory, and in this book the Japanese word is retained.

*16. Hammered bronze shapes and pati-
nated bronze sheets are arranged in a series
of teakwood boxes, creating an interplay
of shapes and textures*

In the Shōwa period (from 1926 to the present) the Moribana style
has given birth to still freer and more imaginative forms, such as
Jiyū-ka (free flowers), and Zen'ei-ka (avant-garde flowers). In this
volume, the latter is called the Abstract style.

Abstract arrangers observe few, if any, rules. In addition to all kinds
of living plants and flowers, they make use of dried materials, both
painted and unpainted, and of pieces of metal, glass, stone, concrete,
and the like. Many abstract arrangements contain no flowers at all
and might, but for the fact that they are put forward by flower arrangers, more properly be classed as abstract sculpture (Figures 15,
16). This has led some people to complain that Ikebana is being
killed by iconoclastic modernists, but a more judicious view is that the
art of flower arranging is growing and expanding to meet the require-
ments and satisfy the creative urges of our time. But the fact remains
that the wildest of the abstractionists are grounded in the fundamental
techniques of the ancient tradition, and many of them perform the
vital task of transmitting these principles to large numbers of followers.
Moreover, the abstract designers are as much concerned with the
fundamental problem of producing an aesthetically satisfying design
as are the sternest traditionalists.

The aim of this book is to give the reader a complete introduction
to Ikebana and a firm foundation in the use of Moribana techniques.
The part immediately following presents a thoroughly illustrated sur-
vey of the five principal styles—Rikka, Nageire, Seika, Moribana, and
Abstract—together with their most important variations. For each of
the classical styles there is a section on the modern version, for all
five styles are still in wide use today, although the aristocratic Rikka
is rarely seen except in exhibitions. Many of the arrangements reproduced were prepared for exhibition; others were made especially
for this book by the author and his colleagues.

In later sections the reader will find illustrated discussions of the
stands and vases used in Japan, both in the past and at present; detailed instructions concerning the selection and preparation of materials; a practical course in the fundamental techniques of Moribana;
and suggestions as to the many paths that open up when the basic
lessons have been mastered.

In Japan today there are literally millions of people studying Ikebana and delighting both themselves and others with their work. In
the large cities there are almost constant exhibitions by one or another
of the many schools of arrangement, and the publications devoted
entirely to the floral art are legion. No other art displays such vitality
on both the professional and the popular levels. This vitality is rapidly
being transmitted to countries other than Japan, and in several
Western countries there are nationwide organizations of flower arrangers. Ikebana is rapidly becoming not a Japanese but a world art.

PART TWO

Ikebana Styles

through the Centuries

THE RIKKA STYLE

THE TRUE RIKKA STYLE OF FLOWER ARRANGEMENT, long in evolving, reached a form recognized as distinctive in the fifteenth century, and by the end of the same century the basic concepts had been developed into an articulate system by one of the masters of the oldest school of flower arranging, called Ikenobō. Arrangements of plant material were carefully chosen to represent the enduring elements of a scenic landscape inspired in part by the traditions of Chinese landscape paintings of the Sung period.

In the sixteenth century Japan was disturbed by wars between ambitious military rivals out of which there gradually emerged a new class of military rulers, less cultured than the Ashikaga shoguns but eager to be leaders in devoted patronage of the arts. The Rikka style, which was on the whole big, bold, and ornate, appealed to the newcomers, who doubtless saw in it a fitting symbol of their recently acquired affluence, and under their patronage the style became even more elaborate. While there had been many variations in form over the years, in the sixteenth century variety gave way to a relatively strict formula, which was followed with only minor deviations until quite recently.

The classic Rikka arrangement involves the use of many materials and requires a high degree of technical skill. It is a beautiful and well-ordered entity, in which each element helps to bring out the beauty of the other elements. Today, a number of artists are experimenting with new types of Rikka, but the style remains both formal and difficult in comparison with other styles of arrangement.

Sunamono

Sunamono (literally "sand object") is a variation of Rikka. Although it is as rigidly formal as other Rikka arrangements, it has greater boldness and breadth. It is made in a shallow container, and is generally wider than it is high.

The strictness of the Rikka style can easily be overemphasized. Actually, it allows for considerable variation, even in the choice of floral materials. When the lordly chrysanthemum is in season, for example, the entire arrangement may consist of chrysanthemums of various colors and sizes; indeed, it is not uncommon to see Rikka arrangements made entirely of Japanese irises or daffodils of the same color and size. Despite these variations, however, the names of the nine main branches do not change, nor is the basic form altered.

17. Rikka style. Now commonly called the seven-nine branch system of flower arrangement, the Rikka style always required at least seven principal branches. By the late eighteenth century the hikae (F) *and* dō (H) *had also become important enough to be considered principal branches, making nine in all. The* kidome (J) *and* kusadome (K), *although not principal branches, are also important, and varying other flowers and smaller branches may be added. (L) is Euonymus japonica and (M) is Japanese cypress.*

shin *(main branch)*	A	*pine*
shōshin *(center main branch)*	B	*gentian*
mikoshi *(overhanging branch)*	C	*bittersweet*
uke *(receiving branch)*	D	*pine*
nagashi *(running or flowing branch)*	E	*chrysanthemum*
hikae *(waiting branch)*	F	*pine*
mae oki *(anterior, or introducing branch)*	G	*boxwood*
dō *(body, or trunk, of the arrangement)*	H	*Japanese iris leaves and chrysanthemum*
soe *(supporting branch)*	I	*chrysanthemum*
kidome *(last branch material added)*	J	*tea bush*
kusadome *(last flower or plant material added)*	K	*small chrysanthemum*

OPPOSITE: *18. Rikka style. The Rikka style, steeped in tradition and symbolism, is the oldest systematized form of arrangement known. Here we see a formal, or Shin, arrangement, in an antique bronze vase with handles in the shape of phoenixes. Its red-lacquered base is edged with gold*

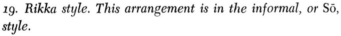

19. *Rikka style. This arrangement is in the informal, or Sō, style.*

shin	A	*pine*
shōshin	B	*pine*
mikoshi	C	*hypericum (St.-John's-wort)*
uke	D	*Chinese bellflower*
nagashi	E	*pine*
hikae	F	*Japanese cypress*
mae oki	G	*boxwood*
dō	H	*iris, cockscomb*
soe	I	*iris*
kusadome	J	*small chrysanthemum*
kidome	K	*Euonymus japonica*

20. *Rikka style. The basic form of a Rikka arrangement is a large scalene triangle within which there are numerous smaller triangles. The basic reason for the triangular form is simply that trees and flowers in their natural state usually assume such a form: typically, they have a wide base that gradually tapers to a point at the top. A second reason is that the scalene triangle has a basic stability that is well suited to the large Rikka arrangements*

OPPOSITE: *21. Rikka style. The dragon-handled bronze vase stands on a red-lacquered base which in turn stands on a gold-trimmed, footed base. The use of two bases together denotes that the arranger has achieved high rank in the Rikka style*

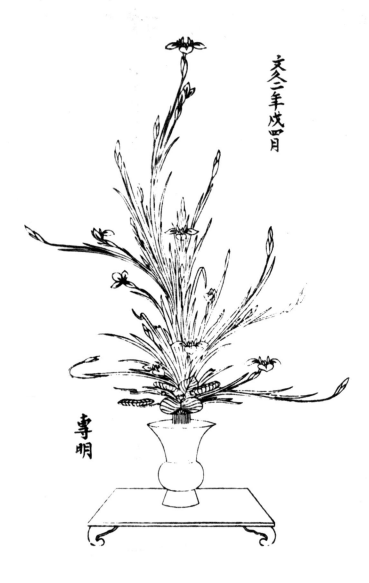

22, 23, 24. *Rikka style. These figures are from wood-block prints of the Edo period (1615–1868). Figure 22 shows an arrangement made entirely of Japanese iris and lotus and is classed as* kusa-isshiki, *or style using only flowers. In Figure 23 we see an evocation of the phoenix, a symbolic bird well known in Japan and the West. During the Edo period designers often strove to evoke birds and landscapes. Here the designer utilized driftwood, willow, flowers, and evergreens in a dragon-handled vase. The extraordinary arrangement pictured in Figure 24 is of a type known as double-shin. Two entirely different sets of materials are used in the two sides, yet they balance to make one whole. A hand held sideways can be passed from top to bottom down the center*

天保六年歳在乙未夏四月曹
勢列来令於東御坊所立錮之
哀元四十一世

OPPOSITE: 25. *Rikka style. The most elaborate form of Rikka requires three arrangements to complete the setting; an arrangement in this* sugushin, *or straight-main-branch style, is placed in the center (see Figure 10). It represents a rugged landscape of very tall pine trees, with rhododendron, chrysanthemum, and auratum lilies growing close to the ground, and weathered deadwood branches scattered here and there. The antique bronze vase stands on a lacquered base inlaid with mother of pearl*

27. *Rikka style. It is interesting, in comparing this arrangement with the one in Figure 26, to notice that the heavy and the delicate branches have interchanged position with a consequent shift in emphasis. Here we have fasciated willow, three sizes of chrysanthemum, a branch of the bittersweet family, Japanese yew, and Euonymus japonica. The leaves in the center are a variety of oleander*

26. *Rikka style. Here again we find the phoenix, this time on the handles of the antique bronze vase. The arrangement consists of tall cedar branches, pine, fasciated broom at center left and bottom right, boxwood leaves in the center, Euonymus japonica, chrysanthemum, and Japanese iris leaves*

43

28. *Rikka style. This very traditional arrangement, made with traditional materials, yet has a modern feeling, partly because of its ceramic vase. The designer has used medium- and long-needled pine branches with their cones, forsythia, a variety of cypress with dark, linear branches, chrysanthemums, white calla lilies and irises, boxwood, and loquat leaves*

OPPOSITE: 29. *Rikka style. The grand scale and luxurious feeling of this arrangement in the semiformal or Gyō style is typical of Rikka. It stands almost six feet high on its simple lacquered base. Green cypress, wisteria stems, white lilies, and driftwood are combined with blue bellflowers, reddish-brown enkianthus leaves, and balsam (the bottom evergreen). The vase is white ceramic*

30. *Rikka style. Old, lichen-covered plum tree branches and the gray-patterned white ceramic vase give this arrangement a serene and nostalgic quality. Large white, and small pink and yellow chrysanthemums; flowers of the lily family at middle right and lower left to center; azalea and rhododendron leaves at the center; a variety of cypress at the bottom. The three large, striking leaves at lower right are loquat*

31. *Rikka style. The use of cypress for its texture and linear qualities gives this elegant arrangement the look of a phoenix in flight. The other materials are Euonymus japonica at the bottom, white iris flowers, leaves of the azalea and rhododendron families, and, at the right, Chinese asters. The modern Rikka vase is of creamy-white ceramic with brown dripped-glaze decoration*

NEW-STYLE RIKKA

THE CLASSICAL IDEAS AND BASIC SKILLS of the Rikka style are today being reinterpreted and created in what is called New-Style Rikka, a revised version of the older form. The accompanying illustrations of some typical arrangements show how the classic beauty of the older style is being expressed in fresh, vivid forms.

It may be that the materials are different from those used in traditional Rikka arrangements. One need only remember that Japan was

32. New-Style Rikka. This arrangement is in the formal style.

shin	A	*weathered branch*
shōshin	B	*chrysanthemum*
mikoshi	C	*Japanese cedar*
uke	D	*Japanese cedar*
nagashi	E	*gladiolus*
hikae	F	*mountain Chloranthus glaber*
mae oki	G	*chloranthus leaves*
dō	H	*driftwood*
soe	I	*bittersweet*
kusadome	J	*chloranthus*
kidome	K	*chloranthus*

closed to the West until the late nineteenth century, to realize that hundreds of the plants, shrubs, and trees used and loved by the Japanese today were unavailable then—materials from Europe and Africa, and from the New World, which had just been discovered at a time when the rules of Rikka were being codified.

Then, too, New-Style Rikka arrangements are usually placed in containers of ceramic, while classic Rikka arrangements are almost always presented in bronze vessels of very traditional shapes, often decorated with traditional motifs. The names of the principal parts of these arrangements are the same as those of classic Rikka, but the style is not restricted to the hard and fast rules of form or position that typify the classic. Rather, New-Style Rikka gives new life to the formal magnificence of the older style. The sweep of the branches or the combinations of colors may follow newer concepts of Ikebana. And, finally, the New-Style Rikka arrangement usually stands on a far less elaborate base than those used for classic Rikka—in harmony with the less formal ceramic containers. In essence, the new style seeks to preserve the noble character of the traditional form while at the same time adding a fresh and modern touch.

It should be noted that the modern versions of the Rikka Style are as difficult to prepare as the classic. Indeed, it may take a skilled Ikebana artist two days of labor to create one arrangement, and often two to four men will work together to ready a single large arrangement in one day. A great amount of training is required, and so is the amount of sheer physical strength needed to manipulate the heavy main branches, which may be six feet, or more, high. On pages 220 to 222 the reader will see how some of these branches are built up from smaller pieces of branch, as carefully dovetailed as a fine piece of furniture. Fresh leaves or pine needles are then tacked to these branches, creating exactly the lines and shapes the designer requires. Needless to say, the Rikka Style is almost entirely confined to professional arrangers creating magnificent displays for public places, and to the major Ikebana shows, where they are always one of the main attractions.

33. New-Style Rikka. Only three materials are used in this arrangement. The lichen-covered pine branches, symbols of timelessness, contrast with the evanescent quality of pure white lilies, accented by small pink rhododendron flowers. Another note of color is introduced in the blue-and-green dripped-glaze ceramic vase

OPPOSITE: *34. New-Style Rikka. The glowing colors and luxurious scale of the Rikka style are well illustrated in this semiformal arrangement. Pink gladioli and carnations, purple and red anemones, orange calendulas, and the brilliant yellow of mimosa are set off against bare branches and evergreens. The leaves extending out at the left are oleander. The brown-and-white-striped modern vase stands on a three-piece lacquered base*

35. *New-Style Rikka. Using traditional Rikka materials and ideas, the arranger adds his own element of dramatic movement to make this a New-Style Rikka arrangement. Spruce, smilax, oak, large chrysanthemums, deep-pink camellias, and New Zealand flax leaves are combined in the light- and dark-brown ceramic vase. The base is a traditional black-lacquered Rikka stand with gold decoration*

OPPOSITE: 36. *New-Style Rikka. Weathered deadwood creates the dramatic sweep of this handsome arrangement. The other branches are Japanese maple and cedar, and Nandina domestica, the sacred bamboo. The only flowers used are gentian and iris, with the blue of the gentians echoed in the light-blue overglaze on the white ceramic vase*

37. *New-Style Rikka. Holding to the traditional forms of the Rikka style, the arranger here uses a great variety of materials untraditional in color and shape. This gloriously springlike arrangement is made of flowering forsythia, eucalyptus, canna leaves, asparagus fern, Clivia miniata, carnations, Aloe arborescens, daisies, Euonymus japonica, and cherry branches. The ceramic vase is white with light-brown dripped-glaze decoration*

OPPOSITE: *38. New-Style Rikka. The sculptural strength of bare branches is combined with cedar, yellow chrysanthemums, and Easter lilies. At the left of the lilies there is a clump of tender new fir tips. The leaves on the bottom are Nandina domestica, the sacred bamboo. Both the handsome vase and the base on which it stands are made of natural wood with a clear lacquer finish*

39. *New-Style Rikka. Some usual and some very unusual materials create a thoroughly modern mood. Red Anthurium andraeanum flowers, New Zealand flax, palm and rhododendron branches, and the berries of mountain chloranthus are combined with the split bases of coconut palm leaf stems and, in the center, roots that were dried and split apart. The New-Style Rikka vase is of light-brown ceramic*

OPPOSITE: 40. *New-Style Rikka. A rich and subtle effect is achieved through the use of many different leaves, among them the dark brown of Japanese maple and the varying greens of mountain laurel and azalea. Delicate pink azalea blossoms contrast with the gnarled shapes of deadwood and driftwood. The ceramic vase stands on a base of dark wood finished with clear lacquer*

41. *New-Style Rikka. The basic Rikka form is still followed in principle in this modern arrangement of Nandina domestica, rhododendron, weathered wood, and dried, split-open roots. The brown ceramic vase is painted with black*

THE CHABANA STYLE
OF NAGEIRE

CHABANA (tea flowers: *cha*, tea; *bana*, flowers) is a style intimately associated with the tea ceremony, a ritual which came to Japan from China together with Zen Buddhism. Chabana arrangements were originally created to adorn the tiny tearooms and teahouses used for this ceremony. As such, they reveal the same simplicity and austerity typical of the ceramic vessels and other implements employed by tea masters, and of teahouse architecture itself. Because these arrangements are usually made in a fairly tall and slender container, rather than in a shallow bowl or urn, Chabana is considered to be a subtype of the Nageire style which developed from it. Chabana calls for a very natural treatment, frequently using only a single flower. The arranger has a good deal of leeway in the overall plan and design, but it is considered improper to bend or cut the flowers into artificial shapes.

As the Chabana style reverts to the pre-Rikka period, when no set rules or forms existed, the greater freedom allowed makes it most popular today.

Chabana arrangements are constantly created by people who have never heard the term. A single rose placed in a crystal vase is essentially a Chabana arrangement. And yet, as in a *haiku* poem or a matched string of fine pearls, the very simplicity of the form requires absolutely perfect execution.

The proportions of the flower in relation to the container must be just right, the stem must be turned so that major and minor points of focus have their proper value, and everything else must be ruthlessly trimmed away. When a feeling of complete serenity and "rightness" is achieved, the Chabana arrangement is successfully completed. It is one of the forms in which delicacy of feeling and a sensitive eye are indispensable, the amount of technique required is very small. The best way to learn how to create Chabana arrangements is to study beautiful examples—some are illustrated in the pictures that follow —and then to experiment with a simple vase and a blossom or two.

42. *Chabana. The simplicity of the Chabana style of Na-geire designs puts special emphasis on the beauty and ap-propriateness of the container. Here a ring-handled bamboo vase holds one sedum flower (stonecrop) and a spray of wild grass*

43. *Chabana. Aster tataricus and Polygonum orientale make a rustic picture in a bamboo water bucket*

OPPOSITE: 44. *Chabana. The elegant simplicity of this single camellia and its leaves is echoed in the graceful shape of the vase and the delicate swirling patterns of the natural-finish cedar base*

45. *Chabana. The roughly-carved wooden handles give this woven split-bamboo basket vase an oddly formal grace. A double spray of toad lily (Tricyrtis hirta) and a stalk of sedum complete the arrangement*

46. *Chabana. One New Zealand flax leaf has been split halfway down its length to create the illusion of two. A single hibiscus blossom with its leaf complete this classic arrangement*

47. *Chabana. A dragon and clouds decorate the white Chinese porcelain vase. Polygonum filiforme vine, cockscomb, and agapanthus (African lily) are used*

48. *Chabana. Pink cockscomb and yellow smilax berries make a colorful combination in a light- and dark-blue ceramic vase*

49. *Chabana. A single zinnia, two thistles (Cirsium purpu-*
ratum), and two sprays of Tremeda triandra grass make a
graceful picture in this unglazed, deeply ribbed container

OPPOSITE: 50. *Chabana. Purple clematis and white bell-*
flower are combined in this symmetrical black ceramic con-
tainer. The austerity of Zen Buddhism is the essence of the
Chabana style

51. Chabana. Dark-blue and pink asters and light-blue aga-panthus complement the tones of a brown ceramic jar with blue-purple overglaze. The bunching of the masses creates a very modern feeling

52. Chabana. The ceramic vase is formed to looked like bamboo. Yellow patrinia on the left and a lavender-pink toad lily with its green leaves on the right. Two strands of Japanese pampas grass fill in the space

OPPOSITE: *53. Chabana. This scene is a typical setting for a tea ceremony during special holidays such as New Year's Day. The willow is symbolic of long life, and the painting pictures never-changing pine trees. The single camellia in its bamboo container stands directly on the floor*

54. *Chabana. The bamboo basket, one of the most appealing of all flower containers, here holds miscanthus, veronica, toad lily, and patrinia—evoking the spirit of autumn*

THE NAGEIRE STYLE

THE FUNDAMENTAL PURPOSE OF THE NAGEIRE STYLE is to preserve the beauty of nature as directly and simply as possible. The names of the principal branches and flowers are the *shin* (first main branch), the *soe* (second main branch), and the *tai* (third main branch). Each of these has a complementary flower or branch, *ashirai*, which we will call the *shin* complement, etc. Besides these essential parts a small cluster of material, usually flowers, is often added to fill out the arrangement or, in other styles, to hide the kenzan (needle-type holder). Arrangements can be made in *hon-gatte* (right-hand) or *gyaku-gatte* (left-hand) form, and in the *Shin* (formal), *Gyō* (semiformal), or *Sō* (informal) mood. These terms apply to the Seika and Moribana styles as well as to the Nageire. Detailed information on these terms is provided in Part Five, as well as specific instructions for making Nageire arrangements based on the principles of the Moribana style, in which case the difference between the two styles is that the Moribana style employs a shallow container, while the Nageire style uses a deep one.

The almost endless kinds of possible arrangements run the gamut from the simple arrangement of a single flower for a tea ceremony to arrangements as dominant but not as formal as those of the Rikka style, capable of holding their own in huge halls to be decorated in the most sumptuous manner.

Methods for securing branches and flowers in place and position are unique to the style. Detailed instructions for these techniques will be found on pages 226 to 228. Although the fixing of the various materials may seem at first to require little more than elementary skills, large arrangements require a high degree of technical ability. Once the fundamentals have been mastered, however, and building on the basis of the established forms, one can experiment with color and design to produce a purely personal expression of beauty or mood.

55. *Nageire.* The shin (A), soe (B), *and* tai (C) *are, in that order, the first, second, and third main branches used in the Nageire style. The* ashirai, *or complements, are related in length to their respective main branches and follow their lines. Auratum lilies and jasmine foliage are used here*

OPPOSITE: 56. *Nageire. The crystal vase used in this arrangement presents both a problem and the opportunity for an imaginative solution. Eucalyptus branches have been inserted down into the vase itself, thus adding another dimension to the arrangement and also hiding the stem ends of the branches and of the carnations*

57. *Nageire. Often when the container has a striking shape or surface design the flower arrangement can be made to harmonize with it. In this example the bare branches of Euonymus alata (spindle tree) are placed and shaped in such a way as to complement the pattern on the white ceramic vase. Both the branches and the pattern are brown. Spotted purple clematis blossoms are used for accent*

58. *Nageire. The fat, dark-purple fruit on the plum branches echoes the smooth, rounded shape of the dark-brown ceramic vase. This arrangement has a cheerful and rather daring color scheme of brown, purple, and the orange of speckled lilies*

59. *Nageire. There is an interesting contrast between the dark brown of the vase and the bark of the pine, as well as between the gray of the weathered wood and the gray-green pine needles. The mass of orange clivia flowers gives a strong accent to the lower sector of the arrangement. Although this arrangement is essentially naturalistic, as one gazes on it, it takes on a rather abstract appearance. There is a good deal of force here, along with dynamic movement*

OPPOSITE: *60. Nageire. Deep-pink dahlias and smilax with unripe berries combine pleasingly in a tall black ceramic vase*

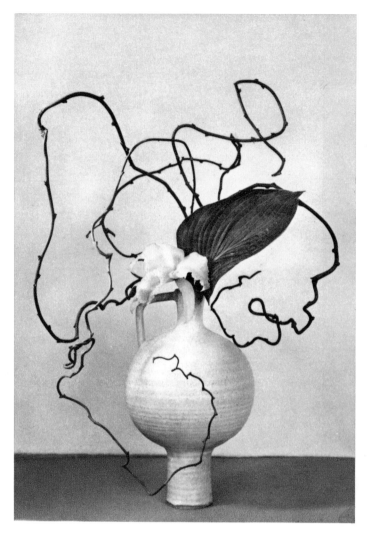

61. *Nageire. The pattern formed by the unusual points on the sides of this light-brown vase is repeated in both the flowers, which are of the bromeliad family, and in the spider plant, giving the whole arrangement a prickly appearance. The dried broom repeats the curve of the vase*

62. *Nageire. Here a lively linear pattern formed by a red vine contrasts with the bulbous form of the vase, which itself is echoed in the shape of the large hosta (plantain lily) leaf. These three elements enclose the white-and-lavender orchid blossom in a frame that recalls* art nouveau

OPPOSITE: 63. *Nageire. Gray-green ornamental onion flowers are made to grow in patterns of the sort seen here by attaching strings at strategic points while the plants are developing. It is often possible to create extremely interesting effects by using "unnatural" materials of this sort. Here the irregular curves of the onion-flower stalks echo the swirling pattern incised on the surface of the vase. Orange gladioli and their buds complete the arrangement*

64. *Nageire. Stripped branches of edgeworthia were cut and glued back together to form the intricate pattern seen here, which is carried out in the sgraffito design on the bluish-purple vase. Green-and-orange bird-of-paradise flowers (strelitzia) combine with the branches to form a design suggestive of action painting*

OPPOSITE: 65. *Nageire. The dramatic sweep of camellia branches is accented by white chrysanthemums. This arrangement would also be particularly effective made in a low Moribana-style container*

66. *Nageire. Here the unusual shape of the vase does much to create the overall mood. The combination of the winding ornamental onion-flower stalks and the spiral design on the vase suggest a fountain in arrested motion. The materials are lavender onion flowers and Easter lilies. The vase is turquoise*

OPPOSITE: 67. *Nageire. An interesting linear design, balanced though asymmetrical, is used as a background for a small cluster of brightly colored flowers. A good many of the leaves of the lower eucalyptus branch have been stripped off to avoid excessive weight on the right side of the arrangement. The gerbera flowers are crimson, and the vine is also red*

68. *Nageire. The somewhat rakish branches of the variegated spider plant falling off to the sides balance what would otherwise be a top-heavy and somewhat massive arrangement of pink and lavender orchids. The blue vase is of recent design*

THE BASIC SEIKA STYLE

WHEN THE PLAN OF THE JAPANESE HOUSE was altered in the fifteenth century it included the tokonoma, a recess or alcove at one side of the living room for the display of art objects. At this time a type of simplified Rikka, the Seika or *shōka* style, appeared. One of the conspicuous differences between the Nageire and Seika styles is that whereas in Nageire the flowers recline against the mouth of the vase, in Seika they rise from the center of the container and clear the rim by a few inches. The mouth of the vase is regarded as the ground from which the flowers sprout straight up. The crotch of a branch or a framework formed of several branches firmly fixed inside the vase serves to secure the plant material in place. Although branches or stems of several different floral materials are combined, they are placed so close to one another that they appear to be the stem of a single plant. This feature sets off the Seika style from other types of floral

69. Seika. These diagrams illustrate the basic form of the Shin, *or formal, style of Seika at the left; the* Gyō, *or semiformal, style at center; and the* Sō, *or informal, style at the right*

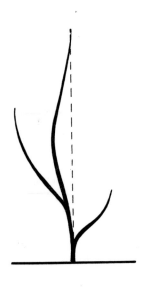

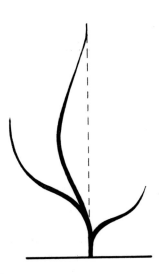

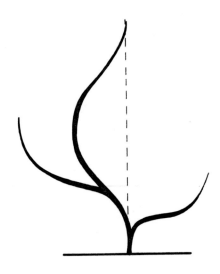

Shin – Formal

Gyō – Semiformal

Sō – Informal

design and contributes greatly to the neatness and precision which distinguishes it.

In the Seika style, as in others, great care is taken to achieve a subtle balance between the faces and the backs of branches and leaves, reminding us of the effect in nature, when one side of a plant is exposed to the sun for more hours than is the other, and we think of it as the "right" side. The proper treatment of these contrasting parts lends both vitality and reality to the arrangement. The leaves facing the observer represent the south or sunny side; those facing away from him represent the north. A detailed lesson in the making of Seika arrangements is presented in Part Six of this volume.

Bronze containers of traditional shapes are most often used for arrangements in the basic Seika style, just as they are in the classic Rikka from which it derived. Containers for formal Seika and Rikka are interchangeable. For the semiformal Seika style the *usubata*, one of the most characteristically Japanese of all containers, is utilized. Figure 71 shows an arrangement made in an *usubata*. Informal Seika arrangements are often made in hanging baskets, boat-shaped vases, and half- or full-moon containers. Pages 165 to 172 illustrate many of the vases used for traditional arrangements.

70. Seika. A right-hand Seika of aspidistra leaves arranged in the formal style. Note that the faces appear only at particularly vital points in the arrangement. Such a balance between face and back is not always easy to achieve, but it is of great importance. In this picture, A indicates the shin, or first main branch; B, the soe, or second; and C, the tai-saki (a term used only in Seika), or third. The bamboo vase stands on a three-piece base of clear-lacquered teak

OPPOSITE: *71. Seika. Flowering forsythia branches are combined with blue iris in a bronze vase with a flat, rimmed, detachable upper section. Vases of this type, traditionally used for semiformal Seika arrangements, are known as* usubata. *The overall height of the arrangement is about four feet*

73. *Seika.* **The legs of this bronze vase, which is a copy of an old Chinese helmet-shaped libation tripod, are very similar to the tips of the Japanese single-petal narcissus flowers. The three-piece base, of vermillion-lacquered wood, is a perfect foil.** *Left-hand arrangement*

74. *Seika.* *Willow fronds are used here for the two main units, shin and soe. Pink chrysanthemums with threads of willow are used in the nejime, a cluster used in place of the tai-saki unit to strengthen the form when the shin and soe branches have no blossoms. Right-hand arrangement*

OPPOSITE: *72. Seika. A left-hand arrangement in the Shin, or formal, style, with the tip of the main branch standing vertical over the center of the container. The leaves of the worm-eaten branch contrast with the fresh lavender Chinese bellflowers. The bronze vase is a copy of an early design*

75. Seika. Millet and small chrysanthemums are used in this beautifully balanced right-hand arrangement. The circular motif of the antique bronze flat-topped vase is repeated in the two-piece black-lacquered base

76. Seika. A right-hand arrangement made in the Gyō, or semiformal, style—somewhat more cursive and open than the Shin, or formal, style. Three materials are used—spirea, fasciated willow, and pink chrysanthemum. The formal, classic Japanese bronze container with three feet has ringed, animal-headed handles, and is inscribed with a Chinese landscape. The stand is of teakwood with convex turned ends

OPPOSITE: 77. Seika. The hanging full-moon arrangement pictured here has its counterpart in a semicircular, half-moon shape. Thistles and sprays of clematis vine are combined in the partly-silvered glass container

78. Seika. This arrangement is especially interesting for the shape and line of its branches. Using one large branch of pine for both shin and soe units, the designer has trimmed excess material from it selectively and well. Cream-colored roses with a small spray of pine for the nejime unit add freshness. The gray-green of the modern ceramic vase echoes the color of the pine

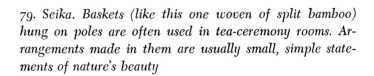

79. Seika. Baskets (like this one woven of split bamboo) hung on poles are often used in tea-ceremony rooms. Arrangements made in them are usually small, simple statements of nature's beauty

80. *Seika. A sailboat moving in the wind is pictured in this hanging bamboo boat. One Japanese quince branch (shin) represents the rippling water behind the boat, the other (soe) its billowing sail*

81. Seika. The image of an old boat left by the waterside so long that plant life has grown up through its rotted bottom is created in this miniature of an ancient boat. Sometimes arrangers use flowers as the mainmast in bamboo-boat arrangements. Made with millet and chrysanthemum in the informal style

OPPOSITE: 82. Seika. This dynamic arrangement is reminiscent in mood of the Rikka style. Note the harmonious interplay of the naturally shaped branches with the contrasting willow and purple statice. The modern ceramic container stands on a black teak base

83. **Seika**. *An old Chinese ink painting of a landscape is evoked in this arrangement made in the semiformal style. This is the most open and cursive form. Weathered wood, cypress, and azalea seem to grow out of the flat bronze vase set on a three-piece, black-lacquered stand*

THE TWO-LEVEL SEIKA STYLE

EVEN THE SEIKA STYLE, with its emphasis on purity and simplicity, underwent many changes in form over the years. There appeared, on the one hand, large and elaborate Seika arrangements suggestive of the Rikka style and, on the other, small and graceful arrangements similar to Chabana. One of the most unusual variations on the Seika form is known as *seika-niju*, or Two-Level Seika.

In Two-Level Seika an attempt is usually made at the upper level to suggest a tree hanging over a cliff, its branches sweeping down in a rhythmic, dramatic curve. Because of this effect, the style is also known as the *kengai* (literally, "cliff-hanging" style). At the lower level a small upright arrangement is added. In the orthodox Seika arrangement the main branch, *shin*, rises almost straight up, while in Two-Level Seika *shin* is the branch that curves downward. Often this branch is of wisteria or some óther vine.

Sometimes, however, the larger arrangement is made in the lower level, thus creating a *nobori-ike*, or climbing, arrangement. A smaller arrangement is then added to the upper level.

Containers for the Two-Level Seika style are traditionally made of bamboo, in several variations. Sometimes two weathered wood containers made in the shape of old water buckets are used, one placed on top of the other but turned slightly on its axis so that openings are created between the upper and lower buckets. Indeed, there is a one-level container, in which only one arrangement is made, that nevertheless is part of the Two-Level style. This is so not only because of the basic character of this arrangement, but also because of the similarity in the containers. And sometimes only the lower part of a two-level container is used, in which case the upper level is filled with water.

Modern potters have created ingenious variations on the two-level theme, but these containers, unless they follow the basic pattern of the Two-Level Seika style, are generally used for free-style creations.

84. *Two-Level Seika. In the Two-Level Seika style, the* shin *branch reaches down toward point A. Point B indicates the* soe, *or second main branch, and point C is the* tai-saki, *or third main unit. Here, small chrysanthemums are placed at point D as the* nejime *accent, because the main units are without blossoms*

85. *Seika. Compare this arrangement with the one shown in Figure 84. Shin and* soe *have exchanged places, and* soe *does not curve downward as* shin *does in the next figure. But the numbered secondary branches emphasize the great structural similarity between the two arrangements.*

A	shin	1	*branch added behind the* shin
B	soe	2	*frontal branch added to the* shin
C	tai-saki	3	*branch added to the* soe
		4	*branch added to the* tai-saki
		5	*frontal branch added to the* tai-saki

OPPOSITE: 86. *Two-Level Seika. Yew branches are placed in the upper and chrysanthemums in the lower level of the bamboo container. One of the rules of the Two-Level style is that the flowers in the lower level must not touch the "window frame"*

87. *Two-Level Seika. A typical example of a right-hand Two-Level arrangement. The "tree" (shin), here a bitter-sweet vine, hangs over the cliff in a graceful sweep. The soe, or second main branch, is made of jasmine branches, the tai-saki of bittersweet. Purple gentians as nejime are completely framed in the window. The bamboo vase stands on a three-piece lacquered base*

88. *Two-Level Seika. Here, in this left-hand arrangement, we have an interesting contrast between the bold, heavy lines of the yew (shin and tai-saki) and the delicate lines of the fasciated willow (soe). Note shin sweeping down to the right and tai reaching out to the left. Following the line of the tai, the pink chrysanthemums of nejime, on the lower level, curve up to meet it*

89. *Two-Level Seika. Deep-purple irises and small white chrysanthemums are the only materials used in this classic arrangement. Following the classic rules, two or three kinds of materials may be used, but only two varieties of flowers, and the materials on the upper level should differ from those on the lower. The iris is an exception to this rule—it may be used alone on both levels*

90. *Two-Level Seika. Japanese quince and small yellow chrysanthemums seem to be growing naturally out of these bronze copies of old wooden water buckets. The three-piece black-lacquered stand is edged with vermillion*

OPPOSITE: 91. *Two-Level Seika. Although this arrangement of forsythia and chrysanthemums is made in a one-level container, it is very definitely in the Two-Level style. This type of container is also known as a two-window vase, from the fact that it is open on two sides*

93. *Two-Level Seika. Stripping all the leaves from flowering pink-and-white Japanese quince branches emphasizes the delicacy of this design. Notice how the triangular form of the pine branch tip on the upper level is echoed by the blue irises on the lower level*

92. *Two-Level Seika. A close look at this arrangement reveals the skill and artistry with which each twig and each leaf has been trimmed or curved. Flowering spirea and azalea branches on the upper level, Japanese iris on the lower*

94. *Two-Level Seika. When the larger arrangement is made in the lower level, the whole becomes known as a nobori-ike (climbing arrangement). These are always in the Sō (informal or cursive) form. Here* shin *and* soe *are of arbor-vitae,* tai-saki *of large yellow chrysanthemums. Small pink chrysanthemums on the upper level arranged in a left-hand, or mirror image, echo the larger arrangement*

95. *Two-Level Seika. Willow branches and rape flowers on the lower level (*soe *and* tai-saki*), quince on the upper (*shin*), make this climbing arrangement. Here the smaller grouping does not mirror the larger—its* shin *branch stretches out to the right*

96. *Two-Level Seika. Although technically not made on two levels, Seika arrangements in containers of this type are classed with them. (When only one level of a two-level container is used, the other is filled with water.) Here we have fasciated willow for shin and soe, pink tulips for tai-saki. The vase is called* ichiju *(single-mouthed)*

OPPOSITE: 97. *Two-Level Seika. Japanese flower arrangers are much more accustomed than are their Western counterparts to utilizing buds as major elements in their designs, but the symbolism of youth and hope for the future is universal. In this arrangement all the lily blossoms are in the bud stage, the small yellow chrysanthemums are in different stages of development. Shin and soe are juniper branches*

98. *Two-Level Seika. In this left-hand arrangement the* shin *branch, instead of sweeping to the left, curves to the right, and the* soe *is to the right of it. These parts are fasciated willow, the* tai-saki *is made of deep-pink chrysan-themums*

THE KABUWAKE STYLE

KABUWAKE IS A SUBTYPE OF SEIKA. It calls for a large flat container with a heavy holder or *shizumi* of hollowed stone or straight-sided metal fitted with a cradle of sticks to hold firmly such plant material as is found in and around water: the willow, the lotus, the Japanese iris. The general aim is to re-create indoors the mood of a quiet wooded shore, either lake, stream, or river. (Many schools now substitute a large, heavy kenzan for the *shizumi*.) In most Seika arrangements the designer strives to achieve the effect of a single plant rising from a given point and spreading out at the top. In the Kabuwake style, however, there are usually two groups (the word *kabuwake* means divided roots), and the emphasis is on the richness and abundance of plant life at the water's edge.

Despite its great beauty, Kabuwake is limited in scope, as comparatively few plants are considered suitable for it, and even these are available only in certain seasons. Kabuwake arrangements are particularly effective in late spring, when they express the freshness and beauty of this season to perfection.

In this connection it must be emphasized—and we will repeat it—that not only the Kabuwake style but flower arrangements in general should accord with the season. Flowers being seasonal, this is a fairly easy rule to follow, at least in so far as materials are concerned. Whether the mood of the arrangement is appropriate to the season is, of course, another matter, and one that depends largely on the sensitive taste of the arranger.

Actually, in this age of hothouse plants the arranger can, if he wishes, make a summery arrangement in the dead of winter. This temptation should be avoided, although the arranger can hardly be blamed for a deviation from time to time.

A detailed lesson in the creation of a Kabuwake arrangement is provided in Part Six of this volume. The reader who wishes to understand the principles involved in this style should also study the Seika lesson which precedes it.

99. *Kabuwake. Arrangements made of two separate parts, one composed of* shin (A) *and* soe (B), *the other of* tai-saki (C), *are called Kabuwake (kabu, stump; wake, to separate). They are composed of water plants or of water and land plants, and are most appropriate for late spring to summer, when the sight of cool water is refreshing. Shin and soe are called* o-kabu (male stump), *tai-saki is called* me-kabu (female stump). *Low containers are always used*

OPPOSITE: 100. *Kabuwake. The larger group of iris in this classic Kabuwake arrangement is the* o-kabu (male), *the smaller group is the* me-kabu (female). *The taller group suggests the sturdiness of the Yo (male principle), while the smaller one suggests the gentle loveliness of the In (female)*

101. *Seika. The Kabuwake style evolved from this simple Seika design. If the irises (tai-saki) are separated from the cattails (shin and soe), a Kabuwake arrangement of male and female groups results. The marshlike atmosphere evoked by the choice of materials is further enhanced by the worm-eaten wood of the container*

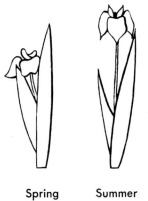

Spring   Summer

102. *Seasons are symbolized not only by the kind of flower used, but by the stage of its development. This does not mean, however, that only flowers in bud may be used to symbolize spring. In the schema for spring, an iris and its leaves have been separated so that the flower is partly hidden. To symbolize summer the flower is taller than the leaves*

103. Kabuwake. The space between the male and female groups is called the "way of the fish," and sometimes small fish are put into the water to emphasize the pondlike mood. New Zealand flax leaves are here used for the male, iris for the female group

104. Kabuwake. This evocation of an early summer morning uses strong, clear colors. The irises are deep purple, and the spirea branches, with no flowers of their own, are accented by bright-red star lilies near their base. The light-blue ceramic vase would be equally appropriate for arrangements in the Moribana style

105. Kabuwake. In this left-hand arrangement shin and soe are on the right, tai-saki on the left. The former are made of Nandina domestica (sacred bamboo) branches, and tai-saki is composed of spirea leaves and aconite (monkshood)

OPPOSITE: 106. Kabuwake. Here the subtle gradations of height in the cattails complement the compactness of the calla lilies. The beautiful old bronze container is the same one used in Figure 100

107. *Kabuwake. Compare this arrangement with the one shown in Figure 104. The same materials have been used to entirely different effect. Here the shin and soe are of spirea branches, still with their accent of star lilies. The irises, so lordly in their tall, full-bloom state, here take on the delicate grace of the female role*

OPPOSITE: *108. Kabuwake. In this arrangement we have three types of material—fasciated willow, blue gentian, and, on the right, forsythia. Note how the small stones in each of these arrangements not only perform their function of hiding the kenzan, but contribute positively to the beauty of the whole*

109. *Kabuwake. The* shōbu *iris (Iris ensata, var. hortensis), with its leaves growing tall and straight as a sword, in Japan symbolizes boyhood. The blossoms in the larger group are lavender, those in the smaller group, white. Pebbles at the bottom of this copy of an antique bronze vase cover the* kenzan *(needle-type holder) and add to the pondlike illusion*

THE KENZAN SEIKA STYLE

As THE NAME INDICATES, this style is a development of Seika. The chief technical difference is that the wooden framework fitted into the straight-sided, broad-rimmed cup of Seika vases, or the *shizumi* classically used for Kabuwake forms, has been replaced by the kenzan. Placed in the bottom of a container, the kenzan permits much freer and more easily manipulated placement of flowers, for to affix a stalk or branch to the kenzan it is only necessary to impale the lower end of it on one or more of the needles.

The use of the kenzan opened up new paths for development. Despite the emphasis on natural beauty of the Seika style, the wooden framework fitted to the sides of the tall container or to the *shizumi* in flat ones to hold the flowers in place limits the choice of vases to a fairly narrow range. The typical Seika arrangement is made in a tall bamboo or bronze container with a relatively small mouth or a straight-sided cup. As a result, the Seika arrangement is usually elegantly formal in feeling. The kenzan makes it possible to use flat, open basins and shallow, wide-mouthed vases, and to achieve freer, more casual effects.

Among arrangements of the Kenzan Seika type, one of the most beautiful is the *kusa-isshiki* (one kind of plant), using a single specimen: the chrysanthemum, the iris, or the daffodil. Flowers may vary in size, shape, and color, but should all belong to one family. A similar type is the *boku-isshiki* (one kind of tree). Often these two types are combined, with the *shin* and *soe* formed of branches, the *tai-saki* (the term for the *tai* in Seika) and the *nejime* (an added part that often serves to tie together the arrangement) made of flowers.

Studying the Seika and Kabuwake lessons provided in Part Six of this book will enable the reader to create Kenzan Seika arrangements like the ones pictured in the illustrations that follow. Pages 223 to 225 give instructions on how to secure materials on a kenzan. The reader should be warned, however, that Seika arrangements of every type are considerably more difficult to make correctly than would appear at first glance. The beginning flower arranger would do well to start with the Moribana course presented in Part Five before going on to this more advanced form.

110. *Kenzan Seika. This type of ceramic container is most commonly used for Kenzan Seika arrangements.*

A   shin *unit*
B   soe *unit*
C   tai-saki *unit*
D   nejime

OPPOSITE: *111. Kenzan Seika. Tulips and eucalyptus branches seem to be growing from a common stump. The modern vase stands on a three-piece lacquered base*

113. *Kenzan Seika. In this left-hand arrangement shin and soe are composed of a variety of bulrush (Scirpus lacustris); tai-saki, extending toward the left, is a carefully trimmed enkianthus branch; the nejime is red gerbera blossoms and their large leaves. Red is repeated in the two-piece lacquered base, contrasting with the modern white bubbly-glass vase*

112. *Kenzan Seika. The Kenzan Seika style is distinguished from Seika by the use of modern vases and the kenzan, and by an essential difference in scale. It is much smaller and lighter in feeling than the traditional Seika. Here we have an example of kusa-isshiki (one-kind-of-plant style), the flowers in this instance being Siberian flag iris*

114. Kenzan Seika. New Zealand flax leaves, tall green spikes with creamy edges, are carefully bent and fitted into place to make shin *and* soe. *Lavender lisianthus flowers form* tai-saki

115. Kenzan Seika. Spirea branches, heavily trimmed to allow the graceful curves of the branches to show, form shin *and* soe. *The single iris leaf bent to the left is* tai-saki, *while the other leaves and their purple blossoms form* nejime

116. *Kenzan Seika. The black ceramic vase on its red-lacquered base makes an elegant foil for this kusa-isshiki (one-kind-of-plant arrangement) of red gerbera flowers and deep-green leaves*

OPPOSITE: *117. Kenzan Seika. The massive strength of black-berry lilies (gemmingia) is well suited to the irregularly shaped, coarse ceramic vase*

118. *Kenzan Seika. All three major elements in this arrangement are yellow patrinia, with the* nejime *composed of chrysanthemum. Note how in all these Kenzan Seika arrangements the flowers seem to grow out of the center of the container*

119. *Kenzan Seika. Willow branches and two sizes and colors of chrysanthemum—small yellow and large pink—make this semiformal right-hand arrangement. A comparison with Figure 74 will show similar materials used in a taller container*

OPPOSITE: *120. Kenzan Seika. Red gerbera flowers and spirea branches combine in this arrangement. Note how the leaves on the branches have been thinned out to emphasize the upward sweep*

121. Kenzan Seika. Stalks of Chinese pampas grass (Miscanthus sinensis) seem to grow out of the blackberry lily (gemmingia) leaves, adding a crispness and lightness to the heavier curves below

OPPOSITE: *122. Kenzan Seika. In this charming arrangement agapanthus seems to be growing out of a black ceramic flowerpot. Contrast this colorplate with the preceding one to see how different the moods created within one style can be*

123. *Kenzan Seika. In this right-hand, semiformal arrangement* shin *and* soe *are both composed of pampas grass and have* ashirai *(complementary sprays) of chrysanthemum;* tai *is also composed of chrysanthemum*

THE MORIBANA STYLE

THE MORIBANA STYLE ORIGINATED toward the end of the nineteenth century, and is thus comparatively new. Yet it has shown itself to be so adaptable and so satisfying that it quickly gained an overwhelming popularity and has achieved the status of a national tradition. In Part Five of this book a complete course in the study of Moribana is presented.

The Moribana style resembles Rikka and Seika in that the flowers and branches have the same names and positions in relation to one another. It differs from the older styles, however, in its degree of freedom. While Seika arrangements always follow an established form, once the fundamentals of the Moribana style are mastered there is complete freedom of expression in both design and color, so that an atmosphere of adventuresome spontaneity can prevail. At the same time a strong sense of proportion and composition is developed as a natural by-product of the study of this artform.

As with the Rikka and Seika styles, a Moribana arrangement may be formal, or *Shin*; semiformal, or *Gyō*; or informal, or *Sō*. Within each of these divisions there are a basic arrangement and three variations. These twelve designs, which are *hon-gatte*, or right-hand forms, can also be made with all their parts reversed, in which case they become *gyaku-gatte*, or left-hand forms, making a total of twenty-four master arrangements within the Moribana style.

Moribana arrangements are always made in shallow containers, and the kenzan holder is always used. Kenzan Seika bowls are about the deepest that would normally be employed, and the most typical container is a large round ceramic dish of the kind pictured in Figure 124.

But it is also possible to adapt Moribana designs to taller vases, by cutting the stems of the materials longer and by using other methods to hold them in position. The result is a Nageire arrangement made to a Moribana pattern. In the Moribana course presented in Part Five, a number of such arrangements are illustrated, and step by step instructions for creating them are provided.

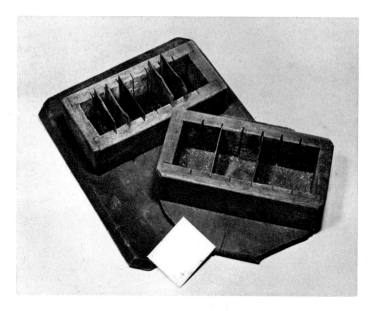

125. *This old-style holder was used before the needle-point kenzan was developed. It is easy to see how much less freedom it granted the designer*

124. *Moribana. In the Moribana style the familiar terms for dominant units, shin (A), soe (B), and tai (C), are used, as well as the term ashirai (1,2,3) for complementary branches added to these units. Thus, ashirai no shin means a flower or branch which follows the line of shin and whose height is determined in relation to it. We shall refer to them as the shin, soe, and tai complements. Pictured here is the basic arrangement of the formal style, with an added cluster of asters*

OPPOSITE: 126. *Moribana. Yew branches, candytuft, and mimosa are here combined in the semiformal style of Moribana. The black ceramic vase is one of the classic shapes designed for this style*

127. Moribana. Precise instructions for creating each of the arrangements in the following plates illustrating the Moribana style will be found in Lesson One of Part Five. Here we illustrate the basic arrangement in the formal style. The materials used are straight pine branches and chrysanthemums

128. Moribana. This is the basic left-hand arrangement in the formal style which we saw in the preceding plate. The parts have simply been reversed in position, and the kenzan shifted from the left to the right of the container. Note, however, that the designer has cut the gladioli a little longer, so that the open blossoms are in pleasing relationship to one another. Shin and soe are of plume grass, tai is a Monstera deliciosa leaf. Instructions for this arrangement may be found in Lesson Four of Part Five

130. Moribana. *This arrangement of Euonymus japonica and chrysanthemum is detailed in Lesson Three. It is in the third variation of the basic style. Note how the kenzan is always hidden from view by the materials*

129. Moribana. *Soe and* tai *and their complements reverse position from the basic form to make this second variation in the formal style. It is somewhat more open than the basic form and lends itself to the phoenix branches which make shin and soe here. Orange-red gerbera flowers make the complements, and one of their large leaves is used as* tai. *The making of this arrangement is detailed in Lesson Two of Part Five*

131. *Moribana. Here we have the basic arrangement in the semiformal style. The* shin, *instead of being nearly vertical, slants at an angle of about 45 degrees, creating a broader, more open arrangement. Enkianthus branches are used for the main parts and dark- and pale-purple gentians for the complements. Because of the nature of the materials, a few small, deep-red chrysanthemums were added to fill out the base of the arrangement and to hide the* kenzan. *Instructions are given in Lesson Five*

OPPOSITE: 132. *Moribana. Gladioli and cockscomb, arranged in the formal style, are seen in a vase almost identical in shape to that in Figure 126*

132

133. Moribana. The left-hand arrangement in the same basic form of the semiformal style illustrated in Figure 131. Here the thicker stems of the castor-oil plant and the chrysanthemum leaves make it unnecessary to use extra material, but otherwise this arrangement is simply the reverse of the other. Instructions are given in Lesson Six

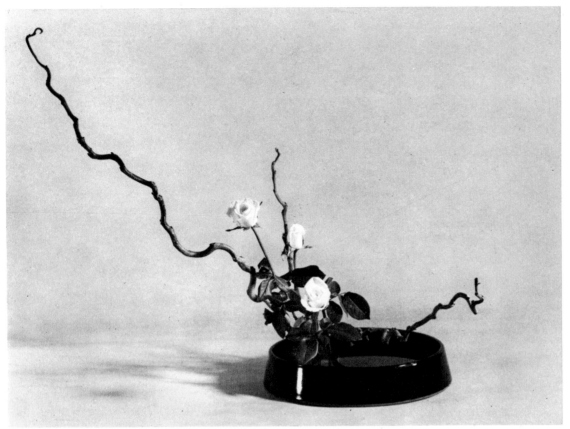

134. *Moribana. The second variation in the semiformal style approaches the informal style in its breadth and sweeping lines. The bare mulberry branches here used for the main parts emphasize this open feeling. The roses, complements to the main branches, are ivory-yellow. Note how the leaves have been removed from the upper stems of the two taller ones in order to retain the airiness above and concentrate the fullness below. Instructions are given in Lesson Seven*

135. *Moribana. Sweeping out both to left and right of center, the informal style is the broadest and freest of all. Here forsythia branches and cockscomb are combined in the basic form of this style. Instructions are given in Lesson Nine*

136. *Moribana. Here we see the third variation of the informal style, made with bare willow branches, pine, and red-and-white dahlias. Because the container has a curved bottom, the kenzan has been placed in the center, an unusual position for it in the Moribana style. Instructions are given in Lesson Eleven*

OPPOSITE: 137. *Moribana. Here we have a freer interpretation of Moribana, using a modern vase that separates the tai group from the others. But the basic lines of the informal style can still be clearly followed. The materials are eucalyptus, candytuft, and mimosa*

138. *Moribana. Here we have the left-hand arrangement of the third informal variation—compare it with Figure 136, the right-hand version. The bottom of the container being flat, the kenzan is in its normal position for a left-hand arrangement—on the left side of the vase. Spirea branches combine with pink carnations in a graceful and delicate pattern supplemented by carefully added branches and flowers of the same material. Instructions are given in Lesson Twelve*

CONTEMPORARY ARRANGEMENTS, OR, FREEDOM WITHIN TRADITIONAL STYLES

WHILE ONE RECOGNIZES THE ESSENTIAL FORMS of Nageire, semiformal Seika, and Moribana in certain "free-form" arrangements, there are differences, notably in mood. Flower masters of prominent schools emphasize that modern compositions should have bold striking contrasts, and that the arranger should be daring. Naturalistic effects are exaggerated or even in some cases abandoned—the artist is in search of the extravagances of nature, its idiosyncrasies, and its awesomeness. Angular, active, even agitated effects are sought—rushes that once were arranged to stand serenely upright are now bent at sharp angles with shifting diagonals about a cluster of short-stemmed blossoms or a flowering branch, to suggest the rain of a sudden spring squall. The fine roots of rape or other plants, washed clean, manipulated into swirling forms as they are drying, and sometimes sprayed with paint, are used with colorful flowers to create an animated, windswept scene. The old ideal of a floral composition as a tranquil refuge no longer holds in the new style—it must arouse, startle, and amaze the eye.

There is now an emphasis on volume and on sculpturesque forms rather than on line and on the spatial effects attempted, symbolically in Rikka and realistically in Moribana, to create foreground, middle ground, and distance. The techniques evolved to achieve these effects of mass and volume are truly ingenious: Leaves of grasses and other swordlike foliage are looped from tip to base, pinned together, and fixed to a kenzan; or perhaps a piece of driftwood is used to make a burgeoning form, and flowers of rounding form are built around it. There is no end to the imaginative exploration of the expressive possibilities of every known variety of plant, stone, rock, feather, shell, butterfly, and man-made bead and plastic bauble.

But the true essence of a style can be discovered only after its fundamental forms have been mastered and a freer hand is given for creative expression. When a beginner sets out to fashion free-style arrangements, he may be at a loss to know how to proceed with his materials. At that point it is wise to follow one of the established forms and then to experiment with various possibilities in harmony with that form until the desired effect is achieved.

139. *Contemporary. This elegant free-style Moribana arrangement is composed of purplish-pink orchids (Cymbidium insigne) and their leaves. The interplay of lines is given solidity by the mass of the modern vase, which is white ceramic with areas of light-green glaze*

OPPOSITE: 140. *Contemporary. Pampas grass, blue gentians, and yellow valerian express a rustic yet slightly formal mood in their handled bamboo vase*

ABOVE LEFT: *141. Contemporary. Two New Zealand flax leaves are folded to create a sharp horizontal plane in opposition to the strong verticals of the body of the arrangement. The two diagonally folded leaves subtly create another plane. White calla lilies and a round brown ceramic bowl relieve the angularity of the leaves, which are reminiscent of* origami, *the Japanese art of paper folding*

ABOVE: *142. Contemporary. When materials such as these ostrich ferns are dried, they lose their identity and become a new element. Here they are combined with red Anthurium andraeanum in an unusual ceramic vase which brings to mind a pair of scales. The total effect is of a modern painting*

143. Contemporary. A blue glass bowl masked with fish net to simulate a floater makes a most effective container for these white, pink, and red cosmos. Some of the flowers are inside the bowl itself. A contemporary interpretation in the Nageire tradition

144. Contemporary. Anthurium andraeanum combined with stripped branches of Euonymus alata (spindle tree) make arresting horizontal and vertical patterns. Note how the lower anthurium fits into the cutout in the vase

OPPOSITE: *145. Contemporary. Sea fern, other ferns, and calla lilies, arranged in a champagne goblet, call forth a sophisticated and festive mood— gaiety emerging out of the veiled and mysterious*

146. Contemporary. Here the designer has used dark-green thorn branches (Aegle sepiaria) tied together to repeat the concave motif of the vase. Gray-green ornamental onion flowers and pink ananas blossoms complete the composition. The blue glaze on the upper portion of the ceramic vase drips onto the unglazed lower part. Vase and form are in the Nageire tradition

147. Contemporary. The black solidity of the vase contrasts with the airiness of the bleached broom and the gray-green ornamental onion flowers, but they all have in common their animated curvilinear qualities. Although the broom may appear irregular at first glance, a closer examination will show that every frond has been carefully bent, and even the curves in the onion-flower stalks reflect the indentations of the vase. Entirely contemporary in its wind-blown yet self-contained form. The modern vase would serve a Nageire arrangement

OPPOSITE: *148. Contemporary. The spiky ananas blossoms and the smooth planes of the anthurium leaves contrast boldly and brilliantly with each other, the veins of the leaves repeating the spirit of the petals. The vase of white bubbly glass has the smoothness of texture that characterizes both plant materials. A fine modern variant in the Moribana tradition*

149. *Contemporary. Strands of wisteria vine, stripped of bark and carefully hand-coiled in hot water, are closely bunched with compact pink hydrangea blossoms in a tall vermillion vase. A striking modern arrangement owing its form to the Nageire tradition*

OPPOSITE: 150. *Contemporary. Dried asparagus fronds, sunflowers, and trimmed Fatsia japonica reinterpret the shape and decoration of their container*

151. *Contemporary. The rugged quality of this vase, welded of old iron by the designer of the arrangement, with its spiky point thrusting up, is accentuated by the soft, rounded form of the pitcher plants. Small red anthuriums add spots of color*

THE ABSTRACT STYLE

Abstract arrangements have ushered in an entirely new atmosphere, one in which the range of material and its manipulation are limitless. For example, iron may be used to express a cold, impersonal feeling, or, if it is rusted, its color and texture may suggest the corrosion of time and weather. If a rock is used, its texture and hardness express the rugged endurance of the "bones" of nature. The various aspects of wood—old and weathered, washed by the sea to a silken surface as is driftwood, peeled to its white inner surface, twisted by the wind, or coiling in natural growth as is the wisteria—all have expressive possibilities.

These countless possibilities are open to the designer who can see new expressions of feeling in a wide variety of materials. At the same time, if there is no particular material which meets the needs of the image he wishes to mold, the designer is free to create his own materials. In this way, entirely new elements have found their way into the age-old art of Japanese flower arrangement.

While adapting such materials as iron and rocks to the expression of one's feelings is a very different thing from using plants and flowers, the basic desire—the expression of feeling—is the same. And, as is true of every one of the artforms that have in this century moved so dramatically beyond the previously established rules, freedom to experiment does not mean that no value judgment on the finished creation is possible or necessary. There are good and bad Abstract Ikebana arrangements, just as there are good and bad abstract paintings. Also as in the case of the other arts, a thorough grounding in the traditional forms is the best guarantee of success in the freer styles.

The Japanese people, who are so thoroughly familiar with the standards of excellence in traditional Ikebana, have shown a tremendous amount of interest in the new forms. Exhibitions of Abstract Ikebana attract great crowds, and the greatest artists in it are treated as matinee idols—surrounded by bodyguards and assistants, and pursued by hordes of admirers.

152. *Abstract. This two-part abstract, titled "Life of the Stamen," stands about fifteen inches high. Made of heavy tin, thin wire, and colored waxes, it illustrates how closely the art of sculpture and the art of flower arrangement are intertwined*

153. *Abstract. Whimsical and witty, this creation is fashioned from beaten tin which has been welded together and painted, and metal rods. Cactus and a single orchid complete the form*

OPPOSITE: 154. *Abstract. "Computer Man," of welded iron, is garlanded with bittersweet vines which echo the color of the oxidized metal and provide a touch of nature*

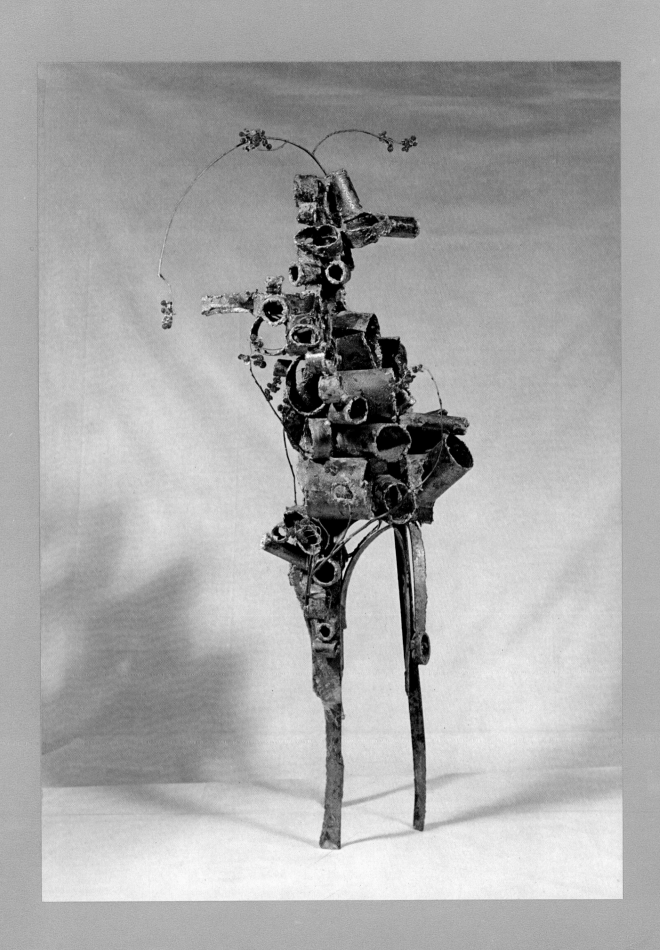

155. Abstract. The round shape of the large brown ceramic vase was the point of departure for this powerful arrangement, titled "Egg of a Tree." Ripe red pomegranates hang from young oak branches and flowering Japanese quince

156. Abstract. Silver-colored wire mesh creates an effect of blurring motion, aptly titled "Move!"

157. Abstract. "Endless Flight," made of beaten bronze in blue, gold, and bronze color, measures about a yard in each direction and weighs 130 pounds

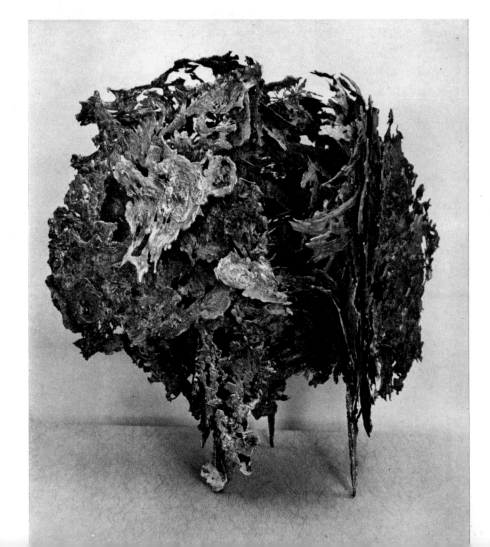

158. *Abstract. A tree root carved and partially painted with colored plaster creates a fascinating series of sculptural planes*

159. *Abstract. "House of the Moon," carved out of plaster and sprayed with paint, combines an architectural solidity with rectangles in subtly varied planes of great delicacy*

OPPOSITE: *160. Abstract. "Iron Flower," finished with aluminum paint, receives a pink rose and a few lemon leaves. Several of the segments of pipe are sealed at one end so that they can be used as vases*

161. Abstract. "Story of a Crown," made of tin welded, hammered, and painted the color of antique gold. Melted red and blue glass creates a jewel-like effect

OPPOSITE: 162. Abstract. Tin, hammered and welded into a gracefully flowing form, is titled "Fawn." Inserted into a vaselike piece of stone, it makes an arresting, sculptural form

163. *Abstract. The very handsome "God of the Wind" subtly evokes the most formal tradition of the Rikka style. Black-painted sheets of steel are combined with wood covered in red bronze*

OPPOSITE: 164. *Abstract. White-bleached coconut stamens, Chinese lantern berries, and dried pitcher plant are combined in a lively and colorful work composed solely of dried natural materials*

Equipment

GATHERING CONTAINERS is a never-ending collector's delight—searching out the right vase for the right place and for one's favorite flowers and style of composition. Ideally, containers should include a selection from the various shapes pictured in the next pages, of bronze, pottery, possibly porcelain, basketry, and wood. Dull copper and rough-surfaced iron, too, are excellent for informal arrangements, but silver or polished brass vessels do not lend themselves to the classic styles. If glass is chosen, it should be opaque or very thick, rather than thin. Bases should be chosen to complement these containers and to blend with favorite color schemes. For modern arrangements, the designer's skill in matching his materials to his containers is the only limitation.

It is more important to have a few tools of high quality than to collect a large number of gadgets. Those illustrated are all that are needed for any arrangement taught in our lessons.

CLASSIC VASES

VASES OF VARIOUS TYPES ARE NECESSARY for arranging flowers in the classic Rikka and Seika styles. In one sense, the history of classic vases is essentially the history of flower arranging itself, and therefore we illustrate them in rough chronological order of style.

Bronze containers whose shapes and decorative motifs are based on ancient Chinese bronzes are shown in Figures 165 to 174. Some of the original Chinese vessels were used as wine containers, others to pour ritual libations, still others were used as drinking cups. The ones illustrated have all been fitted with *izutsu* (straight-sided cups) to accommodate the *kubari*, a forked stick used in Seika arrangements to secure the materials.

Bronze containers of the *usubata* type, designed by the Japanese for use in various capacities, are shown in Figures 175 to 178. The broad-rimmed cup can be removed and used as a separate container for Seika arrangements, leaving the round lower part suitable for Nageire forms. Put together they form the classic Seika vase for semiformal arrangements. The bronze bowl in Figure 179, fitted with a cup for Seika arrangements and held aloft by a frog, is a variant of this type.

Bronze containers suitable for Seika or Nageire forms are pictured in Figures 180 to 182.

Bamboo one-level (*ichijū-giri*) one-window containers and two-level (*nijū-giri*) two-window styles are used for Seika compositions (Figures 183, 184). Two "water buckets" of worn wood lined with copper are also used for two-level arrangements (Figure 185).

Low bronze or wood containers of the *suiban* type are used for informal arrangements in the *sunamono* Rikka and in the Seika styles and for any Moribana arrangement (Figures 186 to 189).

Boat-shaped vases are very popular with the Japanese. Figures 190 to 192 show them made of bamboo, worm-eaten, and worn wood. All are fitted with copper linings and are used for informal Seika arrangements.

Bronze moon-shaped containers, either crescent or full, are also popular for Seika arrangements. They are usually suspended by a chain (Figures 193, 194).

Baskets of woven split bamboo, fitted with liners, are used for informal arrangements, and especially for arrangements of peonies (Figures 195, 196). Traditionally, a base is never used with basketry containers.

165

166

167

165. *Copy of an ancient Chinese wine container*

166. *Animal-handled container of blue bronze, decorated with dragons in low relief*

167. *Modern version of an early animal-handled vase decorated with a stylized geometric pattern*

168. *Ancient Chinese wine cup*

169. *Ancient Chinese wine cup*

169

168

170

171

172

170. *Fish-handled vase in blue bronze*

171. *Ancient Chinese libation tripod*

172. *Vase of blue bronze decorated with demon masks*

173. *Vase of blue bronze decorated with stylized bird and flower patterns*

174. *Ancient vase with handles in the shape of arrow feathers*

174

167

173

175. *Three-legged vase of the* usubata *type, with handles in the shape of elephants' heads*

176. *Three-legged* usubata *with legs shaped to represent waves*

177. *Three-legged* usubata *with legs in the shape of Chinese children. The dripped-glaze effect represents melting snow*

178. *Simple* usubata *vase. Dripped-glaze effect represents melting snow*

179. *Variant of the* usubata *vase, representing a frog blowing the container as though it were a bubble*

175

176

177

168

178

179

180

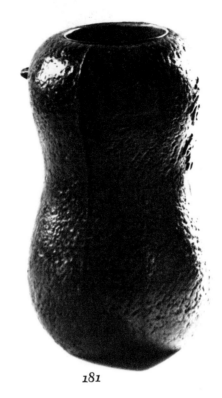

181

182

183

184

180. *Vase with gourd-shaped knob handles*

181. *Cocoon-shaped hanging vase made of iron*

182. *Cylindrical vase of blue bronze decorated with clouds and dragons in relief*

183. *Bamboo one-level (ichijū-giri) one-window container*

184. *Bamboo two-level (nijū-giri) two-window container*

185. Two-level container made of "water buckets" of worn wood

186. Copy of an ancient container of the suiban type, decorated with a turtle and a Chinese unicorn sporting in the ocean

187. Shallow container of the suiban type, decorated with a combination of geometric patterns

188. Copy of an ancient ring-handled round container of the suiban type

189. Rectangular container of the suiban type, made of water-worn wood

186

187

185

188

189

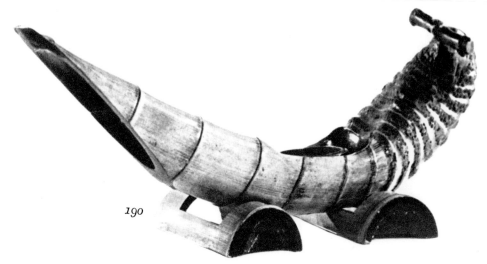

190

190. *Bamboo boat-shaped vase of worm-eaten wood. It can stand or be hung*

191 *Boat-shaped vase of worm-eaten wood with a chain for hanging*

192. *Boat-shaped vase of worn wood*

191

192

193

193. *Vase of blue bronze in the shape of a crescent moon. It may be hung*

194. *Vase of blue bronze in the shape of a full moon*

195. *Basket vase of woven bamboo, fitted with a metal container*

196. *Basket vase of woven bamboo which may be attached to a wall*

195

194

196

VASES FOR ARRANGEMENTS IN THE MORIBANA, NAGEIRE, AND KENZAN SEIKA STYLES

THE SHAPE AND STYLE OF VASES down through the years have been important factors in the history of flower arrangement. An examination of the vases in the preceding section on classic vases will show that in the early years of this art most vases were fashioned in the shape of jars. These were the forerunners of the vases used for Nageire arrangements today (see Figures 197 to 201). With the advent of *sunamono* in the Rikka style, however, wide-mouthed, tray-shaped containers made their appearance. These in turn were simplified

197. Hexagonal ceramic Nageire vase, with classic decoration in relief

198. Multicolored, highly glazed Nageire vase

199. Dripped-glaze Nageire vase in a classic jar shape

200. Stylized geometric pattern in a modern Nageire vase

201. Simple white Nageire vase with brown rims on top and bottom

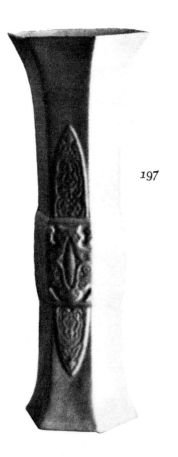

197

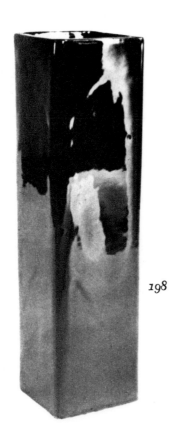

198

199

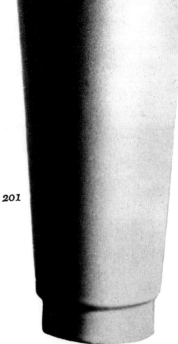

201

to produce the low, basinlike vases in common use to-day. The use of these new vases, along with the kenzan, gave birth to the Moribana style (see pages 127 to 138 and Part Five). Designs in this style are arranged in vases similar to those in Figures 202 to 206. Vases of both Moribana and Nageire style are today made of pottery.

Modern vases which are actually designed for Kenzan Seika arrangements may also be used for arrangements intermediate between Moribana and Nageire (Figures 207 to 211).

205

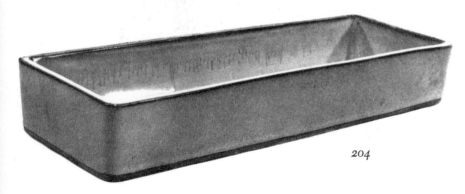

202

203

206

202. *Moribana vase inspired by the shape of a raft*

203. *Triangular Moribana vase*

204. *Rectangular Moribana vase*

205. *Round vase. This is the most commonly used shape for Moribana arrangements*

206. *Moribana vase with sides slanting sharply to a small center*

204

207. *Modern Kenzan Seika vase of heavily ribbed, rough-textured ceramic*

208. *Footed bowl designed for Kenzan Seika arrangements*

209. *Kenzan Seika vase similar to the one shown in Figure 207, but in a glazed finish*

210. *Heavily textured Kenzan Seika container*

211. *Stylized sunburst pattern decorates a rough-textured Kenzan Seika container*

209

207

210

208

211

VASES IN CONTEMPORARY FLOWER ARRANGEMENT

VASES PLAY A MAJOR PART in the feeling produced by an arrangement. It may even be said that the vase establishes the mood for the entire arrangement, and this is particularly true in contemporary designing.

212. Ceramic containers for contemporary arrangements

Figures 212 and 213 show some of the vases in popular use today. Artists are now creating containers that can stand with the finest pieces of modern sculpture, and exhibitions of them are becoming increasingly popular in Japan. When an arrangement is made in such a vase, the object is to enhance the sculptural effect—the materials must not compete with the vase.

213. *Crystal and glass containers for contemporary arrangements. Concealing the mechanics of the arrangement in such cases requires an extra measure of care and ingenuity*

214. *An underwater arrangement capitalizing on the transparency of the crystal vase*

Among the newer styles of vases are those made of crystal or glass, materials rarely used in older styles of Ikebana. Thus, they lend themselves to the creation of a completely different mood. Employing a vase of this type, the designer may experiment by sinking flowers or branches into the water and then bending and molding them to achieve his effect. The transparency of the container pictured in Figure 214 lends great charm, and the fact that the materials are in water not only enhances their colors, but makes the linear elements appear to bend and curve in accordance with the design of the vase. The arrangement is composed of two gerbera flowers and a sprig of fern.

215. *Two brandy glasses create an unusual container*

Household Articles as Vases

At times the designer may choose to utilize very ordinary containers he finds around the house as vases for his arrangements. Many commonplace household articles take on surprising beauty when used imaginatively. All too often, students in Western countries bother too much over finding a container of Japanese appearance. The fact of the matter is that they might better reconsider the possibilities of the objects they are accustomed to seeing every day. Ordinary teapots,

crockery bowls, and crystal ware can spring to life when given the proper chance.

In Figure 215 we see two brandy glasses placed one atop the other to produce a novel design. The bottom glass is filled with orange, violet, and white fruit of an ornamental pepper plant. Yellow patrinia blossoms have been placed at a forward-leaning angle in the top glass. The delicate lines tying the masses of flowers together at the center of the arrangement give the impression of a skyrocket bursting in the night.

The arrangement in Figure 216 is composed merely of a champagne glass and a single giant chrysanthemum flower—an easy way of prolonging the life of an attractive blossom. The dead leaves and outer petals were discarded.

216. *A hollow-stemmed champagne goblet is ideal for a single large blossom*

217. *A vase inappropriate to the arrangement*

Choice of Vases

The selection of a vase to harmonize with an arrangement is always very important. How important is shown in a negative way in Figure 217, in which stalks and leaf, attractive in themselves, lose some of their appeal when placed in a container with sharp, definite angles. A more appropriate vase for this material is shown in Figure 218. Here the base of the container is rounded, so that it does not introduce confusing corners to the

218. *The same arrangement in an appropriate vase*

219. Roses and bare mulberry branches in an arrangement inspired by the vase

arrangement. Its mouth, however, has angles that blend in with the natural flow of the plants. In effect, the curving base harmonizes with the gently bending stems of the flowers, while the angular mouth emphasizes the cut of the monstera leaf.

The materials are three flameflower stalks (tritoma) and a single monstera leaf. The vase in Figure 217 is pale green, that in Figure 218 jet black.

Figure 219 is perhaps an extreme example, but with the wealth of interestingly designed vases available today, the designer will frequently find it possible to permit the container to play a more active role than is usual in traditional arrangements. The crinkly branches of a mulberry bush were aligned with the stripes of the long narrow vessel, and then pink roses, their leaves partly stripped off to reveal the straight lines of the stems, were added at appropriate points. The basic pattern is set by the vase itself.

With a little imagination the viewer can visualize balloons floating toward the sky—a whimsical suggestion that the artist may well have had in mind in fashioning his design.

BASES USED FOR FLOWER ARRANGEMENTS

THE FIRST FLOWER ARRANGEMENTS were simple offerings to the Buddha or deities of the Shinto religion. Since it was considered disgraceful merely to lay such flowers on the floor or on a shelf before the object of worship, pedestals on which the offering could be placed came into use. The type of stand utilized for this purpose is illustrated in Figure 220. Buddhist altar furniture influenced this type of stand, on which votive offerings of flowers were and still are placed.

Pedestals in these early years denoted varying ranks, and when a person of high social standing wished to display his status, it was customary to place a smaller base on top of the principal stand, as illustrated in Figure 221. In some Japanese schools, the use of the two stands now denotes the rank of the arranger.

Two variations of bases used with formal and semi-formal arrangements are shown in Figures 222 and 223. Stands were later drastically reduced to form bases like those in Figures 224 to 230. These simple, versatile bases are made in a variety of shapes and colors, and are commonly used today in the Seika and Moribana styles of arrangement. A basket, it may be noted, is never put on a base, a custom explained by the story of an early emperor who was so delighted with baskets introduced from China that he decreed them worthy to stand alone.

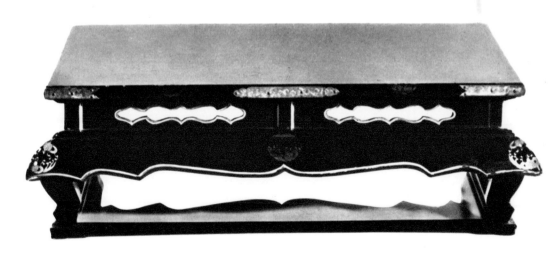

220. Black-lacquered, footed base of a type called kaban

221

222

221. *Vermillion-lacquered set of bases. The small top one is called an* usuban

222. *Black-lacquered stand of a type called* kadai, *inset with pieces of blue shell*

223. *Lacquered with gold powder in a technique known as* maki-e, *this type of base was originally used to hold an incense burner*

223

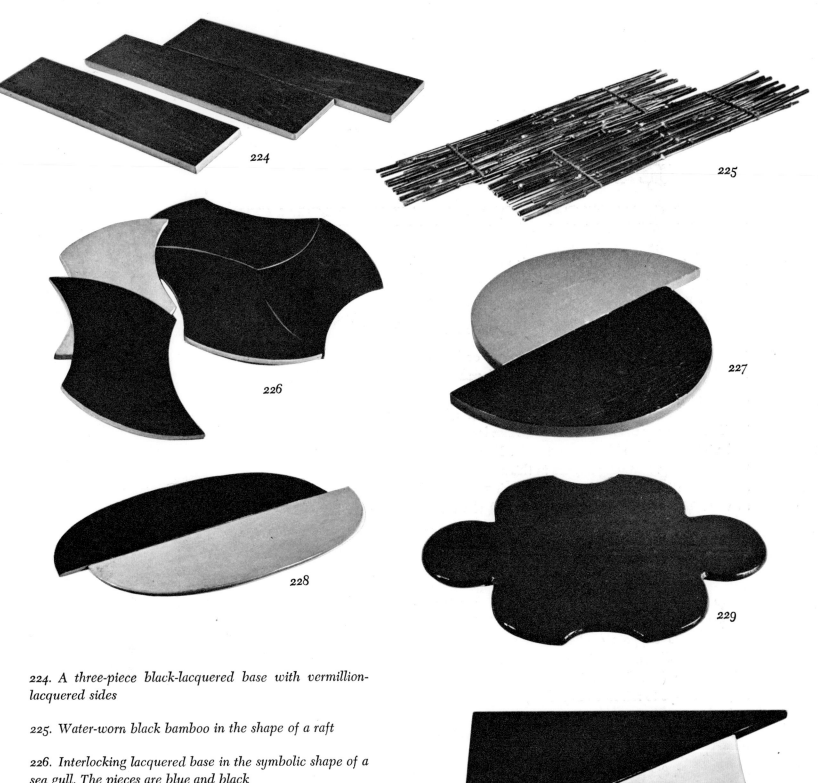

224. A three-piece black-lacquered base with vermillion-lacquered sides

225. Water-worn black bamboo in the shape of a raft

226. Interlocking lacquered base in the symbolic shape of a sea gull. The pieces are blue and black

227. Two-piece lacquered base, black and red, each piece representing a half moon

228. Two-piece lacquered oval base in black and red

229. Flower-shaped vermillion-lacquered base

230. Black and cream interlocking equilateral triangles

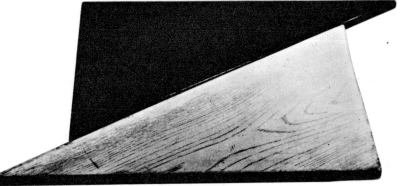

230

USEFUL TOOLS
FOR MAKING FLOWER ARRANGEMENTS

A CERTAIN AMOUNT OF EQUIPMENT is necessary for effective flower arrangement. While a great variety of gadgets and implements is available, the number of necessary tools is small.

On Figure 231, number *1* shows a saw which is particularly useful for cutting large branches or bamboo. A hatchet, numbered *2*, may also be employed for this purpose.

After a design has been completed, water sprayed in a fine mist over the flowers and branches lends a fresh and vivid feeling to the arrangement. Number *3* is a typical sprayer. Spraying flowers in this manner will not only make them look fresh, but will prolong their lives as well. With an attachment (number *4*) the sprayer can also be used to pump water directly into blossoms and stems. Such a pump is generally included in the kits of Ikebana equipment sold by various department stores and specialty shops around the country.

The type of clippers pictured in number *5* is normally used in flower arrangement, but variations of this tool, such as clippers containing a spring or having different handles, are also in common use.

Thin wire (number *6*) is essential. It is utilized in countless ways to reinforce branches, tie up flowers, and so forth.

Kenzan come in various shapes and sizes. The heavier the kenzan, the more useful it will be. Some are shown, numbered *7*, *8*, and *9*. Number *8* is a chain-type holder with detachable links, and number *9* shows also a small tool used to straighten kenzan prongs that are bent out of shape.

Number *10* shows a small sharp knife in an attractive wooden sheath, but any good sharp knife may be used.

A hand-operated siphon pump (number *11*) is used to remove water from large arrangements, so that fresh water may be added.

231. Useful tools for flower arranging:
  1 saw
  2 hatchet
  3 sprayer
  4 sprayer with pump attachment
  5 clippers
  6 wire
  7 large oblong and small round kenzan
  8 chain-type kenzan with detachable links
  9 tool used to straighten bent kenzan prongs
  10 knife
  11 siphon pump

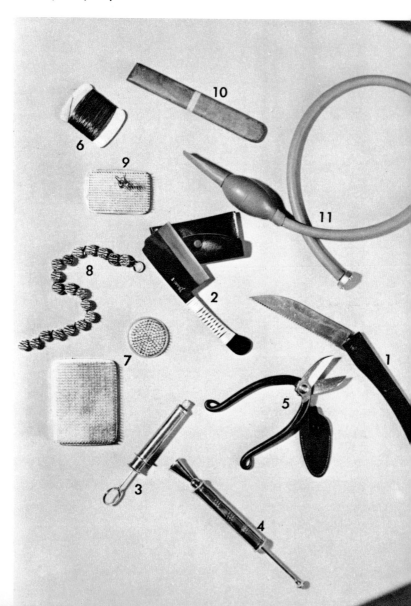

PART FOUR

Techniques and Imagination

in the Use of Materials

Over the centuries Japanese Ikebana artists have developed many methods of handling their materials. In recent years they have gone beyond these techniques and invented new ways of changing the character of their materials. Methods of drying, bleaching, and tinting may be mentioned here, as well as techniques for changing a material that is essentially linear to one that is essentially a mass or a plane—and vice versa. In this portion of our book we will show the reader both the basic necessities—how to bend branches and flower stems, how to secure materials in a deep vase or on a kenzan—and the most modern innovations in the handling of fresh and dried materials. Many of these methods may equally well be used in the creation of floral arrangements in traditions other than the Japanese.

FRESH MATERIALS

Three elements—branches, leaves, and flowers—have always been the basic raw materials for every Japanese flower arrangement, and they remain that today, although in modern abstract designs the branch, traditionally the major element of the trio, is often omitted.

Japan is blessed with four distinct seasons, and is particularly rich in natural materials for flower arrangements. Each season brings with it new flowers and colorful leaves to multiply the host of possible designs, and the Japanese consider an appropriate expression of the season to be of vital importance in any arrangement. But even in places where the seasons are not so pronounced as in Japan, it is possible to express some harmony with the time of year.

Some places have an abundance of beautiful flowers of every shape and color; others have practically no flowers at all. Even where there is a wealth of natural life, however, it is wiser to use only a few specimens in any single arrangement, capitalizing on the peculiar character and interest of those flowers, rather than flooding the arrangement with variety. Two or three leafy branches harmonized with a few flowers in a skillful and articulate manner produce far greater effect than complex and confusing mixtures.

During the winter months, or in areas where flowers are expensive the year round, branches of various types, or dry materials, can be combined with just a blossom or two in arrangements of great beauty.

232. *Key to the fresh materials pictured in colorplate, Figure 233:*

    1 *Enkianthus japonicus*
    2 *willow*
    3 *New Zealand flax*
    4 *hydrangea*
    5 *lily*
    6 *Japanese cypress*
    7 *flameflower (tritoma)*
    8 *fan of iris leaves*
    9 *oleander*
   10 *sunflower*
   11 *pine*
   12 *orange chrysanthemum*
   13 *pink chrysanthemum*
   14 *bellflower*
   15 *white iris*
   16 *asparagus fern*
   17 *bletilla (orchid) leaf*
   18 *liatris*
   19 *dahlia*

OPPOSITE: 233. *Some fresh plants often used in Ikebana. See Figure 232 for key*

SELECTING AND TRIMMING FRESH BRANCHES

IN JAPANESE FLOWER ARRANGING, flowers do not necessarily occupy the center of attention. On the contrary, they are often subordinated to other elements and, even when they form the focal point, they are usually combined with branches, vines, or leaves. Of particular importance are branches. Japanese florists generally prepare attractive leafy branches for quick and easy use by Ikebana designers, but it may be well here to outline the methods commonly employed when the arranger must prepare the branches himself. The branches of any tree may be used, of course, but those with fairly small leaves are generally the most suitable.

In the following pages we will take the reader step by step through the selection, trimming, and arranging of branches from three different trees.

A Japanese Maple Branch

In early spring, the leaves of the Japanese maple tree are a vivid green; in the fall, they are crimson. Green or red, they are full of rich possibilities for Ikebana.

234. A Japanese maple tree. Dotted line indicates the branch selected

190

235. *Dotted line indicates* shin *(the main branch)*

angles may be found on page 233, and instructions on making this variation are given in Lesson Eight of Part Five.)

One of the smaller branches trimmed off in the shaping process is then used as the *tai* (*C*) (third main branch), to produce the essential triangle found in all flower arrangements. It leans 75 degrees to the right and 70 degrees toward the front. To this basic design we have added red star lilies, bellflowers, and patrinia. The arrangement is now complete. Figure 238 shows an arrangement in this variation made in a Moribana-style container.

Careful examination of the tree (Figure 234) reveals that the branch indicated in the photograph would be the best suited to the design we have in mind. The chosen branch is cut away at the point indicated by the dotted line.

As it is, the branch is too long and too full. We must decide (Figure 235) which of the several shoots is to be the *shin* (main branch of the arrangement), and then trim away the rest.

Now the main branch must be fashioned for display (Figure 236). Further trimming is in order, but rather than clip away foliage equally overall, clumps of leaves are left at crucial points along the branch, as shown in Figure 237, in order to reveal and emphasize the main lines of the branch. These lines, along with the clusters of foliage, are the most important factors in this material. The lower shoot in this picture sweeps down below the branch proper. It should not be trimmed away, since it can be used as the *soe* (second main branch).

The branch has now been shaped to serve as the major part of the arrangement (Figure 238). The *soe* (*B*), which, if left alone, would be behind the *shin* (*A*), has been partly cut at the lower end and bent toward the front. The *shin* should slant 45 degrees to the left of vertical as well as 45 degrees toward the front of the arrangement. The resulting design is representative of the third variation of the *Gyō* (semiformal) Moribana style. The *soe* slants 70 degrees left of vertical and 60 degrees toward the front or face of the arrangement. (Detailed information on how to calculate various

236. *Main branch further trimmed. The lower shoot will become* soe *(the second main branch)*

237. *The fully trimmed branch*

238. *Here we see the completed arrangement, with red star lilies, bellflowers, and patrinia added to the design.* A *is* shin (*the main branch*), B *is* soe (*the second main branch*), *and* C *is* tai (*the third main branch*)

A Wild Oak Branch

The branches of the wild oak tree are very flexible, and the leaves are of an ideal shape for use in flower arrangements. The dotted line in Figure 239 indicates the branch to be used for the arrangement.

A close examination of the branch (Figure 240) reveals an interesting crook and a fine curve (*A*). Part *A* will become the *shin* (main branch), and part *C* the *tai* (third main branch). Part *B* can be bent around to form the *soe* (second main branch).

Part *A* (Figure 241) has an unusual abundance of leaves along its entire length. It must be trimmed. In Figure 242 this has been done. The denser clusters of leaves were kept, the lesser sections removed.

The portion of *C* (Figure 243) with the attractive curve is cut out to be used as the *tai*.

In Figure 244 we see the finished arrangement. The branches are in place and tiger lilies have been added to complete the design. The resulting arrangement is representative of the basic arrangement in the *Shin* (formal) style of Moribana, made in its left-hand form, for which detailed instructions may be found in Lesson Four of Part Five.

Several important factors should be kept in mind when searching for raw materials for Ikebana. An overall examination of a particular branch may reveal graceful movements in the branch and attractive clusters of leaves along its length. Attention should be given to the shape of the leaves and to the way in which they are attached to the branch. The natural flow of the branches of almost any tree will usually yield some attractive feature.

It is important to remember that whenever a branch is clipped from a tree it becomes but an insignificant fragment of nature. Through the genius of the arranger it must be fashioned in such a way that it evokes an image of the whole tree.

239. A wild oak tree. Dotted line indicates the branch selected

193

240. *Part* A *will become the* shin, *part* B *the* soe, *and part* C *the* tai *branch*

241. *The* shin *branch (A in Figure 240) shown before the trimming*

242. *The* shin *branch after trimming*

243. *The* tai *branch (C in Figure 240) is cut out as indicated*

244. *The completed arrangement, with tiger lilies added to the design. A is the* shin *branch, B the* soe, *and C the* tai

245. *The branch of a wild silverberry tree before trimming*

246. *The central branch has been cut out, leaving a sweeping arc*

A Wild Silverberry Branch

The wild silverberry tree, with its deep-green leaves and bright-red, ripe berries, offers exquisite material for flower arrangement.

In Figure 245 we see the branch as it was clipped from the tree. It has two distinctive features: the straight, central core that stretches the length of the branch, and the beautifully curved secondary branch that rises upward from the center and then sweeps downward in a graceful arc. Generally a branch laden with fruit presents an interesting curve that should be capitalized on in planning an attractive arrangement.

The central branch having been trimmed away for later use and needless twigs disposed of, the sweeping arc of the curved branch is revealed (Figure 246). Then, leaving as many berries as possible attached to the branch, excess foliage is trimmed away (Figure 247).

In Figure 248 we see the finished arrangement. The long, central curved branch has been used for the *shin*

247. *The fully trimmed branch. Excess foliage has been removed, berries retained*

196

248. *Here we see the finished arrangement, with chrysanthe-mums added to the design. A is the* shin *branch, B the* soe, *and C the* tai

(A). Some of the material clipped from the original branch has been used in forming the *soe* (B) and the *tai* (C), and moderate-sized chrysanthemums have been added as complements. The resulting arrangement is an example of the second variation of the informal style of Moribana, made in its left-hand form. See Lesson Ten of Part Five.

It is important to make the most of any individual and appealing features of materials being prepared for an arrangement. Before any trimming is done, the branch should be carefully studied with an eye to seeking out proper parts for the *shin*, the *soe*, and the *tai*. At the same time, the arranger should be thinking of suitable flowers that will harmonize with the branches.

BENDING BRANCHES AND FLOWER STEMS

WHILE BRANCHES ARE SOMETIMES USABLE in their natural form, more often they must be bent and shaped to achieve the exact angles and shapes desired. Some branches are easily manipulated, but most either break when being shaped or spring back to their original form when the pressure is released. In this chapter we will discuss various methods of making incisions to facilitate bending.

Figures 249 and 250 show a simple way of bending a branch of medium thickness. With a pair of garden shears a notch is cut out on one side of the branch, which is then bent backward on either side of the cut. The gentle arc that results when a series of such notches has been made is illustrated in Figure 251. Leave part of the stem and the bark completely intact. Severing the stem down to the bare bark, or snipping the bark around the circumference of the branch will cut off the supply of moisture to the extremities of the material.

When thicker branches are to be shaped, a large notch such as that shown in Figure 252 may be made with a knife, a saw, or a pair of large garden shears. A triangular wedge larger than the piece removed is then inserted into the notch, forcing the branch to bend to the desired angle (Figure 253). A series of such operations will produce a graceful curve similar to that of our first method, or even a very extreme angle if that is desired.

A variation of this method is to make a diagonal cut in the branch and force a wedge into the slot, as shown in Figure 254.

Since scissors will crush very delicate materials, the stems of flowers and thin branches or leaves must be carefully shaped by hand. Gentle pressure with the tips of one's fingers on the parts to be bent will generally produce the desired effect. Figures 255 and 256 illustrate good ways of handling such stems.

249. Cutting a notch in a Japanese maple branch

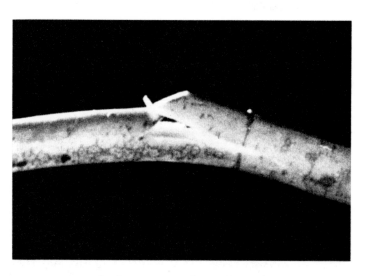

250. Bending the branch on either side of the cut

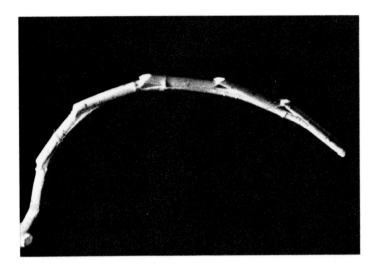

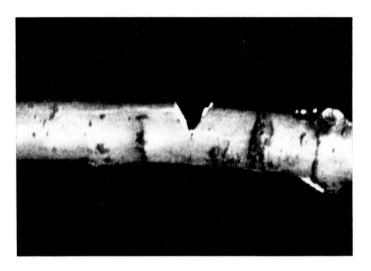

251. *The branch bent into a curve after a series of notches has been made*

252. *A method especially good for thick branches is to cut out a large notch*

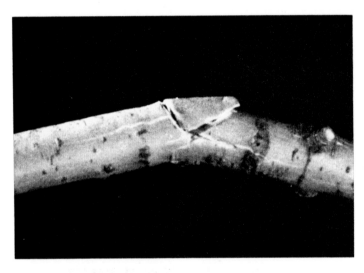

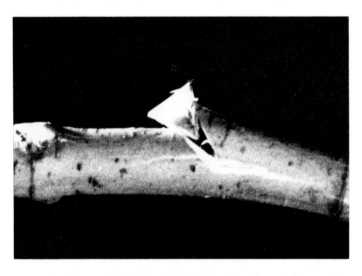

253. *A triangular wedge larger than the piece removed is inserted into the notch, forcing the branch to bend*

254. *Another method for thick branches is to make a diagonal cut and force a wedge into the slot*

255, 256. *Proper ways to bend delicate branches. Flower stems are manipulated in the same way*

THE IMAGINATIVE USE OF FRESH MATERIALS

OFTEN A LITTLE JUDICIOUS MANIPULATION, or even drastic surgery, is required to bring out the best features of a material in the setting for which it is being prepared.

First we see a ti leaf (Figures 257 to 259) that is too large for the kenzan. But trimmed down, a very simple yet very appealing effect is achieved. Experimentation of this sort with various leaves will produce many fascinating results.

In our second group of illustrations (Figures 260 to 262) we have some thistles. The flowers are beautiful, but the leaves are not. The unattractive leaves are removed, revealing that the remaining stems are equally unattractive, so we cut them off close to the base of the

257. *A ti leaf too large for its kenzan*

258, 259. *The leaf cut down to the right proportions*

257

258

259

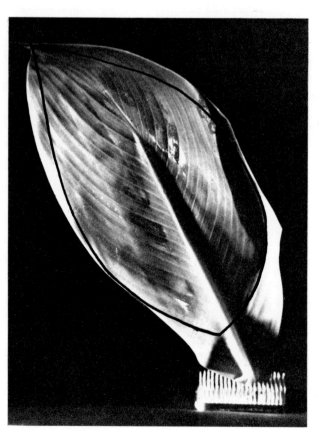

260. *A group of thistles, with beautiful flowers and ugly leaves*

261. *The leaves have been removed, but the stems are equally unattractive*

262. *The stems have been cut down and the blossoms attractively massed*

blossoms, leaving only the flowers to be displayed. To create a mass of color and design, a large number of flowers is needed. If not enough blossoms are available, attractive leaves may be added.

Our next piece of material is the long narrow leaf (Figure 263). The effect of simply splitting the leaf several times lengthwise is pictured in Figure 264. More intricate designs might be produced by bending or curling the delicate strands of the split leaf, or by tying them together in various shapes and forms.

Another attractive way of handling a leaf of this type is to tilt it slightly and place it on a kenzan, as illustrated in Figure 265. Note the manner in which the bottom of the leaf has been cut.

Sometimes leaves that are excellent for arranging are ruined when their flower is cut. Gladioli are a good

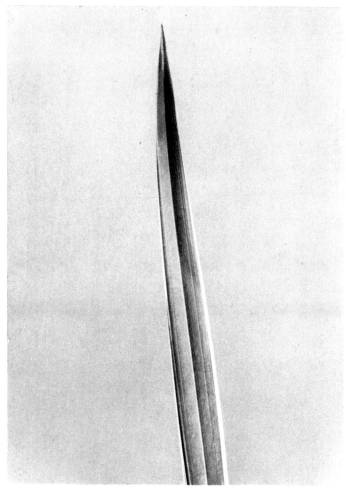

263

264

265

263. A leaf of New Zealand flax

264. The same leaf split several times lengthwise

265. A New Zealand flax leaf cut into a squared-off V-shape at the bottom and placed on the kenzan at a slight tilt

example. Many people snip off the surrounding leaves, as shown in Figure 266, in their haste to get at the flower. The result is a number of useless truncated leaves (Figure 267). It is much wiser to separate the leaves from the stalk and to clip only the flower away, as illustrated in Figure 268. Careful cutting of the flower preserves an abundance of useful leaves (Figure 269).

Our next three figures illustrate what happens when

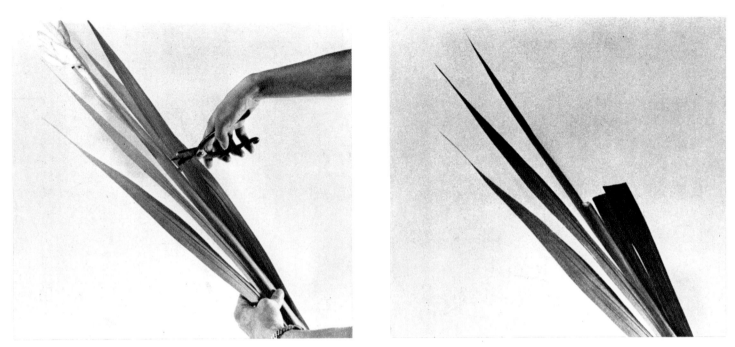

266, 267. *The wrong way to cut a flower. Some good leaves have been ruined*

268, 269. *The proper way to separate flower stems from leaves before cutting preserves a number of useful leaves*

270

271

272

270. *Sprays of cedar forced into an unnatural pattern*

271. *The same cedar leaves attractively arranged*

272. *Emphasizing the stems of small chrysanthemums results in a ludicrous arrangement*

characteristics of the materials at hand are ignored. The designer of the arrangement in Figure 270 had some perfectly good sprays of cedar, but he forced them into an unnatural pattern. A second designer, by bringing out the natural features of the same leaves, produced the attractive arrangement pictured in Figure 271. Even in the creation of a simple design, each flower and branch or leaf should be carefully arranged so that none of the natural beauty and character of the material is lost.

The designer of the arrangement pictured in Figure 272 tried to bring out the definite lines in his materials, but he completely ignored the beauty of the flowers themselves. The resulting arrangement is ludicrous.

The art of Ikebana requires both a love for natural beauty and keen judgment as to what ought or ought not to be preserved. Armed with these qualities, the artist need not hesitate to approach his task with boldness, trimming unflinchingly when trimming is in order, but always with a view to bringing out the best in the plants at hand.

Our experiments with branches of Euonymus alata (spindle tree) will show the wide range of imaginative

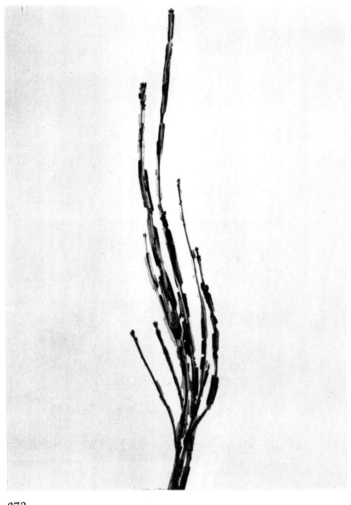

273

274

275

273. *A branch of Euonymus alata (spindle tree) in its natural state*

274. *The smaller branches have been bent and tied together*

275. *The branch is anchored upside down on a kenzan, and some of the smaller branches are bent outward*

ways in which material can be manipulated to express both the designer's wishes and the basic characteristics of the material.

In Figure 273 we see a euonymus branch in its natural state. One approach is to bend the smaller branches and tie a few ends together (Figure 274) Another is to turn the branches upside down, anchor them to a kenzan, and gently bend the smaller branches outward (Figure 275). A third approach is to bend the smaller branches sharply at strategic points (Figure

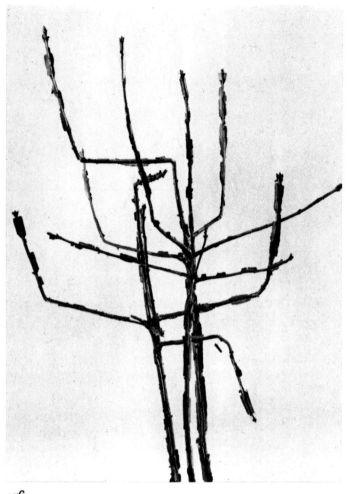

276

277

278

276. *The smaller branches have been bent up at strategic points*

277. *All the smaller branches have been broken off and tied together in a different arrangement*

278. *A combination of all the methods previously illustrated*

276). Still another method is to break off all the small branches and tie them together in a different arrangement (Figure 277).

A combination of all these methods (Figure 278) yields a result that is abstract in feeling and suitable for use in freestyle arrangements.

Arrangements Stressing Lines, Planes, or Masses

There are three basic categories of materials: those that reveal definite line, such as the silverberry branch illustrated in Figure 279; those whose planes are their most arresting feature—a caladium leaf (Figure 280) is a good example; and those that present a mass, either of color or shape, or both. The patrinia in Figure 281 reveals a mass of color.

Before trimming or shaping materials for an arrangement, decide which of these characteristics they will be used to display: If line is to be emphasized, eliminate all leaves or twigs that may hide its movement. If planes are to be stressed, be careful not to allow lines or masses to distract from this. (The leaves of tropical plants are among the most attractive materials for displaying planes.)

In fashioning floral masses there is a wide range of choice. Thin, pliable, linear materials may be wound up into an attractive mass; a cluster of small twigs and leaves may be gathered together; or a colorful bouquet of assorted blossoms may be assembled.

An arrangement based on line is shown in Figure 282. The designer has chosen to emphasize the harmony between the red-brown bark and the silver-soft buds of the pussy willow. The flowing lines of the branches have been crossed and recrossed in interesting patterns to capitalize on their gentle movement. Pale-orange gladioli inserted at the base of the arrangement tie the whole together, and the yellow-brown vase provides balance as well as additional color.

Figure 283 illustrates an arrangement emphasizing planes. A dark-green leaf of a rubber tree occupies the center, where it forms a powerful focal point. Near the base, a pale-yellow rose has been added to provide color, and in the rear, several cattails give contrast to the leaf. Note how the cattails point off at the same

279. A silverberry branch. Line is the main characteristic

280. A caladium leaf, showing an interesting plane

281. A spray of patrinia. Mass is the main characteristic, both in form and in color

279
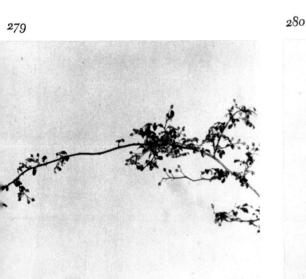

280

281

283

284

282. *Pussy willow and gladioli in an arrangement stressing line*

283. *A rubber tree leaf, a rose, and some cattails in an arrangement stressing planes*

284. *Lycoris blossoms and a New Zealand flax leaf in an arrangement stressing mass*

angle to the right of vertical as the core of the rubber leaf points to the left. The vase is a dull reddish orange.

Deep-red lycoris blossoms have been gathered together to form the principal mass for the arrangement in Figure 284, which emphasizes mass. A green-and-yellow-striped leaf of New Zealand flax has been split lengthwise and placed in the white vase in such a way as to echo the lines of the vase, while at the same time lending a flowing movement. The Nageire vase is of recent design.

Changing
the Natural Emphasis
of Materials

There are many methods by which the natural emphasis of a material can be changed and another characteristic brought out. Once the general idea is understood, the range of possibilities is almost limitless, and in such experimentation the real joy of flower arrangement is born.

While the fatsia leaf in Figure 285 possesses a natural

beauty which is most apparent in its planes, it also offers opportunities for startling departures. In Figure 286 we see one of the patterns that may be created when the designer, wishing to utilize the lines as well as the planes of the leaf, cuts part away. Or the designer, wishing to use only the lines, may cut all but the veins away, producing an entirely different effect (Figure 287).

In Figure 288 we see a branch of the phoenix tree, a member of the feather palm family. The delicate drooping leaves bring to mind the plumage of a peacock. The basic emphasis is linear.

One way in which the many fine leaves of the phoenix may be clipped to fashion an attractive plane is illustrated in Figure 289. Or the same leaf may be used to create a series of planes while still preserving the basic lines of the raw material (Figure 290). A side view of

285. A Fatsia japonica leaf in its natural state. The emphasis is on planes

286. The same leaf trimmed to stress lines as well as planes

287. The leaf further trimmed to show lines alone

285

286

287

288. *A phoenix branch in its natural state*

289. *The same branch clipped to stress one plane*

290. *The same branch further trimmed to create a series of planes while preserving the basic line*

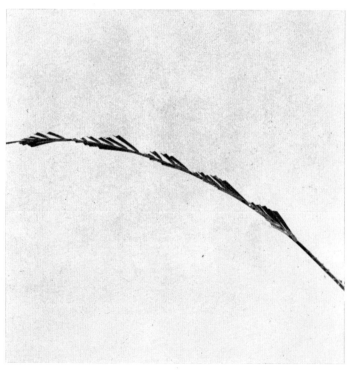

291. *A side view of the branch seen in Figure 290, showing a switch back to pure line*

210

292. *A gladiolus in its natural state. The emphasis is on line*

the same leaf reveals an interesting switch back to the purely linear emphasis (Figure 291).

Now we will see how line can be transformed into mass. In Figure 292 we see a gladiolus. The blossoms of this plant are very beautiful in themselves, but in their natural state they are arranged in a sweeping line which is the basic characteristic of the plant. To eliminate this line we have snipped off the individual blossoms, being careful to cut them as close to the base of the flowers as possible. The best type of cut is demonstrated in Figures 293 and 294. A mass of color and design may then be created by inserting the separate blossoms in a kenzan (Figure 295).

293, 294. *The blossoms are cut from the stem as close to their bases as possible*

295. *The cut blossoms are inserted in a kenzan to make an arrangement emphasizing mass*

211

PREPARATION OF DRY MATERIALS

IN THIS SECTION WE WILL DISCUSS various methods of bleaching, coloring, and drying plant materials.

In Figure 298 a common household spray can is being used to apply lacquer to some ferns. For very large surfaces, to which a considerable quantity of lacquer or paint must be applied, an air compressor may be used, but for smaller arrangements the small sprayer is quite adequate. It applies color quickly and easily, and the treatment prolongs the life of the plant. When a sprayer is not available, a brush like the one in Figure 299 will do the job.

At far left in Figure 300 we see a twig in its natural state. Next to it is one painted white. The last twig was also painted, and popcorn was affixed to it while it was drying. The painted popcorn at far right is attached to wires. All sorts of different materials may be attached to twigs or lengths of wire in this way for special effects.

Leaves from a rubber tree, tassels from millet, and

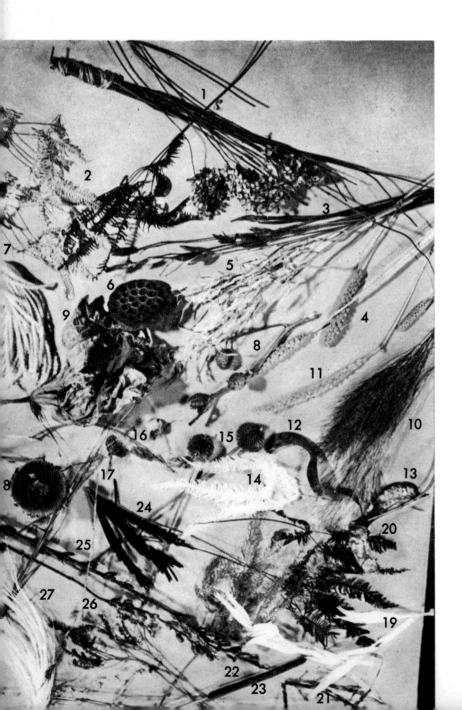

296. *Key to the dried materials pictured in colorplate, Figure 297:*

1 *hydrangea*
2 *fern, bleached and dyed*
3 *Japanese iris seed pods*
4 *millet*
5 *mustard cress seed pods*
6 *lotus seed pod*
7 *miscanthus*
8 *jimson weed (thorn apple) seed pods*
9 *lotus leaf*
10 *broom, bleached and dyed*
11 *millet, seeds shaken off, leaving beards*
12 *honey locust pod, natural color*
13 *honey locust pod, gilded*
14 *fern, bleached and dyed*
15 *globe thistle*
16 *milkweed seed pods*
17 *bearded grasses*
18 *sunflower center*
19 *okra, bleached*
20 *fern, dyed*
21 *Euonymus alata (spindle tree)*
22 *cattail*
23 *bamboo stems, painted gold*
24 *male fern fronds, dyed*
25 *sesame branch with seeds*
26 *coleus branch with seeds*
27 *broom, bleached*

OPPOSITE: 297. *Some dried materials, natural and treated, that are useful in Ikebana. See Figure 296 for key*

298

298. *Ferns being sprayed with lacquer*

299. *Leaves being painted with a small brush*

300. *From left to right: a twig in its natural state; a twig painted white; a painted twig with popcorn attached; popcorn painted and attached to wires*

301. *Leaves from a rubber tree, one fresh, the other two dried in the shade*

302. *Cattails and millet dried in the shade*

299

300

301

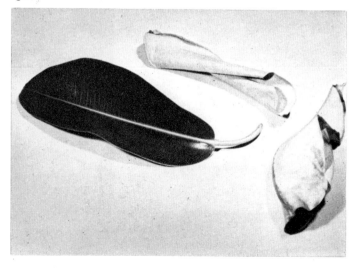

302

303

304

305

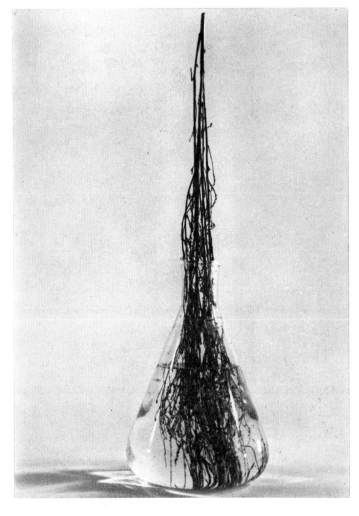

303. *A broom cypress growing by a stream*

304. *A branch of broom cypress dried in the shade*

305. *Broom cypress inserted in a flask of bleach*

stalks of cattail, all dried in the shade, are pictured in Figures 301 and 302. Such materials may also be dried directly in the sunlight or in a dryer, but the best method is to dry them slowly in the shade, letting nature and time do the work.

In Figure 303 we see a broom cypress growing by a stream. Next we see a branch that has been cut from it and dried in the shade (Figure 304). Figure 305 shows the branch inserted into a flask of bleach. Glass, enamel, or plastic may be used, but not metal (full-strength chlorine bleaches will eat through metal). Soak for about twelve hours, until the material turns an off-white, grayish color. Although some materials, such as thick leaves, may take longer to reach this stage, it is wise to watch carefully toward the end of the twelve-hour period. Soaking longer than absolutely necessary tends to decay the material.

To obtain a pure white color a boiling bleach method is used. Great care must be taken to assure proper ven-

215

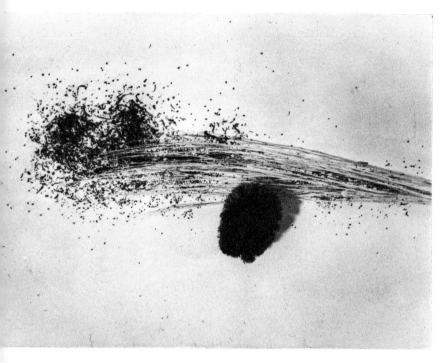

tilation. Sufficient bleach to cover the material completely is brought to the boil, again in an enamel or flameproof glass container, over a medium-low flame. The material is added after the bleach has come to the boil and is cooked for approximately four hours. Add water to replace the bleach as it evaporates.

This method produces a pure white because the heat releases the waxes which otherwise prevent the bleach from penetrating completely.

After soaking or boiling, wash the material thoroughly in cold water and hang it up to dry. The leaves may be left on or, when the material is dry, the branches may be stripped completely with a stiff brush such as the one pictured in Figure 306.

Driftwood scrubbed by swirling ocean waters (Figure 307) and weather-beaten deadwood (Figure 308), pre-bleached by nature, present exciting possibilities for any flower arrangement.

306. Broom cypress bleached, dried, and stripped of leaves

307, 308. Driftwood and deadwood can be used for arrangements in any style

216

THE IMAGINATIVE USE OF DRY MATERIALS

Combining
Dry and Fresh Materials

ALTHOUGH FRESH FLOWERS, branches, and leaves are the staples of Ikebana, the so-called dry materials are of great value, especially in the freer styles of modern flower arrangement. Remember that dry materials include not only withered or dead plants, but all plants that have been artificially bleached or colored.

In recent years, combinations of dry and fresh materials have become increasingly popular in Japan. Proper harmonization of these materials will often produce a work of art that is both original and beautiful.

An unusual orange-red vase with a wide mouth has been used to set the stage for "Fawn," the amusing arrangement pictured in Figure 309. Light-brown dried rubber tree leaves provide weight, cream-yellow roses and yellow-striped, split leaves of New Zealand flax supply color.

In Figure 310 we see wisteria branches stripped of their bark, dried, and hand-curled in hot water. The creamy-white branches are combined with pink thistle flowers in a blue dripped-glaze ceramic container.

Contrasting textures and colors are used to dramatic

309. "Fawn," a contemporary arrangement combining dried rubber tree leaves with fresh roses and New Zealand flax

310. *Dried, curled wisteria branches combined with fresh thistles*

by the vessel, but dry materials may also be displayed without any vase at all. The designer may simply attach legs to his creation or suspend it from the ceiling. Because dry materials do not require water, they open many avenues of expression not possible with their fresh counterparts. Used here are strands of bleached broom, a dried artichoke flower, and the bare stems on which coconut flowers grow.

When dry materials are used in abstract arrangements of this sort, they should not be placed in the way one would use for similar fresh materials. A dried branch, for example, ought not to appear in a natural position; instead, it should be placed upside down or at an unusual angle. Rather than simulate a natural appearance, it should look like the man-made creation it really is.

effect in the arrangement shown in Figure 311. Dried pampas grass and a deep-green, linear kind of cypress are accented with the brilliant colors of the bird-of-paradise flowers at the right. The vase is white ceramic.

Using Dry Materials Alone

Dry materials painted in bright colors are often gayer and more cheerful than fresh materials. At the same time, dried or bleached leaves, branches, or flowers may be used to produce eerie effects of a sort that cannot be achieved solely with fresh materials. The arrangement shown in Figure 312, for example, is almost the negation of natural floral beauty. It resembles some ghostly reptile.

In this case, the mood of the arrangement is enhanced

311. *Dried pampas grass combined with fresh cypress and bird-of-paradise flowers*

218

312. *Bleached broom, a dried artichoke flower, and the bare stems on which coconut flowers grow. Notice the dead fly that has been glued to the coconut stem at top right*

SOME TECHNIQUES FROM
THE CLASSIC RIKKA STYLE, COMBINING FRESH
AND DRY MATERIALS

THE CLASSIC RIKKA ARRANGEMENT pictured in Figure 313 will call to mind Part One, where this and other such arrangements were illustrated and discussed. Here we will briefly outline various principles and techniques used in these, the most difficult of all Ikebana arrangements. Although few readers will attempt to create a six-foot-high classic Rikka, these techniques can be put to good use in many other styles.

The reader may well remember the graceful movement and noble lines of the seemingly fresh young pine branches in the arrangement reprinted here. Although it is difficult to believe, the foundations of such an ar-

rangement are often composed of dead wood to which fresh pine needles are attached.

Figure 314 shows the same arrangement with the *dō*, the main core or body of the design, removed. Once this has been done, it can be seen that the vase is filled with straw to secure the long pine branches.

313. A classic arrangement in the formal Rikka style

314. The same arrangement with its core removed

315. The arrangement completely stripped

313

314

315

316. *The core seen from front left*

317. *Close-up view of the core*

Next we see the arrangement completely stripped (Figure 315), illustrating the extent to which man has used his skills in fashioning the design. The nails that supported slips of fresh pine needles are now clearly visible along the naked branches. To keep the needles from drying out too quickly they are sprayed with sugar water, clear lacquer, or sake (Japanese rice wine).

Figure 316 shows the core of the arrangement as seen from front left. The two black poles in the immediate foreground are composed of aspidistra leaves wrapped around tightly bound bunches of straw. Into these poles the small metal cones shown in Figure 321 are firmly secured. Later they will be filled with water and used as vases to prolong the lives of the fresh flowers. Note also the way in which the many small stubs of pine branches have been wired and nailed together and wedged between the poles.

The points at which they have been joined, as well as the many nails along the way, are clearly visible in Figure 317, which shows some of the twisted branches at close range. One portion of this branch is shown completely disassembled (Figure 318). A careful

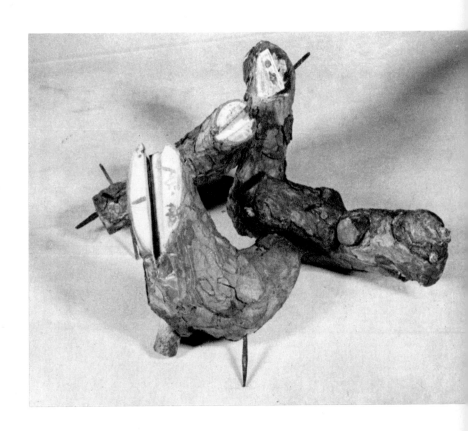

318. *A portion of the core completely disassembled*

examination of the ends of these stubs reveals that "male" and "female" connections have been carved out to assure a perfect join.

Figure 319 illustrates how the beautiful branches of a Rikka arrangement are artificially constructed by the artist. The tiny slips of needles are carefully wired, one by one, to each of the supporting branches. It is difficult to conceive of the time and effort that must be put into such an arrangement. Some notion of the attention to detail that goes into it can be gained from a close study of Figure 320. Beneath the petals of the chrysanthemum, center, a circle of wire prevents the flower from drooping. In addition, a strong wire has been secured along the length of the stem and more wire spiraled up its length to keep it absolutely firm. Finally, each separate leaf was painstakingly wired to the stem. This laborious process was then repeated for each of the branches flanking the flower. The small galvanized steel cones used to hold water for the flowers are shown in Figure 321.

319. One of the pine branches partly assembled

320. Blossom and branches carefully wired into shape

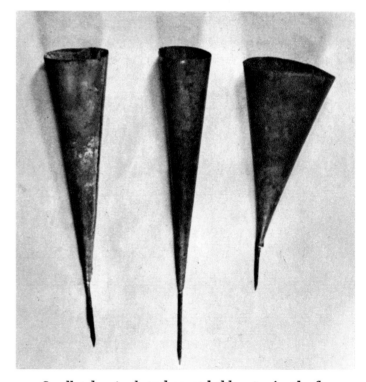

321. Small galvanized steel cones hold water for the flowers

FIXING STEMS SECURELY ON A KENZAN

322. *A branch too thick to be easily placed on a kenzan*

THE USE OF THE KENZAN permits the designer to experiment with all sorts of materials, regardless of their size, weight, firmness, or thickness. Some branches and flower stems are difficult to place securely on the kenzan, but there are many methods of simplifying this task.

To secure a branch as thick as that pictured in Figures 322 and 323, a great deal of strength is required. The task is easy, however, if numerous cuts are made in the end of the branch before it is pressed onto the needles of the holder.

Clipping the end of the branch diagonally (Figure 324) will also ease the job of securing larger branches. When an extremely large branch is to be used, cut out a diagonal notch above the first cut, to achieve a balance in the weight distribution (Figure 325).

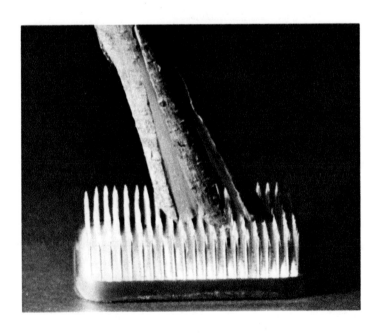

323. *The stem end is split into several sections, making it easy to press onto the needles of the kenzan*

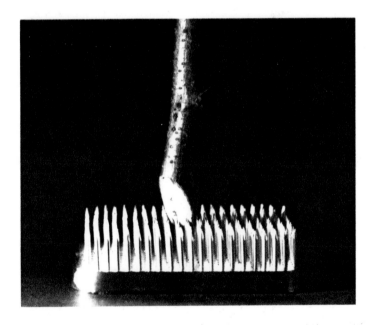

324. *Clipping the stem end on the diagonal is a useful technique when dealing with larger branches*

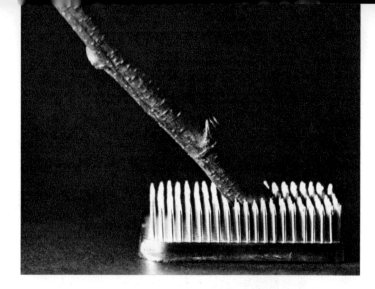

325. *Cutting a diagonal notch above the first cut achieves a balanced weight distribution*

326. *Its stem end cut parallel to the surface of the kenzan, a branch is securely placed at a sharp slant*

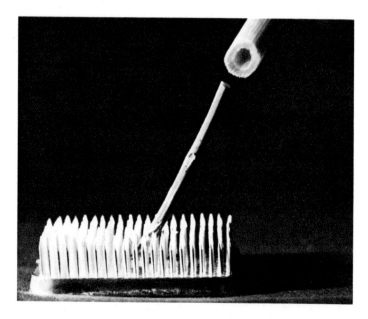

327, 328. *To secure hollow or very soft-core stems, a small solid stick is placed on the kenzan and the stem fitted over it*

When a branch is to slant very sharply, hold it at the desired angle and cut off the end parallel to the surface of the kenzan (Figure 326). This increases the surface of the stem that will be pierced by the needles, making for greater stability. Making lengthwise cuts, as we did in our first method, will make it easier to press the branch down on the needles.

Branches with a hollow or very soft core can be difficult to handle. A small, solid stick, such as that pictured in Figure 327, may be fixed onto the kenzan at the desired angle. The end of the branch to be displayed is then cut at the same angle and fitted over the supporting stick (Figure 328).

A thin, top-heavy branch may be stabilized by reversing our last process. A length of firm, hollow stem such as cane, dahlia, or amaryllis is cut at the proper angle and placed on the kenzan to receive the smaller branch (Figure 329).

If the branch to be displayed has broken or bent, strengthen it by wiring a splint to the main stalk (Figure 330). Should the plant be top-heavy or the stem too weak, wire a supporting stick to it at the base (Figure 331).

When a large number of thin stems are to be placed on the kenzan, bind them together with wire to produce the effect of a single thicker stem (Figure 332).

224

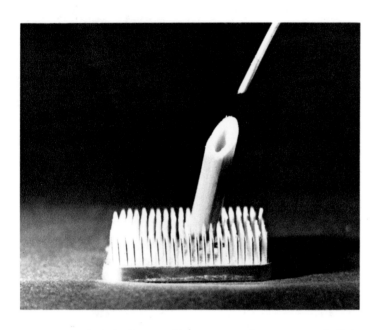

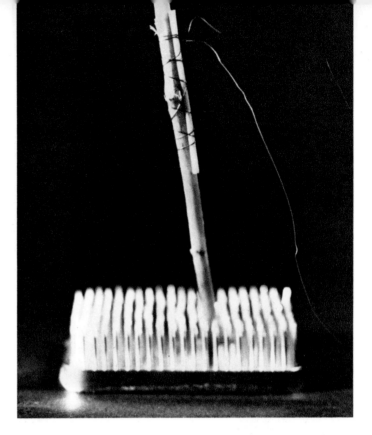

329. *To stabilize thin, top-heavy branches, a firm, hollow stem is placed on the kenzan and the branch fitted into it*

330. *A splint can be wired to a bent or broken stem in order to strengthen it*

331. *A supporting stick wired to the base of a weak or top-heavy branch*

332. *A number of thin stems wired together to form a single base*

FIXING STEMS SECURELY IN A TALL VASE

THE ART OF INSERTING and securing materials in the vase is of vital importance. In this section we shall discuss several of the methods commonly employed. Experimentation along similar lines will yield other useful means for solving special problems.

When a branch or flower is placed in a vase it comes to rest in a stable position (Figure 333). The designer may simply capitalize on the security of this position for some branches and arrange the rest of his materials around them.

Many plants have a natural resilience that can be utilized to keep them in place. In Figure 334 the lower end of a branch has been bent upward to act as a spring holding the upper part of the branch in a fixed position.

When the branch is to lean sharply to the side, the

333. A flower placed naturally in a vase comes to rest in a stable position

334. The lower end of a branch is bent up to act as a spring holding the upper part in position

335. *The lower part of a branch is bent down and wedged against the side of the vase to achieve a sharp slant*

336. *A small forked stick may be used to hold a branch in place*

337, 338. *A small stick may be tied near the base of a stem and fitted snugly into the vase at a point near its mouth*

lower part of its stem may be bent down and wedged against the side of the vase (Figure 335). Or it may be held in place by means of a small forked stick (Figure 336).

A branch can also be firmly secured by tying a small stick across it near its base (Figure 337). The stick should fit snugly into the vase at a point near the mouth. If the sides of the vase slant outward, as in Figure 338, trim the ends of the stick to assure a perfect fit. It is best to position the branch in such a way that its lower end rests against the side of the container. Sometimes, when a single crosswise stick does not provide adequate stability, two sticks may be tied to the main branch (Figure 339). These crosspieces may also be used in securing smaller branches and flowers in the arrangement.

NOTE: A section on keeping cut flowers fresh, which might logically be found here, has been printed as a separate appendix and placed at the back of the volume for the greater convenience of the reader.

339. *A crosspiece made of two sticks assures great stability*

PART FIVE

A Basic Course

in the Moribana Style

THE TWELVE FORMS AND VARIATIONS
OF MORIBANA

THE FIRST STEP IN MASTERING the Moribana style is to learn a series of basic arrangements. These arrangements, which are designed to introduce the student not only to this particular style but to the Japanese approach to flowers as a whole, involve such basic matters as the effective presentation of individual plants; the proper balance between plants and empty spaces; the harmonizing of lines, planes, and masses; and the expression of moods appropriate to the season of the year or to particular occasions.

Three basic groups of arrangements are to be mastered: the *Shin*, the *Gyō*, and the *Sō*. These Japanese terms, which are also used as classifications in other

fields of Oriental art, were originally applied to calligraphy—to the writing of Chinese characters. *Shin* (translated as true, or vertical) refers to writing in which the characters are drawn squarely and without abbreviation. *Gyō* (semicursive) indicates a more open style, in which the corners are often rounded off and certain strokes are abbreviated or eliminated. *Sō* (cursive) refers to writing in which the characters are greatly abbreviated and most of the corners are rounded.

As applied to flower arrangements, *Shin* is formal, *Gyō*, semiformal, and *Sō*, informal. The word *shin* is also used to denote the main branch or flower in an arrangement. In the Moribana style, there are for each

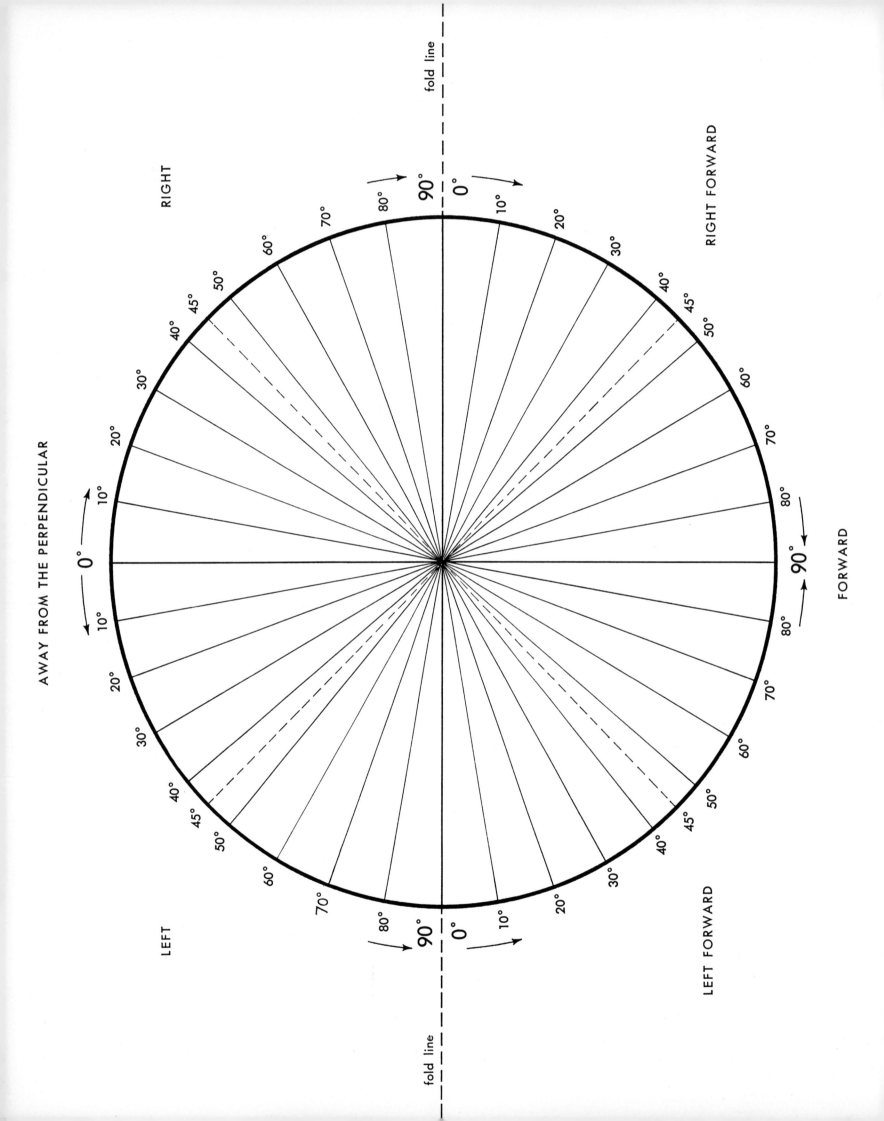

of these three classes a basic arrangement and three variations, making a total of twelve arrangements.

In learning these twelve arrangements the student will not simply be performing a series of practice exercises, but will be making finished flower arrangements. Later he will go on to freer variations on these twelve types, thus gaining mastery of all types of floral material.

For each of the twelve arrangements, which are classified as *hon-gatte* (right-hand), there is a reverse form, *gyaku-gatte* (left-hand), so that in one sense there are not twelve, but twenty-four basic types. The reverse forms, however, are no more than mirror images of the original twelve, and there is little need to study them separately. Beyond this, all twenty-four right- and left-hand arrangements can also be made in a taller vase rather than in the shallow container which distinguishes the Moribana style. This changes the effect completely, and the arrangement is then considered to be in the Nageire style.

The best method is to start the course of study with the basic arrangement in the *Shin* (formal) style and continue with the three variations on it. In studying the variations, it is a good plan to begin each lesson by assembling the basic form anew and then performing the operations necessary to produce the variation. In this way the student will gain extra practice in the preparation of the basic form and will at the same time fix in his mind the relationship between the basic form and each of the variations.

After the student has completed his study of the formal style, he should test himself by making the basic arrangement and each of the variations without reference to the book. When he is satisfied with the results, he may go on to the semiformal and informal styles. In the course of studying each of the twelve arrangements, he should try his hand a few times with its reverse, or left-hand, form.

It should be emphasized that if the plants shown in the lessons are not available, similar ones may be used. Furthermore, a certain amount of leeway with regard to lengths and angles is permissible if the plants used seem to require special treatment. The student may find, for example, that if the main branch he is using is much thinner than that shown here, he can achieve more beautiful results by lengthening it to some extent. If the branch is thicker, he may want to shorten it somewhat. Provided the student does not lose sight of the basic pattern, such variation is to be encouraged.

Finding the Proper Angles and Directions of Materials

In giving directions for arranging flowers, it is necessary to indicate the angle at which each branch or flower slants from the vertical, and the direction in which it points. Figure 340 should prove useful in placing the components. Fold the chart as indicated, so that the upper half is vertical, forming a right angle with the lower half. Holding the pencil vertical, with its point at the center of the diagram, slant the pencil left or right the required number of degrees. Then, keeping this slant, bring the top end forward the indicated number of degrees on the lower half of the diagram. The pencil is now in the position the branch or flower should assume in the arrangement.

As an example, the *shin* of a given flower arrangement is slanted 40 degrees, at 45 degrees left forward. Place the pencil vertically in the center of the folded diagram, then slant it to the left to the position on the diagram marked left 40 degrees. Now bring the end of the pencil around to the line marked left 45 degrees on the lower half of the chart. Remember that flower arrangement is an art, not an exact science; it is not necessary to be mathematically exact in the placement of plants.

OPPOSITE: *340. Fold the diagram as indicated, and place a pencil vertically in its center. Slant the pencil left or right the required number of degrees. Then, keeping this slant, bring its end forward the indicated number of degrees on the lower half of the diagram. The pencil is now in the position the branch or flower should assume in the arrangement*

Locating the Branch
or Flower on the Kenzan

We must consider not only the size, the vertical angle, and the forward angle of each branch and flower, but its location on the kenzan (needle-point holder) as well.

Figure 341 shows the eight basic positions on the kenzan. Four of these, which we will call the front, back, left, and right positions on the *kenzan cross,* are arrived at by drawing a cross dividing the kenzan into equal quarters. The positions are at the ends of this cross. Front is always the side nearest the viewer. The other four positions, which are in the corners of the *kenzan itself,* are called the left-front, right-front, left-back, and right-back positions of the kenzan.

The stems of the three main branches of a Moribana arrangement are always placed so that they form one of the two triangles indicated in Figure 342—back and

left positions on the kenzan cross and right-front on the kenzan (dotted-line triangle); or back and right positions on the kenzan cross and left-front on the kenzan (solid-line triangle)

Proper Lengths of Materials
in the Basic Arrangements

A Moribana flower arrangement has three basic parts: the *shin* (first main branch), the *soe* (second main branch), and the *tai* (third main branch). For each of these there is a smaller complementary part designated in Japanese by the term *ashirai,* which we will call complements. The *shin, soe,* and *tai* are usually branches or leaves, although they may on occasion be flowers. The *ashirai* are almost always flowers.

The size and shape of the container to be used in the

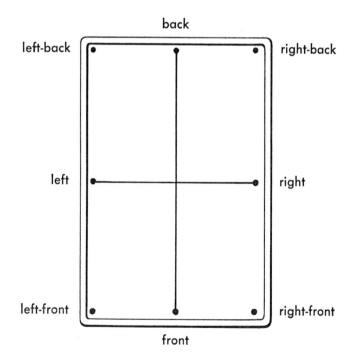

341. *The eight basic positions on the kenzan. Front, back, left, and right are referred to as positions on the kenzan cross, the others simply as positions on the kenzan*

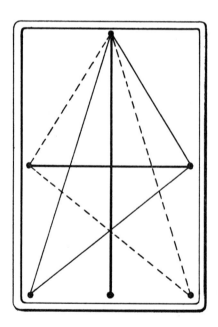

342. *The stems of the three main branches of a Moribana arrangement are always placed so that they form one of the triangles illustrated*

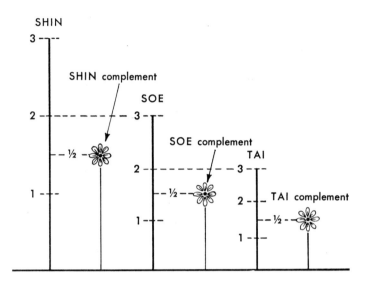

343. *Determining the relative lengths of materials. The soe is two-thirds the length of the shin branch, and the tai two-thirds of the soe. Each complementary flower is half the length of its principal branch*

abundance of foliage stretching off to one side, should not exceed the lower limit. Thinner branches may run to two or three times the measure of the vase, depending on how thin they are.

The relative proportions of the three branches and their complementary flowers are indicated in Figure 344. The *soe* should be two-thirds the length of the *shin*, and the *tai* two-thirds the length of the *soe*. Each of the complementary flowers should be one half the length of its principal branch. If these proportions are preserved, no two parts are the same length, yet there is a subtle, modular interrelation.

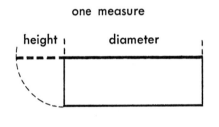

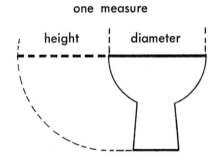

344. *Determining the "measure" of the container—the sum of its height and its outside diameter*

arrangement govern the measurements of all principal parts. These rules are flexible, however, because allowance must be made for the peculiarities of the particular plant employed.

In calculating length, it is useful to speak of the "measure" of the vase, which is the sum of its height and its outside diameter (see Figure 343). The maximum length of the plant to be used as the *shin* varies between one and one-half and three times the measure of the vase. Thick, heavy branches, or branches with an

LESSON ONE FORMAL STYLE:

The Basic Arrangement and Its First Variation

AMONG THE THREE BASIC STYLES of Moribana arrangements, the formal (*Shin*) style is the most vertical in general appearance. For formal arrangements, straight, firm materials are needed. Nothing that droops may be used. The branches of the pine tree in the accompanying illustrations are ideal, but if pine branches are not available, other straight branches will do. Here the green pine branches are accompanied by white chrysanthemums, whose stems are also straight.

STEP 1. Choose the longest and straightest of the pine branches for the role of *shin* (main branch). Cut it to approximately two times the measure of the vase (see Figure 343) and place it at the back position of the kenzan cross (see Figure 341), slanted 10 degrees from the vertical, at 10 degrees left forward (see Figures 340 and 345). The position of the kenzan itself will vary with the shape of the vessel and the arrangement as a whole. Here it has been placed toward the front and near the edge of the container. The placement is unimportant at this point, however, for the whole arrangement can easily be shifted when it is finished.

STEP 2. Cut the *soe* (second branch) to two-thirds the length of the *shin*. Place it at the left position on the kenzan cross, slanted 40 degrees from the vertical, at 40 degrees left forward (Figure 346).

STEP 3. Cut the *tai* (third branch) to two-thirds the length of the *soe*, and place it at the right-front position on the kenzan, slanted 70 degrees, at 70 degrees right forward (Figure 347). The three main branches are now at points on the kenzan corresponding to the apexes of the dotted-line triangle in Figure 342.

To finish the arrangement, cut three modest-sized chrysanthemums to the proper lengths to serve as complements to the *shin, soe,* and *tai.* Each of these flowers

should be half the length of the branch it complements.

STEP 4. Place the *shin* complement vertical and immediately in front of the *shin.*

STEP 5. Place the *soe* complement slightly to the right of the base of the *soe* and tilt it so that it runs parallel to the *soe* (Figure 349).

STEP 6. Place the *tai* complement in the front position of the kenzan cross at a slant of 70 degrees and pointing straight forward.

The arrangement is now complete. The angles, directions, and lengths of materials given here are orthodox for the basic arrangement in the formal style. If the complementary flowers are unusually large, however, shorten their stems; if they are much smaller than the flowers shown here, cut their stems longer. Also, since one of the functions of the *tai* complement is to hide the kenzan, change its angle slightly if necessary to accomplish this purpose.

Figure 351 shows another basic arrangement in the formal style.

The First Variation in the Formal Style

Essentially, the positions and functions of the *soe* and *tai,* together with their complements, have been altered in this variation, and their angles have been reversed (Figure 350). The resulting arrangement has greater breadth and freedom.

STEPS 1 and 2. The *shin* and its complementary flower remain in exactly the same position in the first variation as in the basic form.

STEP 3. The *soe* moves to the left-front position on

345. Step 1

346. Step 2

347. Steps 3 and 4

DEGREES OF SLANT FROM THE VERTICAL

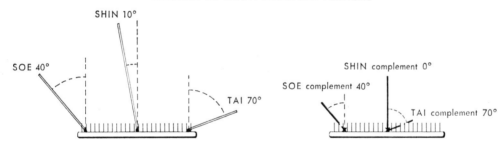

SHIN 10°

SOE 40°

TAI 70°

SHIN complement 0°

SOE complement 40°

TAI complement 70°

DEGREES OF SLANT TOWARD THE FRONT

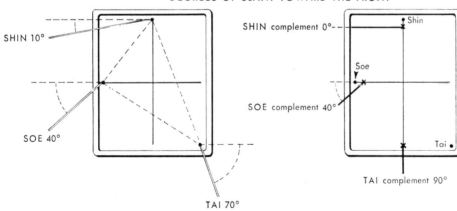

SHIN 10°

SOE 40°

TAI 70°

SHIN complement 0°

SOE complement 40°

TAI complement 90°

Shin

Soe

Tai

348. Positions on the kenzan and degrees of slant for the basic arrangement in the formal style

the kenzan and is slanted 70 degrees, at 45 degrees left forward.

STEP 4. The *tai* is placed on the right position of the kenzan cross, slanted 40 degrees, at 40 degrees right forward.

STEP 5. The *soe* complement is moved to the front position on the kenzan cross, sharply slanted and pointing straight forward.

349. Steps 5 and 6. The arrangement is now complete

STEP 6. The *tai* complement is placed just to the left of the *tai* and runs parallel to it.

Exact angles and directions are not given for the complementary flowers in the variations. They follow the line of their main branches, but greater freedom of placement is permitted.

Figure 353 shows another first variation arrangement in the formal style.

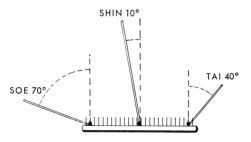

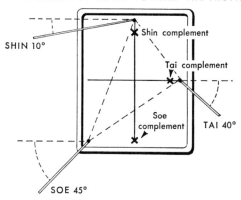

350. Positions on the kenzan and degrees of slant for the first variation in the formal style. The complements follow the general lines of their main branches

OPPOSITE: *351. The basic arrangement in the formal style. Flowering quince is used for the main branches, iris for the complements. As the arranger becomes skilled, more materials than the basic six may be employed to round out an arrangement. Notice that flowers in every stage of development are present—even two wilted quince blossoms have been retained, thus creating a symbolic representation of nature as a whole*

Nageire Style

The basic principles for making arrangements of the Nageire type (in deeper vases) are the same as those for the Moribana style. The formal, semiformal, and informal classifications remain valid for Nageire, and the same rules concerning the lengths, angles, and directions of the parts may be used, although the length of the stem portion to be inserted in the taller vase must be added to the measure. Although the kenzan is not used in Nageire arrangements, in general the positions of the branches with regard to each other remain about the same (Figure 352).

Methods of securing such materials in a vase are discussed fully on pages 223 to 225.

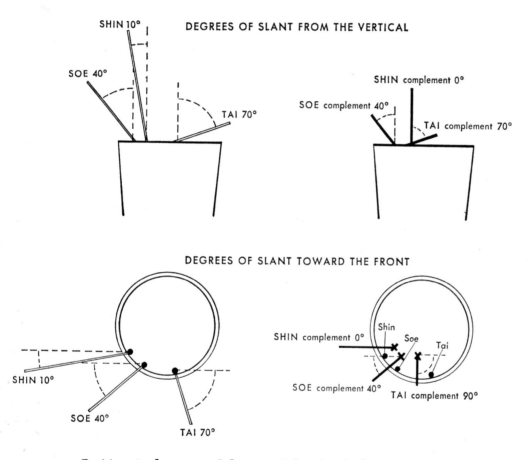

352. *Positions in the vase and degrees of slant for the basic arrangement in the formal style made in a Nageire container*

OPPOSITE: *353. The first variation in the formal style. Lemon leaves and roses create a delicate, open pattern. Insect-eaten and torn leaves serve as a reminder of the forces of nature. A few drops of moisture on the leaves brings soft summer rain to mind*

LESSON TWO FORMAL STYLE:

The Second Variation

FOR THIS ARRANGEMENT rather plain, deep-green phoenix branches have been chosen, along with three orange-red gerbera flowers. Thanks partly to the long graceful leaves of the phoenix branches, this variation has more movement and rhythm than the basic formal arrangement or the first variation. The *soe* and *tai*, and their complements, reverse position and angle.

STEP 1. As in the basic arrangement, the length of the *shin* should be about twice the measure of the vase. When a vessel of the sort shown here is used, care must be taken in calculating this figure, for the depth is rather greater than it appears to be at first glance. In measuring a branch like that of the phoenix, which has long flowing leaves, the length should be taken as the distance from the base of the cutting to the point where the topmost leaf is attached to the stem. If the student will remember first to place his materials in the basic position and then move them to their variant positions, he will see how effectively the slight variations in placement enhance the qualities of the materials used.

The *shin* of this arrangement is placed, as in the basic formal arrangement, at the back position of the

354. *Steps 1 and 2*

355. *Step 3*

kenzan cross and slanted 10 degrees, at 10 degrees left forward. The phoenix branch is most effective when placed so that the stem preserves the directional angle throughout its length. If it is so positioned, the leaves curve gracefully backward (Figure 354).

STEP 2. The *soe* is a second phoenix branch, cut to about two-thirds the length of the *shin*. Place it at the right position of the kenzan cross, slanted 40 degrees, at 40 degrees right forward.

STEP 3. Here, instead of a third phoenix branch, a large leaf from one of the gerbera flowers is used as the *tai* (Figure 355). Substitutions of this sort are frequent, but it is important to remember that as a rule no more than two types of plants are used for the three main branches. In general, the *tai* of the second variation is placed on the left-front corner of the kenzan, slanted 70 degrees, at 70 degrees left forward. In this particular arrangement, however, the angle of slant has been increased a little in order to display the gerbera leaf more prominently. Note that in this variation the placement

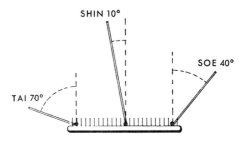

DEGREES OF SLANT FROM THE VERTICAL

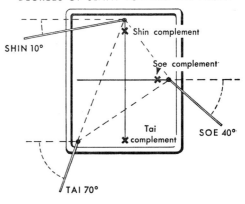

DEGREES OF SLANT TOWARD THE FRONT

357. *Positions on the kenzan and degrees of slant for the second variation in the formal style*

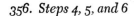

356. Steps 4, 5, and 6

of the three branches accords with the solid-line triangle in Figure 342.

STEP 4. Three gerbera flowers serve as the complements (Figure 356). Place the *shin* complement, which should have a straight stem, on the kenzan in front of the *shin* and parallel to it.

STEP 5. Place the *soe* complement on the kenzan at a point halfway between the *soe* and the *shin* and give it slightly less slant than the *soe*.

STEP 6. Place the *tai* complement on the front position of the kenzan cross, sharply slanted and pointing straight forward. Care should be taken to see that none of the flowers extends to the left of the *shin* branch or droops downward.

STEP 7. This arrangement was completed by adding a number of gerbera leaves to hide the kenzan. If these are skillfully placed, the gerbera flowers will appear to be growing naturally out of the vase (Figure 358).

Figure 359 shows another second variation arrangement in the formal style.

358. *Step 7. The arrangement is now complete*

OPPOSITE: *359. The second variation in the formal style. Ilex branches, laden with berries but stripped of leaves, and elegant spider chrysanthemums create a luxurious effect. The simplicity of the daisies and the restraint of the black vase provide a balancing contrast*

LESSON THREE FORMAL STYLE:
The Third Variation

THE POSITION OF the *shin* remains the same in all variations of the formal style: it is always placed at a slant of 10 degrees to the left and 10 degrees forward. Moreover, although the *soe* and *tai* change positions from one variation to the next, they are always placed at a slant of either 40 or 70 degrees, and their forward angles are normally the same as their angles of slant. In the third variation there is one slight departure from this rule, but the formal style can be remembered as the style of 10, 40, and 70 degrees.

Branches of Euonymus japonica are used for the three principal branches of this arrangement. The centers of the leaves are a fresh yellow-green, and the edges are a bright ivory-yellow.

STEP 1. Place the *shin*, again cut to twice the measure of the vase, in its customary position at the back

360. *Steps 1 and 2*

361. *Step 3*

of the kenzan cross and slanted the same 10 degrees
at 10 degrees left forward (Figure 360).

STEP 2. Place the *soe* on the front-right corner of the
kenzan, slanted 70 degrees, at 60 degrees right forward.
Thus far, the forward angle of each of the main
branches has been the same as its angle of slant, but in
this case, if the *soe* pointed 70 degrees forward, it would
extend too far to the front and would look as though it
were drooping, destroying the crispness of the whole
arrangement. Pointing it only 60 degrees right forward,
or even a little less, gives better balance.

STEP 3. Place the *tai* at the left position of the kenzan
cross, slanted 40 degrees left forward (Figure 361).

STEP 4. One large and two medium-sized chrysanthemums, a deep reddish-purple in hue, serve as the com-

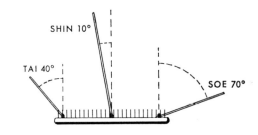

DEGREES OF SLANT FROM THE VERTICAL

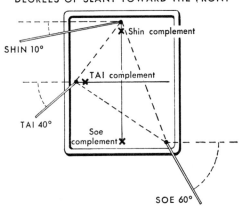

DEGREES OF SLANT TOWARD THE FRONT

362. Steps 4 and 5

*363. Positions on the kenzan and degrees of slant for the
third variation in the formal style*

plementary flowers in this arrangement. As usual, they
are cut to half the length of the main branches. One of
the medium-sized flowers is used as the *shin* complement. Place it immediately in front of the *shin* and tilt
it slightly, straight forward, to set it off somewhat from
the *shin* (Figure 362).

STEP 5. Use the large chrysanthemum as the *soe* complement, placed at the front position of the kenzan
cross, sharply slanted and pointing straight forward.

STEP 6. Place the *tai* complement at the left position
of the kenzan cross, just to the right of the *tai* (Figure
364).

Overall balance is achieved in this arrangement by
placing the largest of the chrysanthemums at the base
of the arrangement and a smaller one near the top. The
large flower at the base not only conceals the kenzan,
but tends to offset the leanness of the tall main branch.

Figure 365 shows another third variation arrangement in the formal style.

364. Step 6. The arrangement is now complete

OPPOSITE: *365. The third variation in the formal style. Echeveria stalks and a monstera leaf make* shin, soe, *and* tai. *The gerbera flowers are their complements, and the eucalyptus branches are added to fill out the arrangement. Note the interplay of shapes and textures*

LESSON FOUR FORMAL STYLE:
A Left-Hand Arrangement in the Basic Form

THE DESIGNS WE HAVE OUTLINED thus far have been of *hon-gatte* (right-hand) arrangements in the formal style. While reviewing these various patterns, we shall now experiment with the *gyaku-gatte* (left-hand) form as well. What we have here is a left-hand arrangement in the basic form.

The classification of an arrangement as right-hand or left-hand depends primarily on the line of the *shin*. The focus of a right-hand arrangement is on the viewer's left. In a left-hand arrangement the focus is on the viewer's right. In the present case, tufts of dry, pale-yellow plume grass, light reddish-yellow gladioli, and

a deep yellow-green leaf of the Monstera deliciosa have been used to achieve a bright, fresh feeling.

STEP 1. The longer of the stalks of plume grass will serve as the *shin*. Cut it to twice the measure of the vase. Insert it at the back position of the kenzan cross, slanted 10 degrees, at 10 degrees right forward (Figure 366).

STEP 2. Cut the second tuft of plume grass to two-thirds the length of the *shin* to serve as the *soe*. Place it at the right position of the kenzan cross, slanted 40 degrees, at 40 degrees right forward.

STEP 3. Cut a monstera leaf, to be used as the *tai*,

366. Steps 1 and 2

367. Step 3

to two-thirds the length of the *soe* and insert it at the left-front position of the kenzan, slanted 70 degrees, at 70 degrees left forward. The face of the leaf should rest on a horizontal plane as shown in Figure 367.

Note that the position of the kenzan in this arrangement is exactly opposite to that in previous ones. In the right-hand arrangement the kenzan is always located at the *left* of the receiver, while in the left-hand form it is always at the *right*. In either case there must be an open space on the surface of the vase, to balance the weight of the *shin* as it stretches off either to the right or to the left of the arrangement. An exception to this rule is the placement of the kenzan in the center when the bottom of the container is not flat. In the arrangement illustrated here, the space to the left of the kenzan balances the sweep of the *shin* to the right.

STEP 4. Cut the gladiolus to be used as the *shin* complement to one-half the length of the *shin* and insert

it immediately in front of the *shin* (Figure 368). Regardless of the shape of the stem concerned, the head or top of the flower should be as close to the vertical position as possible.

Since gladiolus flowers begin to bloom from the bottom upward, the designer will have to snip away two or three of the buds near the top of the stalk in order to elevate the opened flowers to the correct position for the role of *shin* complement. Another peculiarity of gladiolus concerns its length, which in this case should be measured from the base of the stem to the largest or second largest blossom from the top, and not from the base of the stem to its tip.

STEP 5. The *soe* complement should also be cut slightly longer than the standard length for this material, and aligned with the *soe* (Figure 370).

STEP 6. In like manner, cut the *tai* complement a little longer than is usual for this role, and place it at

368. Steps 4 and 5

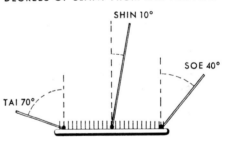

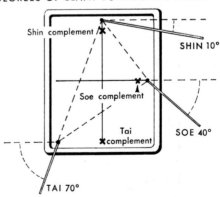

369. Positions on the kenzan and degrees of slant for the left-hand arrangement in the basic form of the formal style

370. Step 6. The arrangement is now complete

the front position of the *kenzan* cross, slanted sharply and pointing straight forward. Peculiarities in the flowers or leaves of the *tai* complement may suggest slightly altered placement. It is quite in order to follow one's own judgment in order to achieve the desired effect.

Be careful not to cut the gladiolus leaves too short, but rather to capitalize on the sweep of their movement to provide action for the arrangement. We would also suggest that the faces of the three flowers of the arrangement be harmonized with each other so that they form a balanced unit. In our illustrated arrangement the *tai* complement faces upward, the *soe* complement points toward the center of the arrangement from its position at the right, and the *shin* complement points directly at the designer, making an appealing, harmonious unit.

The direction in which each of the materials faces is

of great importance. As a general rule, whether the arrangement is in the formal, semiformal, or informal style:

a. Anything inserted at a slant of 10 degrees from the vertical should face toward the designer.

b. Anything inserted at a slant of 40 to 45 degrees should point toward that which is located at a slant of 10 degrees.

c. Anything placed at a slant of 70 to 75 degrees should face upward.

The center points of the three main elements create the base of a pyramid, the apex of which is always the viewer's eye. Figure 371 suggests how this may be done. The feeling of balance and stability that results from this technique is of the greatest importance in all flower arranging. Following these fundamental principles makes for a harmonious and pleasing whole.

Figure 372 shows a left-hand arrangement in the basic form of the formal style, made in a Nageire container.

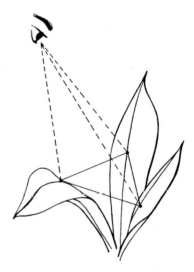

371. A harmonious unit in which the leaves face the center of the triangle they create

OPPOSITE: 372. A left-hand arrangement in the basic form of the formal style, made in a Nageire container. The velvety anemone blossoms set against their background of podocarpus branches are enhanced by the choice of a simple white vase

LESSON FIVE SEMIFORMAL STYLE:

The Basic Arrangement and Its First Variation

THE PRINCIPAL DIFFERENCE between the semiformal *Gyō* and the formal *Shin* styles is in the positioning of the *shin*. While in the formal style the *shin* is inserted at a near-vertical angle, in the semiformal style it slants 45 degrees, giving a feeling of greater breadth to the arrangement. Almost any kind of material may be used in the semiformal style, but naturally curved and sweeping branches or leaves are particularly appropriate. In general, rougher and more unruly material may be used in the informal style than is permissible in the formal.

A host of autumn colors, from yellow and green to a brilliant crimson, is splashed across the face of our arrangement. The designer caught this rainbow of colors in a single branch of an enkianthus tree as it began to clothe itself in its fall robes. To this material he added a combination of purple and pale-purple gentians to lend a feeling of peace and calm, and then completed

374. *Steps 3 and 4*

373. *Steps 1 and 2*

375. *Steps 5 and 6*

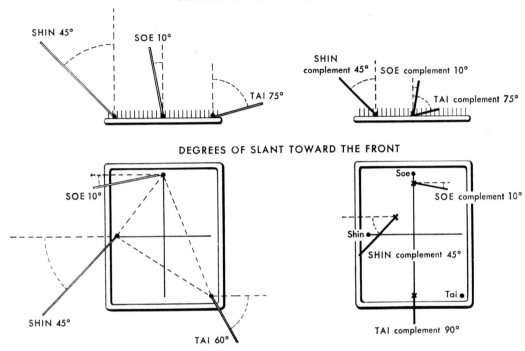

DEGREES OF SLANT FROM THE VERTICAL

SHIN 45°

SOE 10°

TAI 75°

SHIN complement 45°

SOE complement 10°

TAI complement 75°

DEGREES OF SLANT TOWARD THE FRONT

SOE 10°

SHIN 45°

TAI 60°

Soe

SOE complement 10°

Shin

SHIN complement 45°

Tai

TAI complement 90°

376. Positions on the kenzan and degrees of slant for the basic arrangement in the semiformal style

the design with small, deep-red chrysanthemums along with their rich dark-green leaves. This abundance of color produced a brilliant arrangement.

STEP 1. Choose a branch that spreads gracefully to one side for the *shin*, and cut it to two times the measure of the vase. Place it at the left position of the kenzan cross, slanted 45 degrees left forward. Be certain that it looks entirely natural at this 45-degree angle (Figure 373). Branches that must be bent or manipulated in some way to produce the right feeling should yield to those which contain a natural movement or sweep from the base to the top.

This arrangement spreads out over a rather wide area, and therefore the measurements of the various parts must be carefully considered. In the case of the *shin*, use a point midway between the leaves that stretch off to the left and those which face to the rear

at the right of the branch to determine length and angles for the *shin*.

STEP 2. Choose a straight branch for the *soe* and cut it to two-thirds the length of the *shin*. Insert it at the back position of the kenzan cross, slanted 10 degrees, at 10 degrees left forward. Calculate the length and angles of the *soe* from a point at the center of the mass of spreading leaves and twigs.

STEP 3. Choose a branch with natural movement that stretches off to the right for the *tai*. Cut it to two-thirds the length of the *soe* and place it at the right-front position of the kenzan, slanted 75 degrees, at 60 degrees right forward (Figure 374).

STEP 4. A middle-sized flower (here a gentian) with a straight stem is used for the *shin* complement. In this case it is slightly less than one-half the length of the *shin*, because the latter has a very thin stem and the

255

377. *Step 7. The arrangement is now complete*

shin complement is comparatively massive. Shortening the stem of the flower produces the desired balance. It is then inserted between the *shin* and *soe* and aligned with the angles of the *shin*, at the same time filling the space between the two principal branches.

STEP 5. The flower used as the *soe* complement is slightly less than one-half the length of the *soe*, for the sake of proper balance. It stands in front of the *soe* and is slanted a little to the right and forward, to set it off from the *soe* (Figure 375).

STEP 6. Use a rather broad-faced flower for the *tai* complement and cut it to a little less than one-half the length of the *tai*. Place it at the front position of the kenzan cross, at a slant of 75 degrees, and pointing straight forward.

STEP 7. The arrangement as it now stands is not fully balanced. Its top stretches out over a broad expanse, while the base gives a narrow and rather empty feeling. We have used slips of small chrysanthemums to fill in the space near the kenzan, both to hide the holder and

to produce the necessary balance in the arrangement. Care must be taken to see that such flowers do not stand taller than the complements, for this would only serve to detract from the beauty and essential role of the complements in the arrangement (Figure 377).

When inserting these smaller flowers into the holder, we would suggest placing several at the left front and a larger number stretching from the right front toward the center of the kenzan. A flower of brilliant color, such as red or orange, will tend to draw the entire arrangement together into a balanced unit.

Figure 378 shows another basic arrangement in the semiformal style.

OPPOSITE: 378. *The basic arrangement in the semiformal style. Magnolia branches, rubrum lilies, and daisies are carefully balanced against each other, so that the daisies, far from being overpowered by the larger elements, become a focal point*

The First Variation in the Semiformal Style

In the first variation the *shin* and *tai* are unchanged, but the *soe* moves from 10 degrees to the left to 10 degrees to the right (Figure 379). The complements also remain in approximately the same positions they occupy in the basic form, altering the relationship of the *soe* and its complement, but, as in all the variations, their placement is more flexible.

Figure 380 shows another first variation arrangement in the semiformal style.

379. Positions on the kenzan and degrees of slant for the first variation in the semiformal style

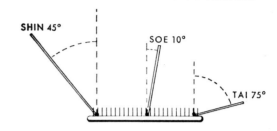

DEGREES OF SLANT FROM THE VERTICAL

SHIN 45°   SOE 10°   TAI 75°

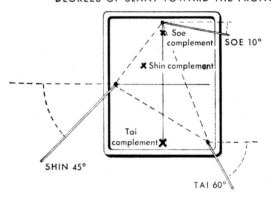

DEGREES OF SLANT TOWARD THE FRONT

Soe complement   SOE 10°

Shin complement

Tai complement

SHIN 45°

TAI 60°

OPPOSITE: *380. The first variation in the semiformal style, in a left-hand arrangement. The addition of candytuft fills an awkward gap in an arrangement that might have been dull had only the pine and tulips been used*

LESSON SIX SEMIFORMAL STYLE:

A Left-Hand Arrangement in the Basic Form

THE REDDISH STALK of the castor-oil plant and its yellow berries and yellow- and dark-green leaves make it ideal for colorful and brilliant arrangements. In our arrangement *shin, soe,* and *tai* are composed of this material, with moderate-sized yellow chrysanthemums serving as the complements.

Since the designer of an arrangement must always use to the fullest any peculiarities and natural movement in his materials, he should first examine them carefully to determine which style and variation of that style they will best fit. He should also decide before setting forth

on his project whether they are best suited to the right-hand or the left-hand pattern. Here we are making a left-hand arrangement of the basic arrangement.

STEP 1. Use the castor-oil branch with the broadest top as the *shin*. Cut it to twice the measure of the vase and place it at the right position of the kenzan cross, slanted 45 degrees, at 45 degrees right forward (Figure 381).

STEP 2. Use an almost straight branch as the *soe*. Cut it to two-thirds the length of the *shin* and place it at the back position of the kenzan cross, slanted 10 de-

381. Steps 1 and 2

382. Step 3

383. Steps 4, 5, and 6. The arrangement is now complete, with the kenzan in the right rear corner of the container

384. *Here the kenzan has been shifted to the left rear corner of the container*

385. *The kenzan in the right front corner*

grees, at 10 degrees right forward. Note the way the designer of this arrangement has utilized to the fullest the natural movement of the top of the branch as it curves gracefully toward the right front. Pointing toward the *shin* preserves the balance of the arrangement while giving it action.

Castor-oil branches are rather heavy, and it may be necessary to counterbalance by using a second kenzan. Turning it upside down and interlocking its needles with those of the principal kenzan at the back will provide the necessary stability. The temptation to use florists' clay to anchor the kenzan should be resisted. Not only does it force the arranger to determine the exact position of the kenzan before the arrangement is completed, but it can be difficult to remove. Most important, the oil in the clay may foul the water.

STEP 3. The *tai* should have a broad face, with leaves that face upward. Cut it to two-thirds the length of the *soe* and place it at the left-front position of the kenzan, slanted 75 degrees, at 60 degrees left forward (Figure 382). Calculate its length from the base of the branch

to a point at approximately the middle of the last clump of leaves, rather than to the tip of the last leaf. Be sure to use this point also when calculating the 75-degree angle. Attempting to place the lines of the *branch* at a 75-degree angle will produce a very strange effect indeed, but if the mass of leaves is used, a very appealing triangle results. It is the angle that is important, not the flow of the branch itself.

Use the broadest of the three chrysanthemums as the *tai* complement, the middle-sized one as the *soe* complement, and the smallest one as the *shin* complement. Although it is the smallest, its leaves and stem are perhaps the most elegant, and as a general rule these are more important in selecting the *shin* complement than the flower itself. The *soe* complement should be fairly straight, and a flower with generous leaves should be used as the *tai* complement.

STEP 4. Cut the *shin* complement to one-half the length of the *shin* and place it just to the left of the *shin* and in approximate alignment with it (Figure 383).

STEP 5. Cut the *soe* complement to one-half the length

262

386. *The kenzan in the left front corner*

387. *The kenzan in the center of the container*

of the *soe* and insert it just in front of the *soe* in a vertical position.

STEP 6. Cut the *tai* complement to one-half the length of the *tai* and place it at the front position of the kenzan cross, slanted sharply and facing straight forward.

Examine closely the arrangement pictured in Figures 384 and 385. Note how the shifting of the kenzan in the container affects the overall balance.

Positioning the Kenzan in the Vase

The kenzan in our arrangement appears at different positions in Figures 383 to 387. In Figure 383 it is in the right rear of the vase; in 384 it is in the left-rear position; in 385 in the right-front corner; in 386 in the left-front corner; and in 387 in the very center of the container.

If the vase has a small dip near the middle, it may be necessary to place the kenzan directly in the center, as illustrated in Figure 387, for the sake of stability. If the bottom is level, however, this cannot be considered a suitable location for the holder.

In this series of possibilities, only Figures 383 and 385 show truly proper placement of the holder. While the kenzan in Figure 383 is located at the rear of the vase, which is perfectly all right, as a general rule the front position is preferable because it is easier to conceal the kenzan there.

In Figures 383 and 385 the kenzan is placed to the right of the vase, leaving a large expanse of water to the left of the arrangement. This balances the weight of the *shin* stretching off to the right.

A comparison of Figures 385 and 386 reveals still another reason for choosing the former: In the latter, the sharp corner of the vase interrupts the bold movement of the *shin* as it stretches off to the right. When the kenzan is shifted to the right, however, as in Figure 385, there is nothing to intercept the stately sweep of the *shin*. The preservation of such lines, as well as the maintenance of an overall balance, is of primary importance in Japanese flower arranging, contributing beauty and stability to the whole.

In brief, in right-hand designs of both the formal and semiformal styles the kenzan should be located in the left front position of the container, while in left-hand designs it should be placed at the right front. This is a basic and important point.

Figure 389 shows a left-hand arrangement in the basic form of the semiformal style, made in a Nageire container.

388. Positions on the kenzan and degrees of slant for the left-hand arrangement in the basic form of the semiformal style

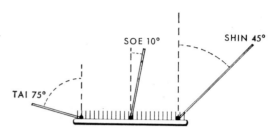

DEGREES OF SLANT FROM THE VERTICAL

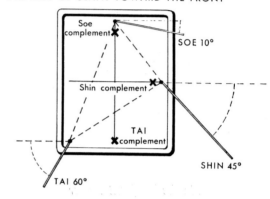

DEGREES OF SLANT TOWARD THE FRONT

OPPOSITE: *389. A left-hand arrangement in the basic form of the semiformal style, made in a Nageire container. The choice of variegated holly instead of the all-green sort makes it possible to carry the red of its berries and the carnations down into the vase, creating a cheerful display for winter*

LESSON SEVEN SEMIFORMAL STYLE:

The Second Variation

A VERY BROAD FEELING is characteristic of the second variation of the semiformal style. We have used extremely thin material to emphasize this breadth, but any material of a similar nature may be used with equal effectiveness.

STEP 1. Choose a branch with free and natural movement for the *shin*. Cut it to approximately twice the measure of the vase and place it at the left position of the kenzan cross, slanted 45 degrees, at 45 degrees left forward (Figure 390).

STEP 2. The *soe* should be slightly thinner than the shin. Cut it to two-thirds the length of the *shin* and place it at the right-front position of the kenzan, slanted 75 degrees, at 60 degrees right forward (Figure 391).

STEP 3. Cut the *tai* to two-thirds the length of the *soe* and insert it at the back position of the kenzan cross, slanted 10 degrees, at 10 degrees left forward.

STEP 4. Cut the middle-sized rose to one-half the length of the *shin* to serve as its complement, and insert it between the *shin* and *soe*. It should follow the general lines of the *shin* (Figure 392).

STEP 5. Use the largest of the roses as the *soe* com-

390. Step 1

391. Steps 2 and 3

266

plement. Preferably it should also have the most leaves. Cut it to one-half the length of the *soe* and place it at the front position of the kenzan cross, slanting sharply and facing directly forward (Figure 394).

STEP 6. Cut the last rose to one-half the length of the *tai* and place it vertically in front of the *tai*. Should the flower conflict with other materials when thus placed, shift it slightly to produce an arrangement that is more attractive.

Figure 395 shows another arrangement in the second variation of the semiformal style.

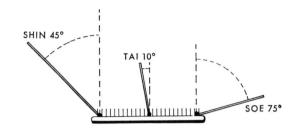

DEGREES OF SLANT FROM THE VERTICAL

SHIN 45°
TAI 10°
SOE 75°

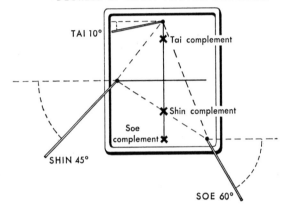

DEGREES OF SLANT TOWARD THE FRONT

TAI 10°
Tai complement
Shin complement
Soe complement
SHIN 45°
SOE 60°

393. *Positions on the kenzan and degrees of slant for the second variation of the semiformal style*

392. *Step 4*

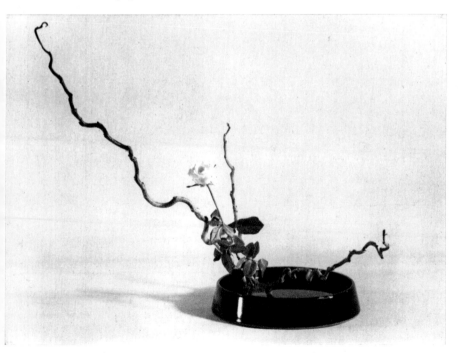

394. *Steps 5 and 6. The arrangement is now complete*

OPPOSITE: 395. *The second variation in the semiformal style. Here the judicious use of extra materials, while not detracting from the main elements, adds much to the charm of the arrangement. It is possible to see in it a gaily caparisoned horse, the tallest iris its head and the graceful curve of mimosa at far right its tail*

LESSON EIGHT SEMIFORMAL STYLE:
The Third Variation, Made in a Nageire Container

MANY ARRANGEMENTS of the Moribana and Nageire styles are precisely the same from the mouth of the vase upward. The only major differences are in the character of the vase itself and in the length of the materials used. Since vases used in Nageire arrangements are always deeper, an additional amount must be added to the length of each material to allow for the hidden stem portion.

Here we picture an arrangement in the third variation of the semiformal style, composed of three branches of flowering quince and three chrysanthemums. The dark-green leaves effectively set off beautiful quince flowers in a mixture of purplish-pink, rose-red, and pure white. Harmonized with these are chrysanthemums of a dark-orange and reddish-yellow blend, which serve as the complements.

For a discussion of the techniques of inserting branches in a vase for Nageire style arrangements, see pages 226 to 228. The kenzan is not used as a holder in the Nageire style except when the vase is exceptionally wide, both at the mouth and at the base.

STEP 1. Use the longest quince branch as the *shin*. The arrangement of the leaves of the branch illustrated is ideal (Figure 396). If other twigs shoot off from the main stem at a lower point, clip them away to give a less complex, cleaner feeling.

Cut the branch to twice the measure of the vase (height plus diameter) plus the length of stem to be inserted in the vase. If the branch is to be bent in some way to secure it inside the vase, add that measurement also.

The proper angle for the *shin* is fixed at a slant of 45 degrees, and leaning forward and to the left 45 degrees. Calculate this angle of slant by lining up the tip of the

396. Step 1

397. Steps 2 and 3

398. Step 4

branch with the mouth of the vase. Follow the diagrams in Figure 399 for the placement of the materials in the vase. Once the proper position has been established, the *shin* may be held in place by using a forked twig (Figure 336) or one of the methods illustrated in Figures 338 or 339.

STEP 2. Cut the *soe* branch to two-thirds the length of the *shin*, plus the length of the stem inside the vase. Slant it 70 degrees, at 60 degrees left forward. In Figure 397, because it leans toward the camera, the *soe* does not appear to be as long as it should be, but in reality it is of the proper size for this role.

STEP 3. Cut the *tai* branch to two-thirds the length of the *soe*, plus the length of stem to be inserted into the vase. Slant it 75 degrees, at 70 degrees right forward. Figures 335 or 338 will be of most help at this point. Since the slant of the *soe* is only 5 degrees different from that of the *tai*, be sure that the *tai* does not rest higher in the arrangement than the *soe*.

STEP 4. Use the longest and straightest of the chrysanthemums for the *shin* complement. Cut it to one-half the length of the *shin* plus the depth of the vase, and align it with the *shin* in angle and direction (Figure 398). We would suggest that the blossom itself stand nearly vertical, at a slant of no more than 30 degrees to the left, at about 50 degrees forward. Insert it all the way into the vase, so that the end rests firmly on the bottom of the receiver. It may be secured either by attaching it to the base of the *shin* or by propping it against the sturdy stem of the *shin*.

STEP 5. Cut the *soe* complement to one-half the length of the *soe*, plus the depth of the vase. The blossom should fill the space between the *shin* and the *soe*, and lean forward slightly more than the *soe* (Figure 400). As the stem has been cut to allow it to rest on the bottom of the vase, it may be wedged into the network of materials there, or propped up against the *soe*. Figure 335 may suggest other suitable methods.

STEP 6. Use the largest chrysanthemum, one with an abundance of leaves, for the *tai* complement. Cut it to one-half the length of the *tai*, plus the depth of the vase, and slant it sharply, facing straight forward, in the

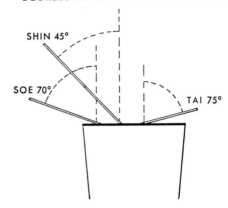

DEGREES OF SLANT FROM THE VERTICAL

SHIN 45°
SOE 70°
TAI 75°

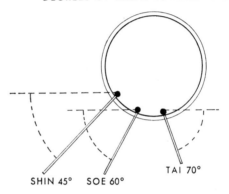

DEGREES OF SLANT TOWARD THE FRONT

TAI 70°
SHIN 45°   SOE 60°

399. *Positions in the vase and degrees of slant for the third variation in the semiformal style, made in a Nageire container*

center of the vase. Figures 335 or 336 may be useful here.

Whenever possible, it is wise to leave one side of the mouth of the vase slightly open, to balance the movement of the *shin*. In the present arrangement, since the *shin* stretches off to the left, the right side of the vase's mouth has been left empty. This is not always possible, for a small-mouthed container may not offer any extra space, but as a principle of proper balance this idea should be kept in mind.

To make this variation in the Moribana style (Figure 401) place the *shin* at the back position on the kenzan cross, the *soe* at the left position on the kenzan cross, and the *tai* at the right-front corner of the kenzan. Figure 402 shows such an arrangement.

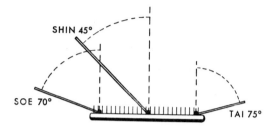

DEGREES OF SLANT FROM THE VERTICAL

SHIN 45°

SOE 70°

TAI 75°

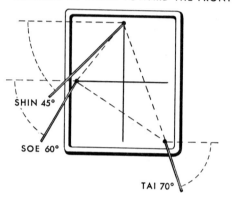

DEGREES OF SLANT TOWARD THE FRONT

SHIN 45°

SOE 60°

TAI 70°

401. Positions on the kenzan and degrees of slant for the third variation in the semiformal style

400. Steps 5 and 6. The arrangement is now complete

OPPOSITE: *402. The third variation in the semiformal style, made in a modern Moribana container whose gray-green matches that of the eucalyptus branches. White candytuft conceals the bare anemone stems at the base, but in other parts of the arrangement the stems are an important element —notice how deliberately the eucalyptus leaves have been stripped*

LESSON NINE INFORMAL STYLE:
The Basic Arrangement and Its First Variation

THE INFORMAL (*Sō*) style is different from either the formal or semiformal styles in the way it spreads out both left and right from the center, and in the very broad and free feeling it produces. Of particular value in this type of arrangement are materials with graceful movements, like branches that stretch out in sweeping arcs in the arrangement illustrated here. Sprays of forsythia, with their light-green leaves, have been attractively combined with the deep red-purple and purplish-red velvet of cockscomb.

Several small changes were made in the elements of this arrangement to enhance their effectiveness. First of all, to better display the gentle sweep of the *shin*, all the leaves on the underside of that branch were removed. Similarly, although less drastically, all the leaves and branches of the *soe* that faced downward toward the *tai* were clipped away in order not to detract from the lines of that material.

404. Step 4

403. Steps 1, 2, and 3

405. Step 5

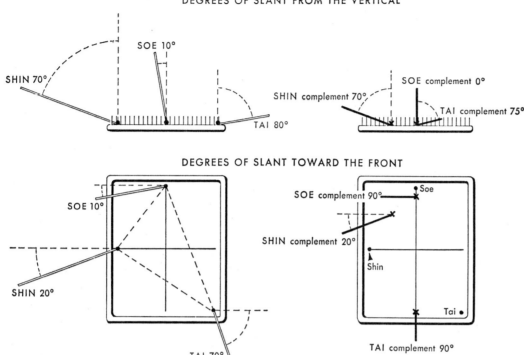

DEGREES OF SLANT FROM THE VERTICAL

SOE 10°

SHIN 70°

SHIN complement 70°

SOE complement 0°

TAI complement 75°

TAI 80°

DEGREES OF SLANT TOWARD THE FRONT

SOE 10°

SOE complement 90°

Soe

SHIN complement 20°

SHIN 20°

Shin

Tai

TAI 70°

TAI complement 90°

406. Positions on the kenzan and degrees of slant for the basic arrangement in the informal style

The *tai* in this case contains leaves that face both upward and downward. Since only one of two such masses may be used as the focal point for the determination of angles and lengths, one of the two must be made to appear the stronger by removing leaves from the weaker of the branches. In the arrangement illustrated here, several leaves were trimmed away from the upper cluster to strengthen the lower branch and make it the guiding point for all calculations.

Also, since the cockscomb flower gives an impression of heaviness, the three complements were cut slightly shorter than usual.

STEP 1. In the basic arrangement of this style, the kenzan is placed at the right-back position of the vase, quite the opposite of the forms outlined before. Our *shin* is reminiscent of the many plants found around lakes and ponds that droop down toward the water, and so we have attempted to preserve that picture by leav-ing the space beneath the *shin* entirely open, allowing the arching branches to be reflected on the surface of the water. Place the *shin* at the left position of the kenzan cross, slanted 70 degrees, at 20 degrees left forward (Figures 403 and 406). To establish the angle of slant, line up the tip of the branch with the bottom of the stem, ignoring the curve of the branch.

STEP 2. Cut the *soe* to two-thirds the length of the *shin* and place it at the back position of the kenzan cross, slanted 10 degrees, at 10 degrees left forward.

STEP 3. Cut the *tai* branch to two-thirds the length of the *soe*, and place it at the front-right position of the kenzan, slanted 80 degrees, at 70 degrees right forward.

STEP 4. Insert the *shin* complement between the *shin* and the *soe* in such a way that it follows the general lines of the *shin* (Figure 404).

STEP 5. Place the *soe* complement vertically at the

407. *Steps 6 and 7. The arrangement is now complete*

back position of the kenzan cross, in front of the *soe* (Figure 405).

STEP 6. Place the *tai* complement at a slant of 75 degrees and directly center at the front of the arrangement (Figure 407).

STEP 7. Leaves of the cockscomb plant may be inserted at the base of the arrangement to hide the kenzan and to round out the completed design.

Figure 408 shows a left-hand arrangement in the basic informal style.

While the formal and semiformal styles are precisely the same in both Moribana and Nageire, the informal design is quite different. The *shin* in the informal Moribana style is slanted 70 degrees, at 20 degrees left forward, but in the Nageire style of this arrangement the slant is 45 degrees, at 45 degrees left forward, and is made to point down and to the left.

The *soe* in the Nageire style is also different; here it would be slanted 45 degrees, at 40 degrees left forward. The *tai* would be slanted 80 degrees, at 60 degrees right forward.

In the next lesson we will make a Nageire arrangement in this basic form of the informal style.

OPPOSITE: 408. *A left-hand arrangement in the basic informal style. The rough strength of the modern container brings to mind trees and shrubs growing out of a hilltop and spilling over its side. The angularity of the quince branches is softened by the drooping mimosa and its fernlike leaves*

The First Variation in
the Informal Style

The first variation in the informal style merely requires shifting the position of the *soe* from a slant of 10 degrees to the left to a slant of 10 degrees to the right (Figure 409). Its complement remains in the vertical position. As in all variations, the positioning of the complements is flexible. Figure 410 shows an arrangement in the first variation.

409. Positions on the kenzan and degrees of slant for the first variation in the informal style

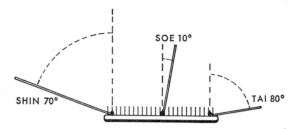

DEGREES OF SLANT FROM THE VERTICAL

SOE 10°

SHIN 70°

TAI 80°

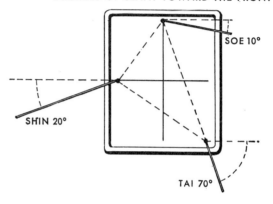

DEGREES OF SLANT TOWARD THE FRONT

SOE 10°

SHIN 20°

TAI 70°

OPPOSITE: *410. The first variation in the informal style. Notice how the simple shifting of* soe *opens up the center of the arrangement and creates a sense of windswept motion. The dried, white-painted birch branches as well as the daffodils have been shaped to enhance this feeling*

LESSON TEN INFORMAL STYLE:

The Basic Arrangement, Made in a Nageire Container, and the Second Variation

THE DARK BROWN BARK and bright red berries of the branches of the Nandina domestica make this ideal arrangement material. In the Nageire arrangement illustrated here, these branches serve as the *shin, soe,* and *tai,* with white lilies used for the complements.

STEP 1. Choose a branch that curves downward in a wide and graceful arc for the *shin.* Cut it to twice the measure of the vase, plus its depth, and slant it 45 degrees, at 45 degrees left forward (Figure 411). See Figures 338 or 339 for ways of holding it in place. Follow the diagrams in Figure 414 for the approximate placement of materials in the vase.

STEP 2. Cut the *soe* branch to two-thirds the length of the *shin,* plus the depth of the vase. Place it behind the *shin,* slanting it 45 degrees, at 45 degrees left for-

ward (Figure 412). Again, the methods shown in Figures 338 or 339 may be used to keep it stable.

STEP 3. Cut the *tai* branch to two-thirds the length of the *soe,* plus the depth of the vase, and insert it at the right, slanting it 80 degrees, at 70 degrees right forward. It may be fixed firmly by using either of the methods shown in Figures 335 and 336.

STEP 4. Use a lily bud for the *shin* complement, and choose a spot approximately in the center of the pod as the focal point from which to determine lengths and angles. Cut it to one-half the length of the *shin,* plus the length of stem to be inserted into the vase (Figure 413). Slant it 50 degrees, at 50 degrees left forward, and secure it by following Figure 334.

STEP 5. Cut the *soe* complement to one-half the

411. Step 1

412. Steps 2 and 3

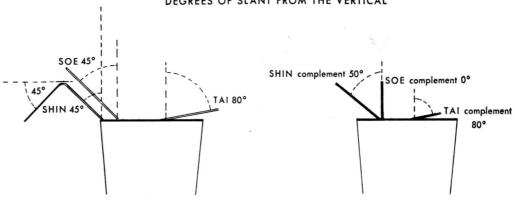

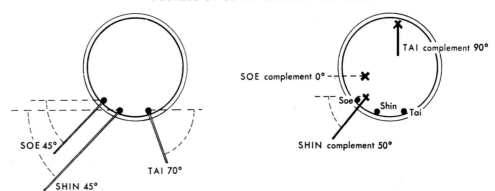

414. Positions in the vase and degrees of slant for the basic arrangement in the informal style, made in a Nageire container

413. Step 4

length of the *soe*, plus the length to be inserted in the vase. The flower should point to the front and stand in a vertical position (Figure 415).

STEP 6. Cut the *tai* complement to one-half the length of the *tai*, plus the amount to be inserted into the vase, and place it at a slant of 80 degrees, at dead center. The flower itself should face upward and to the left, to unite with the other lilies in a balanced triangle. It should never face downward as though independent of that unity. See Figures 335 and 336 for methods of securing it firmly in the vase.

Figure 417 shows a basic arrangement in the informal style, made in a Moribana container.

281

415. Steps 5 and 6. The arrangement is now complete

The Second Variation in the Informal Style

The difference between the basic arrangement and the second variation is the reversal of the *tai* and the *soe* (Figure 416). To make the second variation in the Moribana style:

STEP 1. Place the *shin* at the left position of the kenzan cross, slanted 70 degrees, at 20 degrees left forward.

STEP 2. Place the *soe* at the right-front position of the kenzan, slanted 80 degrees, at 70 degrees right forward.

STEP 3. Place the *tai* at the back position of the kenzan cross, slanted 10 degrees, at 10 degrees left forward.

The complements follow the lines of their main branches.

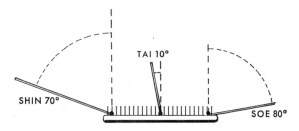

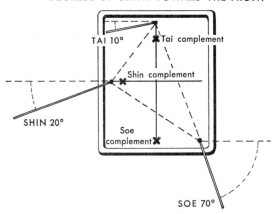

416. Positions on the kenzan and degrees of slant for the second variation in the informal style

OPPOSITE: *417. The second variation in the informal style. This arrangement of cedar and rubrum lilies will reward special study. The perfect balance and harmony which is the goal of Ikebana depends not only on the basic structure of an arrangement, but on the care with which every detail is made to blend into the whole*

DEGREES OF SLANT FROM THE VERTICAL

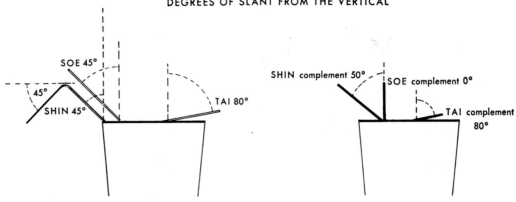

SOE 45°

45°

SHIN 45°

TAI 80°

SHIN complement 50°

SOE complement 0°

TAI complement 80°

DEGREES OF SLANT TOWARD THE FRONT

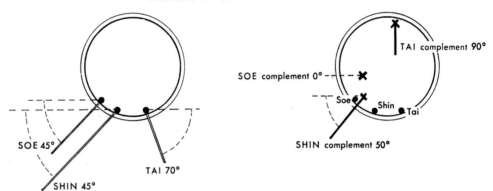

SOE 45°

SHIN 45°

TAI 70°

TAI complement 90°

SOE complement 0°

Soe

Shin

Tai

SHIN complement 50°

414. Positions in the vase and degrees of slant for the basic arrangement in the informal style, made in a Nageire container

413. Step 4

length of the *soe*, plus the length to be inserted in the vase. The flower should point to the front and stand in a vertical position (Figure 415).

STEP 6. Cut the *tai* complement to one-half the length of the *tai*, plus the amount to be inserted into the vase, and place it at a slant of 80 degrees, at dead center. The flower itself should face upward and to the left, to unite with the other lilies in a balanced triangle. It should never face downward as though independent of that unity. See Figures 335 and 336 for methods of securing it firmly in the vase.

Figure 417 shows a basic arrangement in the informal style, made in a Moribana container.

415. *Steps 5 and 6. The arrangement is now complete*

The Second Variation in the Informal Style

The difference between the basic arrangement and the second variation is the reversal of the *tai* and the *soe* (Figure 416). To make the second variation in the Moribana style:

STEP 1. Place the *shin* at the left position of the kenzan cross, slanted 70 degrees, at 20 degrees left forward.

STEP 2. Place the *soe* at the right-front position of the kenzan, slanted 80 degrees, at 70 degrees right forward.

STEP 3. Place the *tai* at the back position of the kenzan cross, slanted 10 degrees, at 10 degrees left forward.

The complements follow the lines of their main branches.

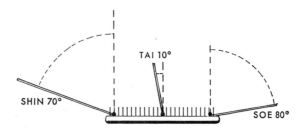

DEGREES OF SLANT FROM THE VERTICAL

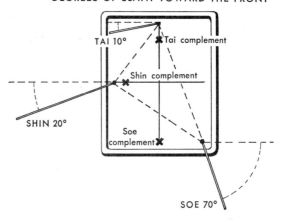

DEGREES OF SLANT TOWARD THE FRONT

416. *Positions on the kenzan and degrees of slant for the second variation in the informal style*

OPPOSITE: 417. *The second variation in the informal style. This arrangement of cedar and rubrum lilies will reward special study. The perfect balance and harmony which is the goal of Ikebana depends not only on the basic structure of an arrangement, but on the care with which every detail is made to blend into the whole*

LESSON ELEVEN INFORMAL STYLE:

The Third Variation

THE ATTRACTIVE HARMONY of a gray-green base and a yellow-brown tip makes the willow branch an appealing material for any arrangement. Here we use willow for the *shin* and *soe*, while a fresh green pine branch for the *tai* lends a note of variety to the design. The complementary dahlias, of a red-and-white blend, provide additional color.

STEP 1. Use the larger willow branch for the *shin* and cut it to two times the measure of the vase. Place it at the left position of the kenzan cross, slanted 70 degrees, at 20 degrees left forward (Figure 418).

STEP 2. Cut the *soe* to two-thirds the length of the *shin* and insert it at the back position of the kenzan cross, slanted 35 degrees, at 35 degrees right backward (Figure 419). This is the first time in our study that we have used the backward position (Figure 422). As a general rule, in such instances the material is measured from the base to the very tip of the branch.

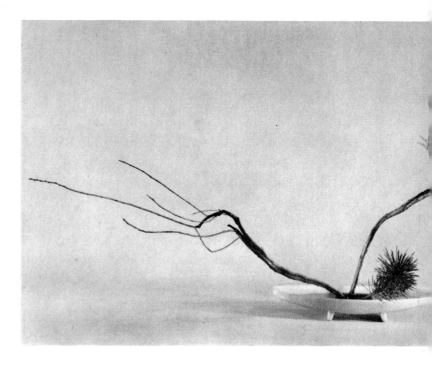

419. *Steps 2 and 3*

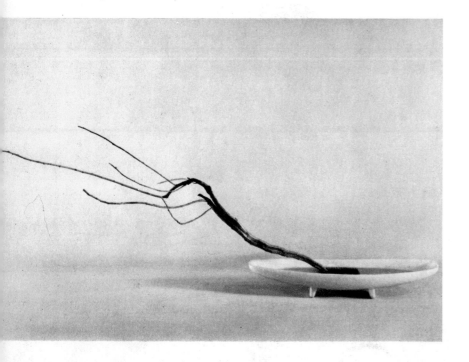

418. *Step 1*

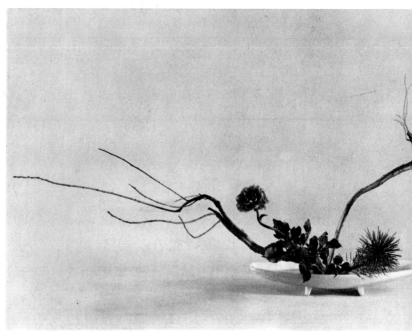

420. *Step 4*

421. *Steps 5 and 6. The arrangement is now complete*

STEP 3. Cut the *tai* to two-thirds the length of the *soe* and place it at the right-front position of the kenzan, slanted 80 degrees, at 80 degrees right forward.

STEP 4. Cut the middle-sized dahlia to slightly less than one-half the length of the *shin*, to serve as its complement. It should be inserted between the *shin* and *soe* and made to follow the general lines of the *shin* (Figure 420).

STEP 5. Cut the *soe* complement to slightly less than one half the length of the *soe* and place it at the back position of the kenzan cross in such a way that it follows the flow of the *soe* in its backward motion (Figure 421).

STEP 6. The largest dahlia, one with an abundance of leaves, should be used as the *tai* complement. Cut it to one-half the length of the *tai*, and insert it at the front position of the kenzan cross, slanted very sharply and pointing straight forward.

Note that since the bottom of the receiver is not flat, the kenzan has been positioned in the center of the vase. This is entirely in order in a case of this sort.

Figure 424 shows another arrangement in the third variation of the informal style.

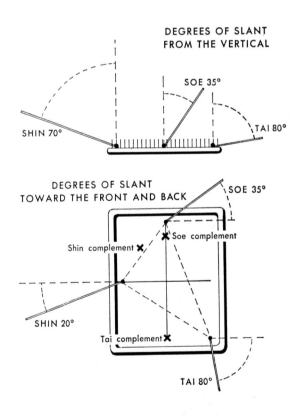

422. *Positions on the kenzan and degrees of slant for the third variation in the informal style*

The Third Variation in the Nageire Style

To make this variation in the Nageire style, see Figure 423:

STEP 1. Place the *shin* branch in such a way that the visible portion lies horizontally at 40 degrees left forward.

STEP 2. Slant the *soe* 45 degrees, at 45 degrees left forward.

STEP 3. Slant the *tai* 80 degrees, at 80 degrees right forward.

The complements follow the lines of their main branches.

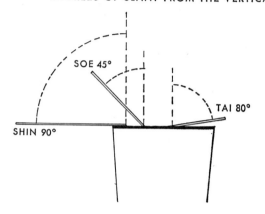

DEGREES OF SLANT FROM THE VERTICAL

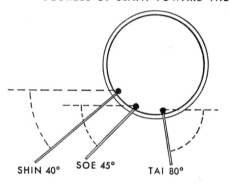

DEGREES OF SLANT TOWARD THE FRONT

423. Positions in the vase and degrees of slant for the third variation in the informal style, made in a Nageire container

OPPOSITE: *424. The third variation in the informal style. Comparison of this arrangement, composed of eucalyptus, anemones, daffodils, and a monstera leaf, with the arrangement detailed in the lesson will demonstrate the variety of effect possible within the seemingly rigid confines of the basic rules, and makes clear why judgment in choice of materials is such an important factor in Ikebana*

LESSON TWELVE INFORMAL STYLE:

A Left-Hand Arrangement in the Third Variation

In this final lesson we shall digress from our usual six basic elements (the *shin, soe,* and *tai,* along with the three complements) and experiment with more material. The elegant movement of spirea branches, with their yellow-green leaves, harmonizes with pink carnations to produce a delicate and charming effect.

STEP 1. Choose the largest and most graceful of the branches for the *shin.* Cut it to twice the measure of the vase and place it at the right position of the kenzan cross, slanted 70 degrees, at 20 degrees right forward (Figure 425).

STEP 2. Use one of the carnations as the *soe.* Cut it to two-thirds the length of the *shin.* Since its stem is naturally very weak, wire a small stick to the base of the stem to assure firm placement in the kenzan. Insert it at the back position of the kenzan cross, slanted 35 degrees, at 35 degrees left backward. Remember the general rule of measuring from the base to the very

426. *Step 4*

425. *Steps 1, 2, and 3*

427. *Steps 5, 6, and 7*

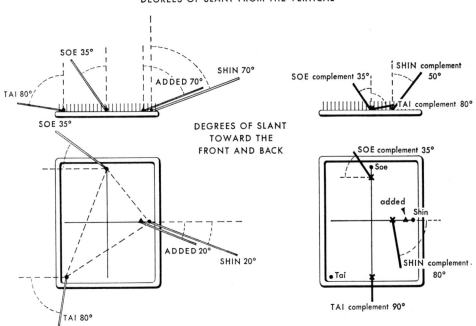

428. Position on the kenzan and degrees of slant for a left-hand arrangement in the third variation in the informal style

tip when material is to be placed at a backward angle.

STEP 3. Use a second spirea branch as the *tai*. Cut it to two-thirds the length of the *soe* and place it at the left-front position of the kenzan, slanted 80 degrees, at 80 degrees left forward.

STEP 4. Insert a third spirea branch, a little more than half the length of the *shin*, into the kenzan in such a way that it appears to shoot off from the same stem as the *shin*. It must follow the general lines of the *shin* except that the tip, or head, of the branch should be clearly separated from the *shin*, and rise slightly higher in the vertical plane (Figure 426).

STEP 5. For the *shin* complement, cut a carnation to one-half the length of the *shin* and place it just to the left of the *shin* and its companion branch. Slant it to about 50 degrees, at 80 degrees right forward (Figure 427).

STEP 6. Cut a carnation to one-half the length of the *soe*, as its complement, and place it right in front of the *soe* in such a way that the two stems follow the same line.

STEP 7. Cut the *tai* complement carnation to one-half the length of the *tai* and place it at the front position of the kenzan cross, slanted 80 degrees and pointing straight forward.

STEP 8. Although we have now used seven pieces of material (Figure 428), the arrangement as it stands still has a lonely look because of the many empty spaces that remain. To fill these and to lend additional balance, several slips of the basic materials may be used to good effect. None of these added materials, however, should appear more prominently in the arrangement than the original seven elements, nor should there be any crossing of lines in adding them to the design. The image of a peacock with his feathers opened in a large sweep at the back of the arrangement is desirable; none of the materials should be of equal length (Figure 429).

This arrangement is also very lovely in the Nageire style. To make it, simply follow the same general pattern we have outlined here.

Another Nageire arrangement in this variation is illustrated in Figure 430.

429. Step 8

OPPOSITE: *430. A left-hand arrangement in the third variation in the informal style. The dramatic impact of the thick clusters of lilac blossoms is heightened by the choice of a Nageire container, and the rich red of the tulips draws the eye back to center*

PART SIX

Advanced Ikebana

Having familiarized himself with the basic techniques of Ikebana in the Moribana and Nageire styles, the student arranger is now ready to meet two different kinds of challenges. On the one hand there are the lovely traditional styles of classic Seika and its variants —Kenzan Seika and Kabuwake. A comprehensive lesson in creating a semiformal Seika arrangement will teach the student new skills and explain the strict rules of this classic style. The Kabuwake lesson which follows will enable the student to create not only this, but also the Kenzan Seika style—for a Kabuwake arrangement is basically a Kenzan Seika arrangement divided into two parts.

Modern arrangements, on the other hand, may be technically simpler to create. Yet they too require a thorough understanding of the techniques and the principles of composition acquired in the study of more formal styles. Beyond this they require the designer to display artistic individuality and imagination, and therefore the creation of a truly successful modern arrangement is an intensely and personally satisfying experience.

MAKING SEIKA ARRANGEMENTS

Having mastered the basic techniques of Ikebana in the Moribana and Nageire styles, the student may well be eager to create the beautiful Seika arrangements pictured in Part Two. Seika includes the Kabuwake style, which is a Seika or Kenzan Seika arrangement divided into two parts.

Part of the pleasure of arranging Seika is that it is like playing a game—there are strict rules, but the living quality of the materials poses new challenges each time. The principle in Seika is the balancing of forms and the expression of the beauty of balance in nature. The creativity of the arranger is expressed in choice of materials, judgment in how best to fit them into the established patterns, and skill of execution.

The Basic Rules

If the *shin* branch is narrow, make it twice the measure of the container. A thicker branch should be cut to a little less than twice the measure of the container; in both cases add to this the length of stem to be inserted in the vase (Figure 431).

Figure 432 illustrates the proper relationship of length among the three main branches. *Soe* should be about three-fifths the length of *shin*, and *tai-saki*, the Seika term for the Moribana *tai*, three-fifths the length of *soe*. These measurements are always determined after the branches have been bent into shape.

Shin is shaped like an archer's bow, curving out to its midpoint and then curving back so that the top is directly above the lower end of the branch, as shown in Figure 433. The ideal proportions of the three main branches and their various complements are illustrated in Figure 434, as well as their proper curving in the formal style. As few as five and an almost unlimited number of branches may be used, but it must always be an odd number. In our discussion we will use nine.

Shin, soe, and *tai-saki* are by now familiar terms for the three main branches. But in Seika the comple-

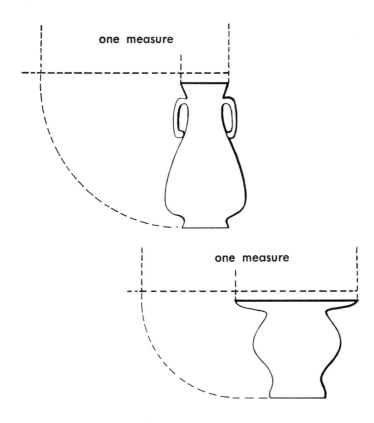

431. *The measure of a vase is its height plus its outside diameter*

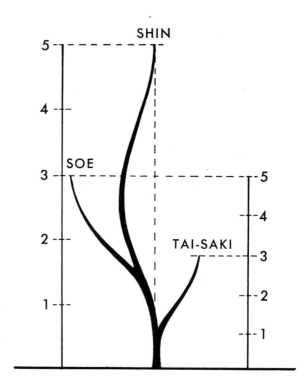

432. *The proper relationship of length among the three principal branches in Seika arrangements.* Soe *is three-fifths the length of* shin, tai-saki *three-fifths the length of* soe

mentary branches have traditional names that will be new to the student, and there are some new parts as well. The *shin* always has two complements, *mae ashirai* (the complement placed in *front*), and *ushiro ashirai* (the complement placed in *back*). We will call these the front and back complements.

Shin and *soe* always have back complements, but they need not necessarily both have front complements. If *soe* has only the back complement, as is true in our examples, it is called simply the *soe* complement. If *tai-saki* has only one, it is called *tani*, which means valley in Japanese. It is always the shortest material used.

Dō, a term borrowed from the Rikka style, follows the body or trunk of the arrangement and is always at or near the center, and about half as long as *shin*.

Tai-mikomi is the last branch added, and is placed at the back of the arrangement.

In raising the number of component parts, the various major branches may all have front and back comple-

ments, and then the complements themselves may acquire their own front and back complements.

Materials used for the *shin* and *soe* groups are usually branches—evergreen, flowering, or even bare. The same material is always used for these two groups.

Tai-saki, tani, and *dō* may be made of the same material as the *shin* and *soe* groups, and when this is the case, flowers are used for *tai-mikomi.* Or it may be composed of flowers or leaves. When flowers are used for *dō*, it is wise to use leaves for *tai-saki* and *tani,* although a smaller flower or bud may be used for *tani.*

In making Seika arrangements in a shallow container and using a kenzan, *shin, soe,* and *tai-saki* may all be of different materials, but it is best to follow the rules of nature. For example, naturally tall material is suitable for *shin*, and the same material may be used for *soe. Dō, tani,* and *tai-mikomi* may be another kind of flower, and *tai-saki* the leaves of these flowers, other leaves, or other low-growing flowers. When a Kenzan Seika arrangement is finished, the kenzan is covered

296

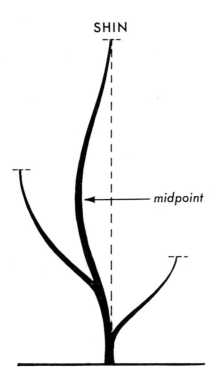

433. Shin *curves out to its midpoint and then back so that its tip stands directly above its lower end*

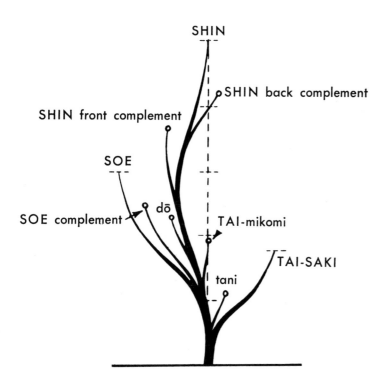

434. *The formal style of Seika*

with small pebbles or sand; the same is true of informal Seika arrangements, which are also made in shallow containers.

As in Moribana, the formal style is slim rather than curving outward, and narrow containers of the kind shown in Figure 435 are the most effective. Figure 436 shows the semiformal style, which is somewhat more curved and open than the formal one. It is perhaps the most graceful and popular, and lends itself to almost any material. The proportions of the complements are the same as for the formal style, but *usubata* vases of the type shown (Figure 437) are effective and traditional.

The informal style (Figure 438), the freest and most animated in its curves, suggests running people, movement, dynamic action. Containers for informal styles are shallow except in the case of Two-Level and hanging arrangements, which are made in their own traditional vases (Figure 439).

The contrast between the faces and backs of leaves, and the amount of the face shown are very important. In the Ikenobō and Ryūsei schools, less of the face is seen than in some of the others. The face symbolizes the future, the back the past or present. Showing less of the face expresses optimism. Figure 440 illustrates how the faces of leaves are presented by teachers of the Ryūsei School, and the directions the leaves assume. (See also Figure 70.)

435. *Suitable vases for formal Seika arrangements*

297

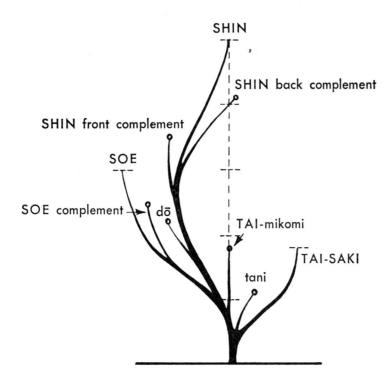

436. The semiformal style of Seika

To make the *kubari* holder pictured in Figure 441, cut two sticks to the inside diameter of the container at the point where the holder is to be positioned. Make a cut on an angle at one end of each stick, to fit the curve of the container, and wire these ends tightly together in two places, as shown. Then fit the holder into the mouth of the container. (It is often possible to find a forked branch, especially from a viburnum, that can be used as a *kubari*.) After the last branch is added to the arrangement, the whole is tightened with a third stick placed as illustrated.

Figure 442 shows the numbered order in which each part is placed in the *kubari* in the classic Seika style, assuming that nine individual stems are employed. When branches are used, however, it is often possible to so trim them that more than one branch on a stem may serve as one of the major parts of the arrangement—for example, the *shin* branch may also include a branch suitable for one or more of its complements. This will become very clear in the later part of our lesson, in which the making of an actual arrangement is illustrated step by step.

The directions in which *shin, soe,* and *tai-saki* will be

bent are indicated in Figure 443. *Shin* stands vertical, curved out to the left and back to center. *Soe* is bent to somewhat less than 45 degrees in the left rear corner. *Tai-saki* is bent to 45 degrees in the right front corner. Figure 444 shows the directions assumed by the complementary materials. *Tani* (2) is vertical. *Dō* (3), which is almost vertical, leans a little into the left front corner. The *shin* front complement (4) follows the line of *dō* approximately. The *shin* back complement (6) goes in the opposite direction to the front complement (4), leaning into the right rear corner. The *soe* complement (8) points toward the left rear corner, and *tai-mikomi* (9), the last branch to be added, leans a little, directly to the rear.

A Semiformal Seika Arrangement

We have discussed the general rules governing Seika arrangements, the names of the various units, and the technique used in securing the materials in place. Now let us see how an actual arrangement is created.

In Figure 445 we see three branches. Branch A is suitable for *shin*, branch B, thinner and less interesting than A, is suitable for *soe*. The lightest branch, C, may be used for *tai-saki*.

When branches are used, it is often possible that more than one element of an arrangement can be found on a single stem, and the judgment of the designer at this point is crucial to the success of the finished ar-

437. Suitable vases for semiformal Seika arrangements

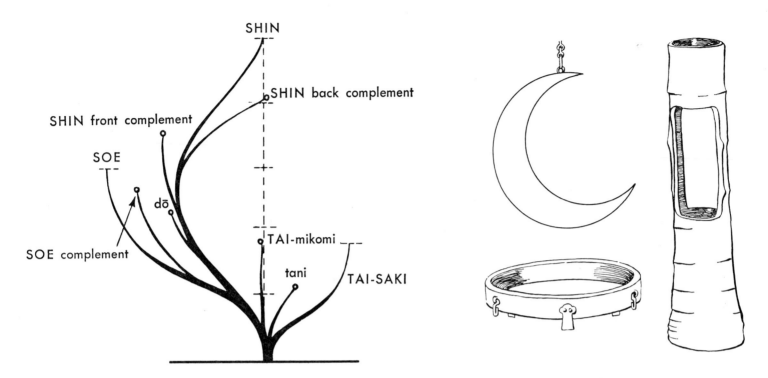

438. *The informal style of Seika*

439. *Suitable containers for informal Seika arrangements*

rangement. In Figure 446 we see branch *A*, the *shin* branch, again. The designer has decided that the portion labeled *1* is to be the *shin* itself, but also that the portion labeled *2* will become its back complement and that labeled *3* its front complement. He must now trim down all the subsidiary branches that are longer than the major ones, removing some altogether in order to emphasize the lines of those that remain.

The trimming has been almost completed in Figure 447. The arranger has kept as many blossoms as possible. Had there been interesting leaves, or fruit that might have lent atmosphere, he would have kept those, too, unless they were large enough to distract attention from the main branches.

Figure 448 shows the *B* or *soe* branch, with *soe* itself labeled *1*. The branch labeled *2* will become its back complement. Branch *B* has been heavily trimmed and *soe* is about to be clipped down to its proper height in Figure 449. Its back complement will then be cut to about two-thirds the length of *soe*, as marked, and the lower part of the stem straightened, using the one-cut technique (see Figures 249, 250).

The *shin* and *soe* branches are now arranged in the

440. *The contrast between faces and backs of leaves as they are presented in the Ryūsei School. Note also the directions the leaves assume—two moving strongly in different directions, the third more weakly*

299

441. *A* kubari *holder, with flower stems held in place by a third stick*

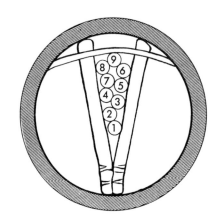

1 TAI-SAKI
2 tani
3 dō
4 SHIN front complement
5 SHIN
6 SHIN back complement
7 SOE
8 SOE complement
9 TAI-mikomi

442. *The positions of materials in the* kubari

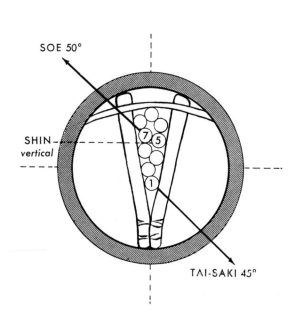

443. *The directions assumed by* shin, soe, *and* tai-saki

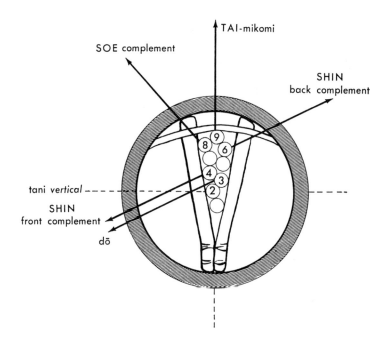

444. *The directions assumed by the complementary materials*

(Figure 453), the arranger carefully examines all the branches and does his final trimming and adjusting.

In Figure 454 we see the completed arrangement. The two tulips make *tai-mikomi*, their smooth curves contrasting with the angularity of the branches. Though following the rules of Seika, the arranger has allowed his materials to retain their own character.

446. *The* shin *branch. The portion numbered 1 will become the* shin *itself, 2 will be its back and 3 its front complement*

445. A *is the* shin, B *the* soe, *and* C *the* tai-saki

vase in approximate position, so that their proportions may be checked (Figure 450). While these branches are in place, the arranger takes the opportunity to measure the *tai* branch against them. He determines its proper length and points of interest (Figure 451), and then trims both from tip and end as may be necessary in order to place the blossoms in just the right areas.

Our three branches are fixed in position (Figure 452). The marked portion becomes *tani*, but the branch curving to the right must still be brought to the left. When it has been shaped and the *dō* branch added

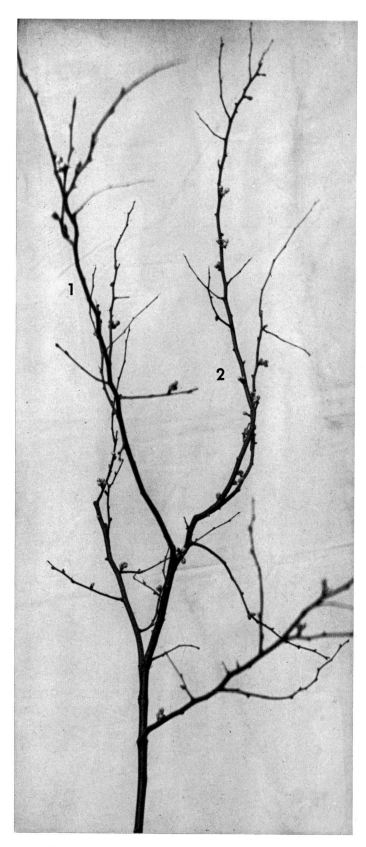

447. *The* shin *branch almost completely trimmed*

448. *The soe branch. The portion numbered* 1 *will become the soe itself, with* 2 *becoming its back complement*

449

450

451

449. *The soe branch heavily trimmed. Soe and its back complement will be cut down and the lower part of the stem straightened as indicated*

450. *The shin and soe branches arranged in approximate position*

451. *The tai-saki branch being measured against the other two*

303

452

453

452. *The three main branches in position. The marked portion will become* tani, *with the branch at the right bent as indicated*

453. *All the branches in place and ready for final trimming and adjusting before the* tai-mikomi *is added to complete the arrangement*

OPPOSITE: 454. *The finished arrangement, with tulips added as the* tai-mikomi. *The three-legged bronze* usubata *vase has animal-shaped handles. Inlaid in gold and silver is a water scene with reeds, an aquatic bird, and tree trunks. Such antique containers are treasured by the Japanese and handed down from generation to generation*

MAKING A KABUWAKE ARRANGEMENT

As we have learned, a Kabuwake arrangement is an informal Seika divided into two parts—a male part composed of the *shin* and *soe* groups, and a female part composed of the *tai-saki* group. As with any of the informal styles, a special degree of freedom is permitted.

This freedom is demonstrated in several ways in Figure 455, which shows the major branches of the male group. Many subsidiary branches have been allowed to remain simply because of their graceful effect. The branch labeled *1* is *shin*, *2* is the back complement, and *3* the front complement. Careful examination will reveal that the front complement is really in back, and the back complement in front, which is possible only in informal arrangements. The back complement remains the back complement because of its greater length and importance. The front complement could be left out entirely if need be, but the back complement must always accompany *shin*. Branch *4* is *soe*, in its proper position in the rear corner. In informal arrangements it is also permissible to have *soe* in the front corner.

Regardless of the shape of the container, the kenzan are positioned according to the principles illustrated in Figure 456. Figure 457 shows the positioning of the *tai-saki* group of materials on their kenzan.

The piece of weathered wood we see added in Figure 458 is called *tai-za*, "borrowing the place of the *tai-saki* group." Its shorter prong, on the left, fulfills the function of complement to the *tai-za*. It is a piece added if it is necessary to hide the bare lower portion of a *shin* branch. Care must be taken to keep it shorter and less important than the *tai-saki* group.

Now an iris taller than the *tai-za* is added as *dō*, and a second, shorter one becomes *tai-mikomi* (Figure 459). Kabuwake arrangements are meant to suggest a water or waterside scene, and the materials used should be chosen accordingly. Both groups may be composed of

455. The major branches of the male group. Branch 1 is shin *itself, 2 its back and 3 its front complement. Branch 4 is* soe

aquatic plants, like water lilies. The *shin–soe* group may be of land-growing material or of tall marsh grasses and the *tai-saki* group of waterside plants or plants that require a great deal of water when growing. If one of the materials is more definitely a water or waterside plant than the others, it should be used in the *tai-saki* group. Both groups should not be composed of land-growing material, although there are a few exceptions to these rules—spirea and lilies, for example, and nar-

row-stemmed, curved branches with small delicate leaves.

In Figure 460 we see the finished arrangement. The fine, curved leaf extending to the right is the *tai-saki* itself. The two other, shorter leaves are its complements, and although both are placed on the kenzan behind *tai-saki*, one spreads out to the front and the other to the back of it. The shortest iris is *tani*. The finishing touch is covering the two kenzan with pebbles or sand.

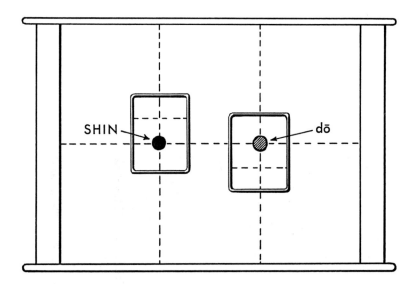

456. The positions of the kenzan in the container and of the shin *and* dō *on their kenzan*

457. The positions of the elements of the female group on their kenzan

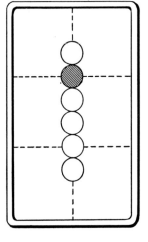

TAI-mikomi

dō

dō complement

tani

TAI-SAKI front and back complements

TAI-SAKI

458. *The added piece of driftwood is called* tai-za, *"borrow-ing the place of the* tai-saki *group." Its shorter prong fulfills the function of complement to the* tai-za

459. *The taller iris is* dō, *the shorter one* tai-mikomi. *It is important that the* dō *be taller than the* tai-za

OPPOSITE: 460. *The finished arrangement. Worm-eaten wood is a favorite material for arrangements suggesting water or waterside scenes. Here it blends especially well with the weathered wood of the* tai-za *and the bare branches, and also serves to sharpen the contrast between them and the fresh, crisp irises*

INTRODUCTION TO MODERN STYLES

THE TECHNIQUES AND PRINCIPLES of classic Ikebana underlie the modern trends, and the student who has mastered them is now equipped to begin creating independent designs.

There are two basic approaches—the naturalistic and the abstract. The student who leans toward the naturalistic will continue to emphasize the colors and lines of naturally growing flowers, but with new freedom. For example, in basic Moribana, branches are generally used for *shin* and smaller leaves or flowers for the complements. Now the student may wish to experiment with complementary flowers that are larger than the branches. There are two essential purposes: to reveal natural beauty as it really is, and at the same time to create a personal expression.

The second approach leads to the creation of abstract forms that may or may not be similar to forms observed in nature. In the Abstract style, the preservation of natural beauty is not so important as the creation of arrangements that will suggest a variety of moods or emotions. The designer may choose to employ only the center of a flower and dispose of petals, leaves, and stem if that suits his purpose. He comes to look upon plants and flowers not as natural objects, but as materials to be handled in much the same way that the abstract painter handles paints or other substances. The resulting arrangements often resemble modern abstract sculpture more than traditional Ikebana.

The designer of the arrangement pictured in Figure 461, entitled "Early Fall," has tried to suggest the cool freshness of the harvest season. He has combined feathery tufts of golden-brown miscanthus with yellow patrinia. Near the base of the arrangement are small twigs of Enkianthus japonicus, whose leaves have already begun to put on their fall colors, and numerous pale purple-blue gentians.

461. "Early Fall." The naturalistic approach. The designer has used materials symbolic of the autumn season

462. *"Red Tears." Here the designer has selected his materials purely for their shape, color, and texture*

This arrangement is one of the more naturalistic in the modern free styles. The artist has not endeavored to reproduce nature precisely, but has attempted, instead, to reveal his own personal feeling with materials used in their natural state.

By contrast, in the arrangement entitled "Red Tears," shown in Figure 462, the only materials used are the right half of a dark-green monstera leaf, branches of bleached ground cherry tree with berries, and two crimson gerbera blossoms. One of the flowers is made to follow the lines of the monstera leaf, while the other emerges from a small hole in the container. From the same hole a red tear appears to have trickled down and congealed on the side of the ivory-white ceramic vase.

Designers of abstract creations in the free style may use both fresh and dry materials at will. The principal difference between the abstract and the naturalistic schools of modern arrangement lies in the way the artist looks upon his materials. The designer of "Early Fall" chose miscanthus as one of his materials because it is an autumn plant. An artist of the abstract persuasion, however, would value this material solely for its tallness and straightness. Again, the abstractionist would look upon tulips not as signs of spring, but as possible providers of colorful round masses and noble straight lines. In brief, the abstract designer is interested in shapes, colors, and designs, rather than in innate beauty or traditional connotations.

THE EXPRESSION OF FEELING

LIKE THE SCULPTOR OR PAINTER, the flower arranger who aspires to rise above the level of the purely decorative must be concerned with the expression of human emotions. In doing so, he must acquire the same feeling for the language of flowers that the poet has for the language of words. The success with which the designer conveys his feelings to the viewer depends to a large degree on the sensitivity of the viewer himself, but the expressive qualities of flowers will often penetrate to the mind and heart where even words would fail.

To a greater extent than in painting or sculpture, the natural propensities of the materials influence the overall psychological effect. Early spring flowers, for example, will naturally suggest youth, freshness, and joy,

OPPOSITE: *463. "Joy." Pink roses and a phoenix branch are arranged in such a way that every line is in complete harmony with the vase. The flowers have been carefully bent to conceal the mechanics of the arrangement, always a necessary consideration when the container is transparent*

464. "Sorrow." Not only the choice of Easter lilies, with their connotation of death, but their combination with the angular, bare euonymus branches, the somberness of the color scheme, and the emphasis on downward lines create the mood

whereas flowers plucked from under a hot summer sun are apt to suggest intense passion. Flowers will often produce an emotional sensation even when the designer has made no conscious effort to achieve one. The arranger must therefore be careful to analyze the psychological connotations of the materials he uses.

To a great extent, mode of expression depends on personal tastes and feelings. The designer will find, however, that there are two general situations with which he must deal. One occurs when he starts with a definite idea or emotion of his own, to which he must adjust the materials he uses. The other occurs when he accepts the traditional symbolism of the plants as his point of departure and adjusts his frame of mind accordingly. In the first instance the arranger will have to pick and choose among a variety of materials to find those that best fit his plan; in the second he must decide what sort of feeling a given set of materials can best be made to express. It is a question of subjectivity or objectivity, but in either case the probable psychological overtones of each material used must be taken into consideration. In the arrangements pictured in Figures 463 and 464 the designer has aimed deliberately at expressing the contrasting emotions of joy and sorrow.

UNUSUAL OBJECTS AS IKEBANA THEMES

ALL OF US HAVE a supply of trinkets and mementos collected over the years—toys or keepsakes from our childhood, souvenirs from a trip abroad, or odds and ends that for some reason or other we do not wish to throw away. Such mementos are customarily hidden away in the corner of a drawer or shelf, but many of them can be used attractively as the focal point of a floral arrangement. There is, in fact, a style called Morimono, in which arrangements are built around objects other than flowers, and such arrangements are often seen in exhibitions.

Heirlooms such as the model of an imperial carriage shown in Figure 465 are treasured, of course, and carefully handed down from one generation to the next. The soft colors of the hydrangeas and the stones used in the arrangement evoke a sense of nostalgia for the glories of the past.

The principal element in the arrangement shown in Figure 466 is a beautiful Japanese fan of a sort often used in the classical dance. The fan is covered with bright silver paper on which there are brilliant red stripes. To emphasize its shiny black-lacquered frame, white lilies have been placed at the back of the design. The freshness of the lilies contrasts nicely with the somewhat artificial elegance of the fan.

The horse in Figure 467 is a folk toy produced in the northeastern area of Honshu, the central Japanese island. Its black-lacquered surface is adorned with brilliant shades of gold, silver, red, yellow, orange, green, and blue. The orange-red gerbera flowers placed in front of and behind the horse make it appear to be in motion. Although Japan has a particular wealth of folk toys for use in arrangements like this, equally suitable toys are to be found in almost every country.

OPPOSITE: *465. This delightful arrangement uses violet hydrangeas, violet-gray stones, and a model of an ancient imperial carriage, suggesting a mood of melancholy remembrance of things past*

466. A beautiful Japanese fan combines with fresh lilies whose leaves repeat the lines of the fan

467. A gaily painted toy horse combines with bright gerbera blossoms

316

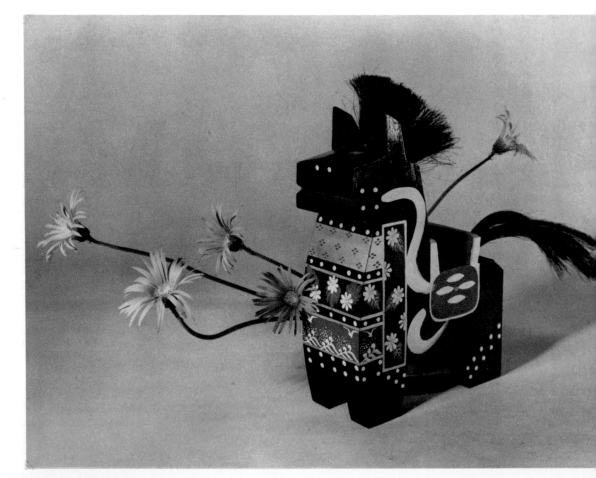

ARRANGEMENTS
CREATED TO FILL DIFFICULT SPACES

FLORAL ARRANGEMENTS ARE usually displayed in prominent settings, but this does not necessarily have to be. On the contrary, awkward corners or empty gaps that one would not ordinarily think susceptible to decoration may suddenly spring to life with the addition of a well-planned Ikebana. Such spaces are often difficult to adorn satisfactorily, but modern techniques of flower arrangement offer many interesting solutions.

Our first arrangement, shown in Figure 468, was designed for a narrow vertical space. Dried brown stalks of fuller's teasel were secured in a vase at the center of the arrangement and made to point both upward and downward from that point. Leaves of dried ruscus, combined with these stalks, also flow both upward and downward from the center. Purple-red liatris flowers add color and balance, and the bold lines of the arrangement are gathered together by this mass of color at the midpoint.

A comparatively large blank space may be decorated with a suspended arrangement of the sort shown in Figure 469. A hole was cut in the blue glass ball that serves as the vase, and inside the ball a vine of Smilax china with bright red berries has been wound up tightly to provide both color and a firm base into which the other materials may be inserted. From the vase, more branches of smilax flow downward, dotting the surrounding space with spots of brilliant color. Yellow and pink gladioli complete the design. If hung properly, this arrangement will swing and turn gently in the breeze, like a mobile.

A narrow horizontal space is ideal for arrangements like the one shown in Figure 470. Although they can be used in a number of ways, they are shown to best

468. An arrangement designed for a narrow vertical space. Dried fuller's teasel and ruscus combine with purple-red liatris

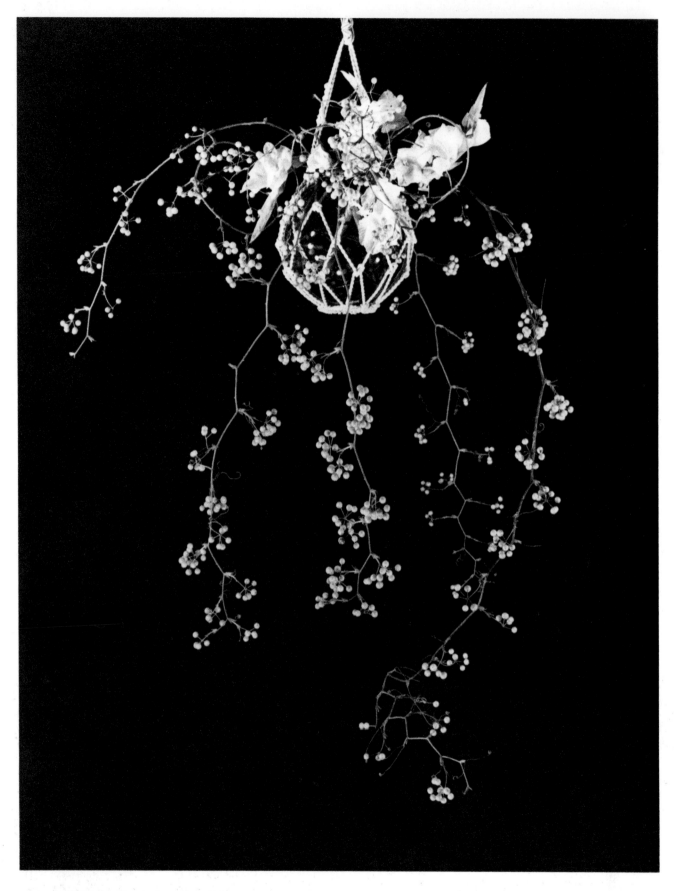

469. *An arrangement designed for a large blank space. Smilax vines with bright red berries and pink and yellow gladioli in a blue glass bowl*

470. An arrangement designed for a narrow horizontal space. A dried lotus seed pod, white-painted stalks of bamboo, and dried hydrangea blossoms are accented by the orange-red of fresh gerbera blossoms

advantage against a blank wall. A section of dried lotus seed pod and dried hydrangea blossoms, placed slightly to left of center, provide the focal point, from which white-painted stalks of bamboo shoot off to left and right. Orange-red gerbera flowers add color and contrast. The addition of a fresh flower or two will sometimes lend needed vitality to a design otherwise composed of dry materials. The advanced student of Ikebana will want to experiment with many combinations of fresh and dry materials.

A low table set in an awkward corner would benefit from the arrangement shown in Figure 471. The designer has tried to suggest a quiet, sequestered pond. He has chosen a low, flat container, in which the arrangement is supported by means of a small kenzan. Water lilies are the principal element, with some of their leaves serving to conceal the kenzan. Other flowers and leaves may be used in place of the water lily, provided their stems are kept short and the impression of floating is preserved. Small pebbles can also contribute to the total effect, if they harmonize with the other elements.

471. An arrangement designed for a low table in an awkward corner suggests water lilies growing in a quiet pond

TRANSFERRING THE BEAUTY OF GARDENS TO IKEBANA

472. A quiet pond in the Kōraku-en Gardens in Tokyo. Compare the large rock with the small one in Figure 476

THE GENERAL PRINCIPLES of Japanese landscape gardening were established by the sixteenth century, if not earlier. Since the latter part of the nineteenth century, certain innovations have been adopted from the West, but even today the typical Japanese garden is far more natural in appearance than its Western counterpart. The reason is simply that Japanese garden designers have always aimed either at reproducing natural landscapes in miniature or at creating a symbolic representation of nature as a whole. In this respect, their approach is similar to that of experts in traditional Ikebana.

There are actually several distinct types of Japanese gardens, and it is somewhat misleading to lump them all into a single class. Still, it would be no great mistake to say that Japanese gardens as a whole differ from their Western counterparts in several respects. In the first place, as we said, they are basically naturalistic. This means, among other things, that they have no regular geometric plan, no symmetry, and no immediate evidence of human tampering with natural forms. A Japanese gardener may go to unheard-of lengths to make a tree or a shrub grow in the shape he desires, but he always tries to make it seem as though the shape developed naturally.

In the second place, the emphasis in Japanese gardens is often on rocks of interesting or unusual shape rather than on statuary or sculptural ornaments (Figure 476). Stone lanterns and water basins are much employed, but when they are, the gardener almost invariably tries to make them appear to have been standing since time immemorial rather than deliberately placed to accord with a master plan.

Finally, Japanese gardens almost never depend on flowers for their beauty. Many of them have no blos-

473. *Carefully tended lawns and shrubs contrast with the natural appearance of the river and its banks. Kōraku-en Gardens, Tokyo*

soming plants whatever, and even when blossoming plants are present, they are placed as they might be in a natural wood or thicket. Most Japanese gardens are designed to be as beautiful in one season as in another —a result difficult to achieve when seasonal flowers are prominently displayed. Japanese gardens are apt to lean heavily on evergreen shrubs.

One of the most beautiful and famous gardens in Japan is the Kōraku-en in Tokyo, which was begun in 1629 by Tokugawa Yorifusa, a feudal lord of the district of Mito. It is an excellent example of the classic "tour garden," a type so named because it is intended to be walked through rather than simply viewed from an adjacent building. Figures 472 to 475, all taken in the Kōraku-en, demonstrate the skill with which traditional gardeners created landscapes almost more natural than nature itself.

Although it is impossible to capture all the beauty, grandeur, and interest of a large Japanese garden in a small Ikebana, the designer may well catch the fundamental charm of the garden. Even a single flower can suggest a magnificent scene. A mountain lily inserted at the proper angle in a simple container, for example, becomes a majestic cliff, while a single flower from an aquatic plant can convey the freshness of a rushing mountain stream or the mysterious charm of a misty marsh. Even more than technical skill, the flower arranger's task requires an eye for beauty.

A small pumice-stone lantern becomes the center of an attractive arrangement in Figure 477. Forsythia branches, complemented by Chinese asters, provide graceful lines and movement. Small stones around the lantern balance the design and complete the suggestion of a garden scene. It is important to keep supporting materials small, so that the main element appears to be larger than it actually is.

Titled "June," the arrangement shown in Figure 478 represents the welcome clear day that sometimes occurs in the midst of Japan's dreary summer rainy season. Umbrellas are drying in the sun, and irises, flowers of the season, are in bloom. Such bamboo baskets are commonly seen along the riverside, which in this design is created by sprinkling lines of white sand on a black base.

475. Steppingstones look as though nature had placed them in position. Kōraku-en Gardens, Tokyo

474. A lake view in the Kōraku-en Gardens. A similar stone lantern can be seen in miniature in Figure 477

OPPOSITE: 476. Brilliant cockscombs seem to be growing quite naturally beside the dark central stone. From behind, sprays of pampas grass stretch their heads as if to look over the top of the arrangement. Small black pebbles at the base of the design complete this model of a spectacular scene

477. *Forsythia branches and Chinese asters complement a stone lantern, some rocks, and a few pebbles*

478. *"June." A summer's day on the banks of a river are evoked in this arrangement*

PERMANENCE AND CHANGE IN IKEBANA

ALMOST FROM THE BEGINNING of history, mankind has expressed its sorrow and its joy through the medium of flowers. In the hustle and bustle of modern times, the natural world of flowers has come to seem very remote from the actual business of living. But even so, who has not taken time to gaze at a lovely blossom and feel refreshed?

Whatever the age, primitive or contemporary, there is within the human heart a silent, often unconscious realization that man and nature are bound together in an inseparable union. To be sure, this union is not a static relationship, but one that shifts and changes in accordance with the times. Revolutions in ways of life and in the types of buildings in which man lives and works have influenced his concept of natural phenomena and, consequently, his mode of dealing with them in the expressive arts, flower arrangement included.

Perhaps the greatest change that has occurred in Ikebana in recent decades is a shift from the purely natu-

479. "Cave." This arrangement, in the Abstract style, is constructed of branches nailed together and painted. Although it conveys no message from the world of nature, it does express power and complexity in the way that the roots of a tree might

ralistic approach to one that might be described as expressionistic. Instead of centering their designs on the innate beauty of flowers and plants, many modern flower arrangers choose to express their own thoughts and feelings in any way that seems effective, regardless of whether they allow their natural materials to retain their original shapes and colors. As a result, the relatively strict forms of classical flower arrangement have given way to freer, abstract forms that are felt to accord more completely with our own changing times.

The effect of modern building methods on flower arrangement cannot be overemphasized. The steel, glass, and concrete buildings of today offer new types of spaces, many of which invite the use of materials that would have been totally out of place in traditional rooms—not the least of these materials being the same steel, glass, and concrete from which modern buildings are constructed.

With the appearance of modern arrangements, many of which contain no flowers at all, there has arisen a need for a new definition of Ikebana. The tender, peaceful Chabana composed of a single flower seems to represent not merely a different art, but a different world from that of the abstract creation put together with hard, rough, modern materials. Is it proper to class these two contrasting types together as Ikebana?

In a historical sense, yes. The Abstract style, after all, was developed by arrangers grounded in traditional Ikebana, and although they may seem to have come a long way from it, they are still closely connected to the great lineage of the art. Furthermore, many of them consciously attempt to employ the broad aesthetic principles that have developed over the ages.

And yet, in comparison with the traditional flower arrangements, modern Ikebana often seem lacking in tenderness or loveliness. A work such as "Cave" (Figure 479), although constructed of branches, conveys no message from the world of nature which the observer can appreciate instinctively. Instead, it represents an attempt on the part of the artist to express a personal, and possibly very complex, emotion of his own. Perhaps, as some have argued, it would be best to find some

entirely new name for this new style and reserve the name Ikebana for the traditional forms. Doubtless, indeed, a suitable name *will* be found if the Abstract style continues to develop and spread, as it shows every sign of doing.

Still, it seems not only unfair but inaccurate to dissociate the Abstract style from the great tradition out of which it in fact emerged, and to confine the term Ikebana to the traditional styles would, in a sense, be to conceal the great scope and potentialities of the art. Even in the past, the art of Ikebana was rich in variety, and it has experienced revolutions of almost the same magnitude as that which has occurred in recent years.

From the first simple floral offerings to Buddhist images the Nageire style was born. Next came the vastly more complicated Rikka style, with its abundance of materials displayed so nobly and luxuriously. In reaction there emerged the Seika style, which was, in essence, a reversion to an emphasis on the natural beauty and character of simple floral materials. In our own century, Seika has been eclipsed in popularity by the Moribana style, which in turn gave birth to the freer methods of arrangement now in fashion. All in all, it seems best to regard the contemporary Abstract style, not as a departure from the art of Ikebana, but as a broadening of its scope, an attempt to accommodate an ancient art to its present-day surroundings.

The history of flower arrangement is essentially the history of mankind. In countless ways, Ikebana reflects the attitudes of men as they faced the crossroads of time. That contemporary flower arrangers have found new forms and inspirations in their own age is a sign, not that their art is dying, but that it has the vigor necessary for survival and growth. And lovers of Ikebana, whether they are strict traditionalists or strictly modern, will always be bound together by one feeling held in common—a quiet, nostalgic love of the simple beauty of a single flower blooming in its natural setting.

OPPOSITE: *480. A zinnia bud and a spray of sorbaria, placed with seeming artlessness in their sumptuous vase, create a picture of timeless beauty*

APPENDIXES

Keeping Cut Flowers Fresh

Your Garden and Ikebana

Suggested Combinations for Ikebana

The Symbolism of Plants and Suggestions

for Their Enhancement

KEEPING CUT FLOWERS FRESH

RUNNING ALL THROUGH A PLANT are tiny conducting tissues which carry moisture and nourishment from the roots to the smallest leaf at the top. A constant flow of moisture is necessary to preserve life. When flowers are cut off from their roots, moisture in the leaves and flowers evaporates and they soon wither and die. A number of steps can be taken, however, to delay the inevitable.

When a flower stem is cut, air seeps into the lower stem and blocks the continuous flow of moisture to the plant. If this can be prevented, the flower will live much longer.

Cutting the stem under water (Figure 481). The simplest way to avoid air in the lower stem is to cut it off under water. When this is done, the vase to be used should be at hand, so that a quick transfer can be made. This method is most effective with lilies, gladioli, daffodils, and other flowers with soft, juicy stems, and is also the safest method to use for most branches.

Flowers that have been displayed for some time and show signs of withering may be revived by clipping a piece from their stems under water. After this treatment, flowers placed in a container of fresh water to a depth of at least one-third of their stems and left in a cool place overnight will generally revive by morning.

The boiling water treatment (Figure 482). This method is particularly effective for flowers such as roses, chrysanthemums, daisies, gentians, liatris, hydrangeas, and dahlias, whose stems are firm on the outside but soft within. After the stems have been cut, immerse them in about two inches of boiling water for five minutes. The boiling water forces the air in the stems to expand slightly and escape. Small bubbles may be seen at this point. The submerged parts of the stems may lose color, but this is not to be feared. They become sturdy once again if put into cold water immediately after the boiling water treatment, as the stems contract and bring up fresh water. The key to this treatment is the quick transfer from hot water to cold.

This method is convenient when a large number of flowers must be cared for at one time.

The burning method (Figure 483). Materials suited to this method include those listed for the boiling water

481. Cutting a stem under water

482. The boiling water method

method, poinsettias, clematis, poppies, maidenhair fern, and, generally, the firmest stems and wood. In this method, about one inch of the stem is held in the hottest part of a flame until it is a glowing red. This turns the juicy stem to charcoal, which, as it is porous, readily absorbs moisture, making it available to the rest of the branch. While the end is still burning, it is thrust into cold water. When using the boiling or burning methods, it is best to wrap the upper parts of the materials in wet cloth or paper to protect them from the heat.

Another simple treatment is to scrape the bottom two or three inches or crush the clipped ends of the stems. Or split them vertically into four parts with a sharp pair of scissors or a knife, so as to increase the water-absorbing area (Figure 484).

The basic principles are to avoid the introduction of air into the stems and to improve the flow of moisture through the arteries. Heat expands the stems of branches and flowers, enabling air to escape from the arteries of the plant; cold water closes these paths to air and assists in forcing life-giving moisture in. Whenever heat is used in the treatment, a quick transfer to cold water is of crucial importance.

Since heat sterilizes the ends of the stems, any of the heat treatments will also aid in preventing decay. A few drops of household bleach or disinfectant in the vase is also very effective. Other helpful steps include changing the water in the vase at least every three days and spraying the arrangement lightly every day. (Spraying the backs of the leaves is more effective than spraying the faces.)

We do not recommend the use of chemicals, for their acidic and alkaline properties and the quantities used must be carefully matched to the materials being treated. Equally good results may be obtained with simpler and safer classic methods. The list which follows provides a convenient guide to the preferred treatment for a large number of plant materials. No such listing can be complete, of course, and the character of the stem is, as outlined above, the determining factor in most cases.

483. The burning method

484. Scraping, mashing, and splitting stem ends

acacia—split stem ends

aconite (monkshood)—cut in water

agapanthus (African lily)—cut in water

akebia—cut in water and crush stem ends

amaranth—cut in water. Burn stem ends or boil for 3 minutes in salted water or water with a little vinegar. Plunge in cold water. Small stalks may be treated by rubbing salt into the freshly cut stem end. If salted water is used, put a little salt in the vase. If vinegar is used, put a few drops in the vase. If foliage is heavy, strip some leaves

amaryllis—cut in water

ananas blossom—cut in water

anemone—cut in water. When they begin to droop, dip stem ends in alcohol for a few seconds, or rub with salt

anthurium—cut in water

artichoke blossom—cut in water. If the leaves droop, stand in vinegar for a few minutes

asparagus fern—use boiling water method

aspidistra—cut in water. If the stems start to bend, recut and rub with salt and stand in water. When they are firm again, recut in fresh water

aster—cut in water. If they begin to droop, crush stem ends and then use boiling water or burning method

azalea—cut in water

babies'-breath (gypsophila)—cut in water

balsam—split stem ends

bamboo—pierce holes down through center to the bottom node, or drill a small hole through the side just below each node. Fill with a mixture of half alcohol and half water, or, if obtainable, sake (Japanese rice wine)

banana plant—cut in water. Apply lemon juice or vinegar to all cut edges to prevent discoloring

begonia—cut in water

bellflower—cut in water. If they start to droop, use burning method

bird-of-paradise (strelitzia)—cut in water

bittersweet—cut in water, or, if it is to be dried, spray with clear lacquer

blackberry lily—cut in water

black-eyed Susan—cut in water. If they begin to droop, recut and use boiling water method

bougainvillea—split woody stems, strip off unnecessary foliage

boxthorn—cut in water or use burning method. Then split stem ends under water

broom—cut in water

burnet (sanguisorba)—use burning method. Be sure to leave in cold water at least 5 minutes afterwards

bush clover—crush stem ends and use boiling water method

caladium—cut in water, insert heavy wire up through stem to support leaves

calendula—cut in water

calla lily—cut in water. Rub stem ends with salt, let stand a few minutes, then recut in fresh water

camellia—cut in water. Press dressmaker's pin through center of blossom into stem to hold it firmly in place, or shake a little salt into each blossom

candytuft—cut in water. If they start to droop, use boiling water method

canna lily—cut in water. If they start to droop, use boiling water method

carnation—cut in water

castor-oil plant—cut in water. If they start to droop, use boiling water method

cattail—cut in water

cherry blossom—split stem ends

Christmas rose—use burning method and stand in deep cold water overnight

chrysanthemum—cut in water, scrape, split, or crush stem ends, or break stems with fingers. For wilting plants, break stems with fingers and use boiling water method, then stand in deep cold water overnight

clematis—crush stems as far up as they will be concealed by the container. If they start drooping, use burning method

clivia—cut in water

club moss—split stem ends

cockscomb—cut in water. When the leaves begin to droop, use boiling water method

coleus—cut in water and split stems

columbine—cut in water. Avoid wetting blossoms

cornflower—cut in water

cosmos—crush stem ends and rub salt, or use burning method

cyclamen—cut in water or use burning method
cymbidium—cut in water

daffodil—cut in water
dahlia—cut in water or use boiling water method
delphinium—cut in water
dendrobium—cut in water
deutzia—use burning method
Dianthus superbus (pink)—cut in water
dogwood—split stem ends, stand in warm water and leave overnight

Easter lily—cut in water
enkianthus—split stem ends
erica—cut in water
eucalyptus—cut in water
evening primrose—use burning method
evergreens—split stem ends and stand in deep cold water overnight. Spray lightly from below with clear lacquer to hold the leaves on the branches longer

fatsia—cut in water
fern—cut in water or use boiling water method
flax—split stems, stand in warm water and leave overnight
forsythia—cut in water or split stem ends
four-o'clock (marvel of Peru)—split stem ends or cut in water
freesia—cut in water
fuchsia—split woody stems. Remove unnecessary foliage and use boiling water method
funkia (hosta; plantain lily)—split stem ends and cut in water

gardenia—cut in water. Spray foliage and blossoms. Submerge in water before arranging
gentian—crush stem ends and use boiling water method
geranium—use boiling water method
gerbera—use boiling water method
gladiolus—cut in water
globe amaranth—use boiling water method
globeflower (kerria)—cut in water, then split stem ends
gloxinia—cut in water
golden bell—cut in water
gypsophila (babies'-breath)—cut in water

hawthorn—split stem ends or use burning method
heather—cut in water
helenium—cut in water
herbaceous peony—use burning or boiling water method
hibiscus—cut in water and split stem ends
holly—split stem ends
hollyhock—split stem ends deeply and use boiling method with salt water
honeysuckle—split stem ends
hosta (plantain lily; funkia)—cut in water and split stem ends
hyacinth—cut in water
hydrangea—use boiling water or burning method
hypericum—split stem ends or use burning method

ilex—split stem ends
inula—use burning method
iris—cut in water

jasmine—split stem ends or cut in water
Job's-tears—use boiling water method with salt water

kerria (globeflower)—cut in water, then split stem ends
kudzu vine—crush stems with salt

laurel—split stem ends
liatris—cut in water
ligustrum—split stem ends
lilac—split stem ends and rub them with salt, or use burning method
lily—cut in water. See under calla lily and canna lily for special instructions
lily-of-the-valley—cut in water
linden—split stem ends and rub them with salt, or use burning method
loquat—split stem ends
lycoris—cut in water
lythrum—cut in water, then split stem ends

magnolia—split stem ends or use burning method
mallow—split stem ends or use burning method
maple—split stem ends or use burning method. Spray backs of leaves with clear lacquer, or spray fronts of leaves with sugar water (3 teaspoons to each quart of water)

marigold—cut in water. When leaves start to droop, use boiling water method

marvel-of-Peru (four-o'clock)—split stem ends or cut in water

mesembryanthemum—cut in water, then crush stem ends, or use boiling water method

mignonette—use boiling water method

millet—cut in water, or use boiling water method

mimosa—split or crush stem ends

monochoria—cut in water

monstera—cut in water

morning-glory—cut very early in the morning or in the evening—not when the sun is shining. Crush or scrape stem ends and rub them with salt, or use burning method

myrica—cut in water

Nandina domestica—crush stem ends and, if in flower, salt the water lightly

narcissus—cut in water

New Zealand flax—cut in water

oak—cut in water, or split stem ends

oleander—split stem ends or use burning method

orange blossom—split stem ends, or use burning method

orchid—cut in water. Avoid wetting petals

osmanthus—split stem ends, or use burning method

pampas grass—cut in water, or use boiling water method

pansy—cut in water

patrinia—cut in water, then crush stem ends

paulownia—split stem ends and dip in vinegar for 1 minute

peony—scrape bottom inch of stem ends deeply, then crush

periwinkle—cut in water, or use boiling water method. If leaves start to droop, use burning method

petunia—cut in water, then crush stem ends lightly

philodendron—cut in water

phlox—cut in water, then crush stem ends

phoenix—cut in water or use burning method

pine—see evergreens

pink (Dianthus superbus)—cut in water

pitcher plant—cut in water and split stem ends

plum—split stem ends

poinsettia—cut in water, then use boiling water or burning method

pomegranate—split stem ends and use burning method

poppy—cut in water and crush stem ends, or use burning method

primrose—cut in water

privet—split stem ends

pussy willow—split stem ends

quince—split stem ends

rape—cut in water

reed—use burning method, then wrap in wet cloth or paper and lay in a cool place for half an hour. Then recut in water

Rhodea japonica—cut in water

rhododendron—cut in water or split stem ends

rose—cut in water, then crush stem ends, or use boiling or burning method

rubrum lily—cut in water

salvia—split stem ends and use boiling water method

sanguisorba (burnet)—use burning method. Be sure to leave in cold water at least 5 minutes afterwards

scabiosa—cut in water

sedum (stonecrop)—cut in water

snapdragon—cut in water or use boiling water method

sorbaria—split stem ends

sorbus—split stem ends and rest in deep water overnight

spirea—split stem ends

slantonia—cut in water

star lily—cut in water

stock—cut in water or use boiling water method

stokesia—cut in water

stonecrop (sedum)—cut in water

strelitzia (bird-of-paradise)—cut in water

sumac—split stem ends. In autumn, when foliage is red, put salt water in vase to prevent leaves from falling (half a teaspoon to each quart of water)

sunflower—cut in water. If leaves begin to droop, use boiling water method

sweet pea—cut in water

sweet William—cut in water, then crush stem ends or use boiling water method *tamarisk*—crush stem ends

thermopsis—cut in water

thistle—cut in water and rub cut stem ends with salt, or use burning method

tiger lily—cut in water

trachelospermum—cut in water and crush stem ends

tree peony—see peony

tuberose—cut in water

tulip—cut in water. To prevent stems from drooping, open blossoms and insert wire down through stems. Then close petals and pinch stems very gently just under the blossoms

verbena—split stem ends and use boiling water method, adding a teaspoon of sugar to each quart of water

viburnum—cut in water and crush stem ends

wallflower—split stems and use boiling water method

water lily—cut leaves in water. Crush stems gently just under each leaf that is to be floated on water, but do not crush the others. Rest flowers in deep cold water half an hour, then use pump (see Figure 231) to fill blossoms and stems with water. Or, carefully run a wire from inside the blossom down through the stem to keep the stem from drooping

willow—split stem ends

wisteria (in flower)—split stem ends and peel back bottom inch of bark, then crush. Stand in alcohol or sake (Japanese rice wine) for half an hour. Use burning method for large branches or for foliage

yarrow—crush stem ends, rub with salt, and use burning method

zinnia—cut in water, remove unnecessary foliage. If leaves begin to wilt, use boiling water method

YOUR GARDEN AND IKEBANA

IN JAPAN FLOWERS FOR ARRANGEMENTS are always available at the ubiquitous florists—exactly those that are needed, branches or blossoms, and all properly treated and conditioned. In America the situation is rather different, but with a little thought and planning one's own garden can be an admirable source of suitable blossoms, leaves, and foliage through a good part of the year. In the house a place to work, properly equipped with shelves for containers and storage space for tools, is desirable. A gardener's workroom would be ideal, fitted with a sink, running water, and an electric hot plate. Containers should include the various shapes, with which the reader has become familiar, of bronze, pottery, possibly porcelain, basketry, and wood. If glass is chosen it should be opaque or poured very thick, rather than blown and thin. Silver or polished brass vessels do not lend themselves to the classic style; dull copper and rough-surfaced iron, however, are excellent for informal classic arrangements. Gathering containers is a never-ending collector's delight—searching out the right vase for the right place and for one's favorite flowers and style of composition. An album or two of seventeenth- and eighteenth-century Japanese flower paintings can be stimulating, too, for they reveal the qualities that flower arrangers try to suggest.

Spring

Among the early spring flowers that flourish in most gardens, crocuses, Jacob's-ladders, Job's-tears, violets, spring-flowering hellebores, and pulmonarias lend themselves to Moribana arrangements made to suggest woodland scenes. When using violets and pulmonarias, take the whole plant, but be sure to wash the roots so as not to muddy the water. The plants will survive and can be planted again. Add light branches of plum or another early-flowering shrub, forced or bare of blossoms, for *shin* and *soe*. Narcissus suit a one-specimen semiformal scheme in a low container, or a formal one in a tall vase or slim basket. When the Japanese use bulbs or iris they remove the leaves carefully and cut them to the length required.

As the heads of many of the later, tall daffodils tend to be heavy, they may be bunched with short stems to achieve a mass of color in the contemporary manner. Set them against a background of heather or an evergreen like Japanese cypress, juniper, holly, or box, grouped and clipped to repeat the round shape of the massed flower heads on a somewhat larger scale. Or place sprays of rhododendron behind and to either side of the blossoms in Nageire style.

Spring-flowering shrubs—Japanese quince, azalea, rhododendron, forsythia, cherry, viburnum—present many possibilities. Select the branch carefully so that the shape of the plant is not marred by its removal. Japanese quince, plum, or azalea, each specimen carefully pruned and used alone, lend themselves to airy arrangements in flat basins, with line the dominant factor. Interesting stones, driftwood, or low-growing foliage like pachysandra or club moss may be used to conceal the kenzan. Rhododendron and viburnum, with their massy, rounding flower heads, will look best in deep, fat bowls. Forsythia and pussy willow can be bent to a semiformal Seika style or used for trailing effects. The Japanese rarely use more than one kind of flowering branch in an arrangement, preferring to accent them with cut flowers and leaves.

The tall Darwin tulips and Oriental poppies are seldom used, but volumes have been published illustrating ways of setting off the princely elegance of various iris specimens. The German iris requires great care in arranging because it is so heavy and the falling petals are

337

so ponderous. Irises like the flags—Siberian, Japanese, and Spanish—Iris ensata, sanguinea, kaempferi, and others that have light, dainty flowers and outspreading rather than downfalling petals—these are favorites. There is hardly a vase shape or a style to which they cannot be adapted. Let the stems be very long to emphasize their grace; if other plant material is to be added to Iris kaempferi, try reeds or bulrushes in a Kabuwake arrangement—this variety likes marshy places.

The Chinese tree peony (moutan), which blooms in late spring, is so striking in itself that just a branch with one blossom and its leaves is all that is needed. Place it in a container set inside a low mahogany-colored basket of split bamboo, with perhaps a single angular branch of weathered wood set upright among the leaves to add character. Broom, too, of which the Japanese are very fond, is tractable and can easily be shaped into lithe, sweeping curves. Blossoms of species tulips or small dwarf daffodils in spring, miniature zinnias in summer, pompom chrysanthemums in fall, can make the *nejime* and *tai* elements. Broom is handsome and adaptable to most garden soils, liking it dry and sunny.

Summer

Unlike most American gardens, no Japanese garden is ever crowded with flowers, except public gardens specializing in iris, chrysanthemum, or some other favorite crop to be "viewed" on special occasions. In their landscaping, blossoming shrubs and trees, foliage plants, vines, rocks, and water predominate and reflect the natural beauties of the country itself. The influence of the ideal landscape is apparent in Japanese flower arrangements, where water and rocks may be as important as branch or bloom. The Chinese say that flowers are too ephemeral for the peace of a garden, and the Japanese feel much the same way. But with the coming of summer the majority of American gardens are ablaze with blossoms from June to November, and almost any library or botanical garden has information that tells us how to keep up the succession of blooms.

If we have said that Darwin tulips and Oriental pop-pies are seldom used, it does not mean that they cannot be used. Hardly a flower grows that cannot be given the vital, living quality or the natural flowing grace that characterize the Japanese style—provided they receive the proper thought and attention. Japanese arrangements are composed as an artist creates a picture, and what we call "rules" are simply aids to achieve a basically good design. It is here that attention to foliage comes in, and it is well worth mastering, for with its artful use half the battle is won. Among valuable foliage plants are the broad-leafed hosta; aspidistra, a tender plant in the North but one with a high survival record as a pot plant; anthurium; banana palm; cyclamen; arum; calla and canna lilies; and the leaves of the tender rex begonia. Narrower and longer-leafed are various grasses: miscanthus (a variety of pampas grass); plume grass; snake grass; bamboo; yucca; New Zealand flax; leaves of the hardy wild orchid, bletilla; and reeds. Feathery foliage and other types are dill; fennel; eucalyptus; grape leaf; porcelain ampelopsis (a hardy, handsome vine with silver-streaked leaves and blue or lilac berries); amaranth; arborvitae and other dainty types of evergreen; and various ferns. Such foliage performs a painterly function by bringing several forms into a unified whole; or it may contribute leaves more congenial than their own to certain flowers. Magnolias, blooming before their leaves come out, can be enhanced with anthurium leaves; the tall, open-faced auratum lily, native to Japan, can be used with sprays of pampas grass, but it also looks handsome set low as *nejime*, with *shin, soe,* and *tai* of large-leafed begonia. Leaves of miscanthus added to roses in Moribana arrangements add grace and liveliness to what might otherwise be a static affair.

The Japanese have great admiration for cockscomb. It appears in representations of Rikka arrangements painted on screens as early as the sixteenth century, making the *shin* component, with stalks of ornamental corn, plumes of miscanthus, branches of acacia stripped of leaves, and sprays of arborvitae for *soe,* and subsidiary branches and leaves of banana palm and box at the base for *tai.* Filmy materials like acacia, babies'-breath, and smoke tree lend a sense of atmosphere—of air and space—to complex forms.

Certain of our summer annuals and perennials have

long stems and rather monotonous lateral leaves, like spiderflower (cleome) and phlox. Spiderflower, which is frail and airy, looks lovely cut rather short and accompanied by maidenhair fern. Phlox bunched in colors ranging from pink to violet can be cut short and arranged, Nageire style, with hydrangea flower heads in soft blue and a trailing spray of its foliage. Sea holly sets off the robust forms of zinnias and marigolds, but this is only one of various foliages that can be used to advantage.

The Japanese often use plants with striking basal leaves and tall spirelike blooms, like callas, cannas, and wild asters. These, with their leaves rearranged, can be composed to look like a single growing plant; they give a sense of serene strength and striking simplicity. Hydrangeas make a handsome display with little effort. Round bowls suit them well, echoing their great round blossoms. Try the Nageire style. Among the vines, which are especially effective in hanging containers or flasks, are the morning glory; varieties of summer-blooming clematis and fall-blooming Clematis montana; wisteria; and trumpet vine. Whether the wisteria and trumpet vine bloom or not, and they are both temperamental, they deserve a place in the garden, for their habits of growth, whether green or dry, make lovely spiraling tendrils to accompany other plant material.

Autumn

While autumn is the time for chrysanthemums, the famous Seven Grasses of Autumn (*aki-no-nana-kusa*) must not be forgotten: miscanthus, patrinia, thoroughwort, Chinese bellflower, bush clover, arrowroot, and Dianthus superbus (pink). These, with the call of the deer and red maple leaves, epitomize the season for the Japanese, and we find reference to them as early as the sixth century. All are perennials, of easy culture, and grow in most old herb gardens or in country meadows. They are always arranged in semiformal Seika style, often in baskets, and sometimes only three or five are used. Sometimes other plants are substituted, such as burnet, kudzu vine, knotweed, or morning glory.

It will be noted that the flowers of these are small, of pastel shades, and often filmy. They suggest the mists of autumn which prevail in the valleys of Japan.

Thanks to the devotion of Chinese and Japanese hybridizers, the variety of color and form in imperial chrysanthemums seems almost legion. The Japanese call it the "year-round flower," as they raise it extensively in pots in stove-houses, lath-houses, and in open ground. It is one of the principal "viewing" specimens. At the turn of the last century, at the Imperial gardens at Akasaka, 160 varieties were on display, each with its own poetic name, such as Companions of the Moon, Waves in the Morning Sun, Sky at Dawn, Golden Dew, and Disheveled Hair.

The traditional rule for chrysanthemums in Seika arrangements is to use white at the top and move down through the darker colors. Variegated blossoms, the least appreciated by the Japanese as being less pure, are placed at the very bottom if they are used at all.

It is well to have a range of sizes and forms in our own gardens, in a run of congenial colors. Small ones growing in clusters make excellent *nejime* or *tai* units with broom or juniper as *shin* and *soe* in formal arrangements. They look well when different sizes, carefully proportioned in relation to one another and monochromatic in hue, are grouped together in formal or semiformal compositions. Artists in the seventeenth and eighteenth centuries painted them so, and flower masters either found inspiration in these works or had the same appreciation of the plant and its expressive possibilities.

Seika arrangements of one kind of huge pompoms or shaggy blossoms can also be very handsome. If any of the leaves have drooped, they may be lightly manipulated into an animated direction at right angles to the stem; the leaves of healthy, well-grown chrysanthemums add character to the perfection of the whole. Indeed, they are often more important than the blossoms, so care could be taken not to remove them hastily. The stems of plants that are allowed to grow freely, without staking, often take on interesting, irregular, windblown curves well suited to a Nageire arrangement. Like irises, chrysanthemums are one of the most versatile, gratifying flowers to arrange and, as with the iris, there are many books in Japanese copiously illustrated for its devotees.

Winter

This is the season for using dried materials, bare vines, bittersweet, and evergreens like holly, laurel, pine, and spruce. Experimenting with a single evergreen specimen can be a most rewarding occupation. Take a branch and study the possibilities of its form, which with thoughtful pruning will become a striking object. Any bare branches, especially those with nice lines, can be used with massed flowers, contrasting line and mass. Weeping willow or birch, for example, make beautiful and graceful forms. The willow, especially, has a pleasing golden color, and is so supple that its branches can be manipulated in many ways. Looping and tying them into circles of different sizes on a single branch creates an entirely new mood.

Flowering plum branches are especially suitable for winter arrangements. They can be forced by putting them in deep water and covering them completely with a heavy cloth, newspapers, or straw mats. Keep the cover moist and put the bucket in a warm place—blossoms will appear in about two weeks.

Camellias, which are a winter flower in Japan and very popular, can also be forced in the same way. The blossoms of forced camellia branches tend to fall off very easily, but a little salt sprinkled into each blossom holds them more firmly to the branches. Although camellias may be used for any style, the contrast between the graceful line of branch and the planes of the leaves should be emphasized.

Pussy willow can be forced or one can simply remove the bud sheaths. It is very easily manipulated—freshly cut it does not even require soaking overnight. Combine pussy willow with hyacinth, narcissus, or any bulb flower, placing the bulbs on the kenzan as though they were stems. Use a vase deep enough to conceal the bulbs. In arranging the branches, let them cross over each other, rather than seeming to sprout in different directions from a single base (see Figure 282). Or combine them with driftwood or dried plant materials in Nageire, Moribana, or Abstract style designs.

Following is a seasonal listing of some of the more common plant materials in the average garden. Obviously, this list will vary according to climate and geographical area, and equally obviously, many of these materials may be bought during most of the year at your local florist. Different parts of the same plant may be used at different seasons, as for example leaves in the spring and blossoms in the summer. Flowers and plants from all parts of the country are grouped together, even though some will be common only to the North, the Southeast and South, or to the warmer parts of the West Coast. In warmer climates, the growing season may extend through two or more calendar seasons.

The list is not meant to be definitive or restrictive, but only to suggest that your own garden, or the countryside nearby, contains an endless variety of growing things that may start you on the way to very personal Ikebana creations.

SPRING

FLOWERS AND LEAFY PLANTS

anemone
arctotis
astilbe
begonia
bleeding heart
bletilla
bouvardia
calceolaria
camass
candytuft
chionodoxa
cineraria
columbine
coral bells
crocus
cyclamen
daffodil
daisy
delphinium
dianthus
forget-me-not
foxglove
freesia
fritillary
geranium
geum
hellebore
hyacinth
iris
ismene (Peruvian daffodil)
Jacob's-ladder
Job's-tears
larkspur
lily
marigold
mignonette
narcissus
nierembergia
pansy
pentstemon
peony

periwinkle
phlox
pimpernel
poppy
primrose
pulmonaria
ranunculus
rose
rue
saxifrage
scilla
snowdrop
spiderwort
sweet pea
tigridia (Mexican shell flower)
trillium
tulip
viola
violet

SHRUBS

abelia
acacia
andromeda
angel's-trumpet
aralia
azalea
bamboo
banana shrub
bayberry
beach plum
blueberry
box
broom
buddleia
buttonbush
camellia
canary bird bush
cassia
Chinese witch hazel
chokecherry
cotoneaster
crape myrtle
currant

daphne
desert willow
deutzia
enkianthus
escallonia
euonymus
flannel bush
forsythia
fothergilla
gardenia
guava
heather
hibiscus
holly
jasmine
kerria
lantana
laurel
lemon bottlebrush
lilac
magnolia
manzanita
mescal bean
Mexican orange
Natal plum
opopanax
pomegranate
pineapple
pittosporum
pussy willow
pyracantha
quince
redbud
rhododendron
sage
shadbush
sky flower
snowball
spicebush
spirea
strawberry shrub
strawberry tree
sweet shrub
tamarisk
toyon

341

tree peony
viburnum
weigela
white fringe tree
wild lilac
witch hazel
yaupon

VINES

asparagus vine
bignonia
bittersweet
bougainvillea
clematis
grape
hoya
ivy
moonflower
passionflower
wisteria
woodbine

TREES

acacia
almond
apple
apricot
banana
bay
beech
birch
cherry
cork
crabapple
dogwood
eucalyptus
fig
gingko
goldenrain
hawthorn
jacaranda
laburnum
live oak

locust
loquat
madrone
magnolia
mimosa
olive
palm
peach
pepper
pittosporum
plum
quince
silver bell
smoke tree
sorrel
tulip
willow

SUMMER

FLOWERS
AND LEAFY PLANTS

agapanthus
allium
amaranth
amaryllis
anemone
anthurium
artichoke
arum
aspidistra
aster
astilbe
babies'-breath
banana palm
bee balm
begonia
bellflower
beloperone
bilbergia
bird-of-paradise
bletilla
caladium

calceolaria
campanula
canna
carnation
cleome
clivia
cockscomb
columbine
coreopsis
cornflower
crocus
cyclamen
dahlia
delphinium
dianthus
dieffenbachia
dill
fennel
ferns
flameflower
forget-me-not
frittilary
fuchsia
gaillardia
geranium
gerbera
geum
ginger
gladiolus
gloriosa
gloxinia
grasses
heliotrope
hosta
immortelle
iris
larkspur
lavender
lily
lotus
lupine
lythrum
magnolia
marigold
miscanthus

monstera
montbretia
New Zealand flax
nicotiana
ornamental onion
pentstemon
petunia
philodendron
phlox
phoenix
plume grass
reeds
rehmannia
rose
rudbeckia
salvia
saxifrage
scabiosa
snake grass
snakeroot
snapdragon
spiderflower
statice
stock
sunflower
tigridia
tritoma
veronica
watsonia
yucca
zinnia

SHRUBS

acacia
azalea
bamboo
berry bushes
box
broom
buddleia
creosote bush
euonymus
garrya
hydrangea

ocotillo
oleander
rhododendron
rose of Sharon
sagebush
salal
sea holly
silverberry
snowberry
spirea
tamarisk
yucca

VINES

bittersweet
cinquefoil
clematis
convolvulus
cotoneaster
creeping thyme
grape
honeysuckle
moonflower
morning glory
myrtle
pachysandra
passionflower
porcelain ampelopsis
scarlet runner
strawberry vine
sweet pea
trumpet vine
watermelon vine (with leaves)
wild cucumber
wisteria
yerba buena

FROM POOL AND WATER

arrowhead
bulrush
cattail
iris (flag)
horsetail

lobelia
lotus
pond grasses
umbrella palm
water hyacinth
water lily
water palm

TREES

arborvitae
aralia
avocado
banana
beech
buckeye
citrus
cork
eucalyptus
filbert
fringe tree
gingko
jacaranda
loquat
olive
palm
paulownia
pepper
persimmon
silk tree
smoke tree
sorbus
weeping willow

AUTUMN

FLOWERS, LEAVES, AND GRASSES

aconite (monkshood)
actinidia
amaranth
ananas
anthurium

arrowroot
artichoke
asparagus fern
aspidistra
aster
babies'-breath
bellflower
bird-of-paradise
burnet
bush clover
caladium
carnation
chrysanthemum
castor-oil plant
cockscomb
cornflower
cosmos
crocus (fall)
dahlia
dianthus
gentian
gerbera
gladiolus
iris
liatris
lily
lycoris
millet
miscanthus
monstera
New Zealand flax
orchid
pampas grass
patrinia
phoenix
plume grass
sedum
snapdragon
thistle
thoroughwort
windflower (Japanese anemone)

SHRUBS

barberry

bladdernut
blueberry
boxwood
broom
enkianthus
euonymus
heather
highbush cranberry
holly
jessamine
mahonia
nandina
ninebark
pearl bush
pittosporum
pomegranate
privet
pyracantha
rose branches (bearing rose hips)
sky flower
smoke tree
snowberry

VINES

asparagus fern
bittersweet
cinquefoil
clematis
convolvulus
cotoneaster
grape
honeysuckle
kudzu vine
moonflower
morning glory
myrtle
nasturtium (climbing)
pachysandra
passionflower
porcelain ampelopsis
scarlet runner
sky flower vine
smilax
strawberry vine

sweet pea
thyme (creeping)
trumpet vine
Virginia creeper
watermelon vine (with leaves)
wild cucumber
wisteria
yerba buena

TREES

birch
box elder
chestnut
crabapple
eucalyptus
hop hornbeam
Japanese cedar
juniper
maple
oak
pagoda
palm
sorbus
sweet gum
sycamore
tulip
white ash
yew

WINTER

BARE BRANCHES, VINES,
AND TROPICAL, HOTHOUSE,
AND HOUSE PLANT
MATERIAL TO BE COMBINED
WITH PURCHASED FLOWERS

agave
aloe
ananas
anthurium
aspidistra

bittersweet
brassaia
burnet
cactus
caladium
camellia (forced blooms or bare
    branches)
chloranthus
cotoneaster
echeveria
evergreens
ferns
forsythia (forced blooms or bare
    branches)

ginger
gourd
grapevine
heliconia
jade plant
kalanchoe
monstera
nasturtium (climbing)
orchid
palm
passionflower
plum (forced blooms or bare
    branches)
plumeria

pussy willow
rape
scarlet runner
sedum
sempirvivum
spirea (forced blooms or bare
    branches)
sugar-cane plumes
sweet pea
Tahitian spinach
ti leaves
weeping willow
wild cucumber
wisteria

SUGGESTED COMBINATIONS FOR IKEBANA

Here we offer a sampling of readily available plant materials that combine well in Ikebana. Choose one material from the left-hand column and one or two from the right. Again, as in the seasonal listing of materials from your own garden, in many areas some of the flowers, especially in winter, will be forced or purchased.

SPRING

broom *and*   daffodil
flameflower
iris
rose
snapdragon
tulip

cherry *and*   daffodil
iris
pine
spirea
tulip

dogwood *and*   daisy
pine
snapdragon
star lily

forsythia *and*   iris
star lily
tulip

lilac *and*   calla lily
rose
tulip

magnolia *and*   candytuft
daffodil
iris
lily
narcissus

mimosa *and*   clivia
poppy
rose
sweet pea
tulip

peach *and*   daffodil
daisy
iris
narcissus
tulip

quince *and*   iris
tulip

spirea *and*   carnation
daisy
geranium
iris
pansy
rose
tulip

weeping willow *and*   daffodil
iris
narcissus

SUMMER

agapanthus *and*   aster
babies'-breath
monstera
phoenix
vines

azalea *and*   aster
canna
gladiolus
lily

blueberry foliage *and*   bellflower
dianthus
lily

bulrush *and*   clematis
Japanese iris
lily
spirea foliage
water lily
weeping willow

caladium *and*   anthurium
bird-of-paradise
broom
carnation
cattail
gerbera
gladiolus
lily
vines

cattail *and*   agapanthus
begonia
bellflower
clematis
dahlia
iris
spirea foliage

clematis *and*   driftwood
miscanthus

eucalyptus *and*   carnation
dahlia
gladiolus
iris
lily
rose

flameflower *and*   aspidistra
dried materials

monstera

gladiolus *and* babies'-breath
broom
caladium
eucalyptus
monstera
New Zealand
 flax
palm
phoenix
pine
spirea foliage
sunflower

hibiscus *and* dry materials
pussy willow
weeping willow
wisteria

iris *and* azalea
spirea foliage
star lily

ornamental
onion flower *and* broom
dahlia
gerbera
gladiolus
lily

sunflower *and* artichoke leaves
aspidistra
gladiolus
vines (dried)
wisteria
 (stripped
 and curled)

water lily *and* bulrush
driftwood
horsetail
rocks and
 pebbles
weeping willow

wisteria *and* bulrush
cattail
 (miniature)
driftwood

horsetail
iris
pine

AUTUMN

actinidia *and* amaranth
artichoke flower
chestnut foliage
chrysanthemum
cornflower
cosmos
dahlia
gladiolus
lily
rose

bittersweet vine
 and bellflower
chrysanthemum
 (all sizes)
cockscomb
Euonymus
 alatus
gentian
Japanese cedar
patrinia
sedum

castor-oil plant
 and aconite
 (monkshood)
bellflower
chrysanthemum
 (small
 or medium)
cockscomb
gentian
lily (calla,
 Easter)
patrinia
sedum

chestnut foliage
 and aster
bittersweet
chrysanthemum
 (all sizes)
cockscomb
miscanthus

patrinia
sedum

enkianthus *and* aster
bellflower
chrysanthemum
 (all sizes)
cockscomb
gentian
lily
miscanthus
patrinia

eucalyptus *and* chrysanthemum
 (all sizes, but
 especially
 spider variety)
cockscomb
gerbera
snapdragon

Euonymus alatus
 and aconite
 (monkshood)
aster
bellflower
bittersweet
chrysanthemum
 (small
 or medium)
cockscomb
dahlia
gentian
miscanthus
patrinia
sedum

heather *and* anthurium
babies'-breath
bird-of-paradise
carnation
chrysanthemum
 (small
 or medium)
cornflower
cosmos
dahlia
gerbera
gladiolus

lily
patrinia
rose

holly *and*
aconite (monkshood)
chrysanthemum
cockscomb
dahlia
gentian
Japanese toad lily
patrinia
rose
sedum

Japanese maple *and*
aconite (monkshood)
aster
bellflower
bittersweet
chrysanthemum (small or medium)
cockscomb
dahlia
gentian
miscanthus
lily
patrinia
sedum

millet *and*
broom
cockscomb
lily (small)
lycoris
rose

miscanthus *and*
bellflower
blueberry foliage
Euonymus alatus
gentian
patrinia

Nandina domestica *and*
chrysanthemum
liatris
rose
thistle

New Zealand flax *and*
asparagus fern
artichoke flower
aster
bird-of-paradise
caladium
dahlia
gladiolus
lily
lycoris
orchid
rose

oak *and*
chrysanthemum
cockscomb
gentian
miscanthus
rose
sedum

pampas grass *and*
actinidia
anthurium
aspidistra
bird-of-paradise
carnation
cosmos
dahlia
gerbera
lily
monstera
palm
phoenix
pineapple
rose
thistle

pomegranate (in fruit) *and*
aster
chrysanthemum (small or medium)
cockscomb
gentian
miscanthus
rose

smilax *and*
aster
cockscomb
dahlia

eucalyptus
gladiolus
lily (yellow calla)
maple
monstera
patrinia
sedum

sorbus *and*
aster
bellflower
chrysanthemum (small or medium)
gentian
patrinia
sedum

sunflower seed pod *and*
ananas blossom with leaves
anthurium
bird-of-paradise
cockscomb
gladiolus
lily
rose

willow (fasciated) *and*
aster
bellflower
chrysanthemum (small or large)
dahlia
gladiolus
iris
Japanese toad lily

WINTER

aspidistra *and*
daffodil
dry materials
gerbera
iris
narcissus
pampas grass
poinsettia
rose
stock

sweet pea
tulip

burnet *and* anthurium
daffodil
gerbera
gladiolus
narcissus
sweet pea
tulip

caladium *and* agapanthus
amaryllis
ananas
anthurium
bird-of-paradise
canna
carnation
dry materials
ginger blossom
gladiolus
heliconia
lily
pampas grass
rose
stock
wisteria
and other vines

camellia *and* daffodil
narcissus
pussy willow
rape
spirea

chloranthus *and* chrysanthemum
daffodil
iris
narcissus
tulip

evergreen foliage
and amaryllis
carnation
chrysanthemum
(all sizes)
daffodil
daisy
iris

narcissus
rose
tulip

forsythia *and* camellia
iris
narcissus
rose
tulip

holly *and* camellia
carnation
chrysanthemum
poinsettia

hydrangea stems
and carnation
chrysanthemum
(all sizes)
daffodil
daisy
narcissus
pine
rape
rose

monstera *and* ananas blossom
anthurium
bird-of-paradise
carnation
gardenia
ginger
gladiolus
lily
magnolia
orchid
ornamental
onion flower
plumeria

plum
(forced blooms)
and chrysanthemum
(all sizes)
daffodil
iris
lily
narcissus
pine
rape

pussy willow *and* carnation
chloranthus
chrysanthemum
daffodil
daisy
rose
tulip

salal *and* babies'-breath
carnation
daisy
iris
lily
rose
snapdragon
stock
tulip

ti leaf *and* ananas blossom
anthurium
babies'-breath
bird-of-paradise
brassaia
candytuft
gardenia
heliconia
lily
magnolia
orchid (large
single or spray
of small)
rose
snapdragon
stock

trifoliate orange
and anthurium
bird-of-paradise
carnation
dry materials
rose
tulip

weeping willow
and camellia
chrysanthemum
iris
narcissus
pine
rose

THE SYMBOLISM OF PLANTS
AND SUGGESTIONS FOR THEIR ENHANCEMENT

IT SHOULD BE EMPHASIZED here that the Western world, and, indeed, all nations or states, have their own symbols and associations for flowers and plants. They may be related to religion (lily: purity, the Virgin Mary), military distinction (oak-leaf clusters), political achievement (laurel), superstition (four-leaf clover), poetry (rose), and so on. American states have their symbolic flowers (sunflower: Kansas), and many European "dynasties" had theirs (fleur-de-lis: France).

The symbolism of plants in Japan derives from many sources: age-old association of flowers with ceremonies, Confucian and Buddhist traditions from China, and Japan's own native lore. Like all symbolism, East and West, it is vague and subject to various interpretations, for it is based primarily on analogies or likenesses between an object—in this instance a plant—and an unseen quality like courage; a desirable state like long life and happiness; or a rare person—tender and beautiful. The Japanese pink, Dianthus superbus, called *nadeshiko*, is one of the plants symbolizing feminine grace, and Japanese women are often called Yamato-Nadeshiko. Similarly, certain irises with tall, straight leaves stand for a promising young boy and are used in arrangements for the Boys' Festival on the fifth day of the fifth month. Specific flowers are identified with the four seasons and with the festivities associated with the twelve months of the year.

Some flowers are male (*yo*)—tall, vigorous ones, and branches and blossoms of bright colors; others are female (*in*)—trailing, bending specimens like the willow, and those of soft, pastel shades. Certain combinations of plant material are dearly loved, like the Three Friends of Winter (*sho-chiku-bai*) or the Seven Grasses of Autumn (*aki-no-nana-kusa*). The Three Friends are pine, bamboo, and plum; or, as variants, plum, green orchid, and chrysanthemum, or bamboo, ardisia (an evergreen with clusters of berries), and club moss. The evergreen character and the strength of pine suggest endurance "even against the winds of adversity," the steadfastness of friends, and long life; the resilience of bamboo, bending with the wind but not breaking, is analogous to pliancy and adaptability, its greenness to constancy, and its spreading habits of growth and ample supply of shoots, to abundance and prosperity. First to bloom in the frosty days of early spring, even before its leaves come out, the plum stands for hardiness and courage, and the delicacy of the petals against the brown bark makes it the symbol of sheer loveliness. This combination is appropriate in arrangements for the New Year, for weddings, and for other embarkings on new ventures where good omens and stanch virtues are to be hoped for.

The Seven Grasses of Autumn are native to the hillsides and banks of streams in the Japanese countryside. They are slender and their flowers, small and muted in color, convey the mood of gentle melancholy characteristic of the season. They are: bush clover, Chinese bellflower, Dianthus superbus, patrinia, kudzu vine, miscanthus, and thoroughwort.

Plum, bamboo, chrysanthemum, and green orchid with pods, associated with four famous Chinese poets and scholar recluses, are called the Four Noble Characters of Four Beloved Ones (*shi kunshi*). The flowers of the Four Seasons are sometimes displayed together with the representation in a painting or perhaps a small sculpture of a bird or animal associated with them:

Spring: peony, moutan, or peach, together with a
nightingale
Summer: lotus, with a duck
Autumn: chrysanthemum or grasses, with quail or
partridge
Winter: plum, with a magpie

The Japanese flower calendar, as presented here, is not rigid, but it provides a general picture:

January: bamboo, narcissus, pine, plum
February: plum, camellia, Adonis, crocus
March: peach, pussy willow, forsythia, anemone
April: cherry, apricot, magnolia, primrose

May: azalea, peony, wisteria, iris

June: iris, peony, lily, hollyhock

July: hydrangea, lotus, lily, spirea

August: morning glory, sunflower, rhododendron, water lily

September: gourd, Seven Grasses of Autumn, aconite (monkshood), gentian

October: maple, dahlia, cosmos, canna

November: chrysanthemum, cockscomb, daisy, bittersweet

December: Nandina domestica, holly, Rhodea japonica, poinsettia

The following list will convey some idea of the kinds of connotations that plants may bring to the Japanese mind. In some instances these will be familiar to the Western reader; in other cases they will be very different. Not every "meaning" is given for every plant, nor can such a list hope to include every variety of plant material in the rich and varied lexicon of Oriental symbolism. Nevertheless, it is hoped that the examples provided and the suggestions for handling and arranging these materials will be helpful to the Western reader who would like to re-create not only the form but the emotional content of Ikebana.

ACACIA *Friendship*
The white and red varieties also symbolize elegance and nobility; the yellow, secret love. It is best to strip most of the leaves from around the blossom, so as to expose the bloom and the lovely line of the stem.

ACONITE (Monkshood) *Animosity, hostility*
The Japanese name means "bird helmet." Purple aconite is attractive in autumn arrangements when combined with golden leaves.

ADONIS (Pheasant's Eye) *Reminiscence, blessing*
The Japanese name means "happy long life plant." This flower is used in decorations for the morning of New Year's Day. Flowers and leaves are ideally combined with bare branches in winter.

AGAPANTHUS *Love letters*
The Japanese name means "purple prince orchid." The showy flowers on their long stems suit agapanthus to the role of *shin* in Moribana arrangements. Its long leaves, like those of the amaryllis, are the best accompaniment, but other green leaves, or dry materials, are also suitable.

AMARANTH *Coxcomb, affected person*
Evergreens add interest to arrangements of amaranth.

AMARYLLIS *Attractiveness, pride*
Light-colored amaryllis also symbolize ravishing but affected beauty; dark-colored ones, chattering talk. Only a few blossoms are needed in an arrangement, and the leaves should be given prominence.

ANEMONE *Truth, sincerity*
The red anemone says "I love you"; yellow indicates loneliness, a breaking-off, as of a friendship; purple symbolizes belief, faith. The beautiful long stems of this flower should be utilized in the design of the arrangement.

APPLE *Righteousness, justice, exactitude*
A flowering branch is ideal for arranging. If you use one with a few tiny new apples, the feeling of harvest time and trees burdened with fruit will be enhanced by the bent, arched line of the branch. If other flowers are used with apple blossoms, be careful that they do not destroy each other's beauty.

APRICOT *Doubt, distrust*
The old Japanese name for apricot meant "old Chinese peach flower." In arrangements, flowering branches are best used in combination with several larger flowers and leaves from another kind of plant. Dark red tulips or daffodils with their own leaves are excellent choices.

ASPIDISTRA *Improving fortunes*
The ideal green leaf for use, alone or in combination with almost any flower, in any style of Ikebana.

ASTER *Sentimental recollections*
Use asters in the same way as chrysanthemums, but on a smaller scale. Cut short they are excellent for hiding the kenzan when used to complement branches.

AZALEA *Temperance, moderation*
The white azalea means "first love," the red one "joy of love." Both flowering branches and foliage alone are excellent material. The lines of the branches of even a short piece look much like a miniature tree, and are therefore ideal for creating natural-looking arrangements.

BABIES'-BREATH (Gypsophila) *Pure heart*
Not used alone, gypsophila combines well with almost any material, as a complement, or as *shin* with one or two bright flowers in a modern design.

BALSAM (Impatiens Balsamina) *Impatience*
"Touch me not" is the message of this plant. Pink balsam is also symbolic of a tomboy. The old Japanese name meant "manicure," for the petals of pink-toned varieties were rubbed on the fingernails to color them. In autumn, the fruit of this plant will pop open and spill its seed if it is touched—thus the name "touch-me-not." This flower is attractive when combined with narrow branches or tall, slender grasses.

BAMBOO *Steadfastness, pliancy, constancy, abundance*
The prince of grasses. Traditionally used for New Year's arrangements. The bamboo must be heavily trimmed to create the familiar clean, open lines.

BEGONIA *Unrequited love*
A representative flower of autumn in Japan, its name means "flower of the autumn sea." A simple Chabana arrangement, contrasting the wide leaf with small pink flowers, is much favored by tea ceremony masters.

BITTERSWEET *Truth*
Such wild-growing materials, with beautiful lines and bright berries, are excellent for both naturalistic and abstract arrangements in the modern vein.

BLETILLA *Patience*
Ideal for making small naturalistic arrangements using no other materials. Bletilla leaves combine well with bright flowers or dried vines.

BLUEBERRY *Prayer*
Excellent for making landscape scenes, because even a small branch has the characteristic bushiness of the whole. The light-green and coppery leaves, and the interesting shape of the branches create miniature trees.

BROOM *Tidiness*
There is great beauty in the fine leafy stems, which are easily bent to form dramatic curves. The Chinese name for these blooms means "golden baby sparrows."

BULRUSH *Loneliness*
Place bulrushes upright and combine them with aquatic or waterside flowers to create a landscape, or bend and tie the stalks to achieve an abstract arrangement.

BURNET *Prankishness, roguery, mischief*
The old Japanese name referred to a sort of sweet dumpling on a stick, with the same connotations of childhood that lollipops have in the West. The long, hard stems with their small, stiff flowers lend themselves especially to modern arrangements.

BUSH CLOVER. *Thoughtful, pensive mood*
One of the Seven Grasses of Autumn. Strip enough flowers and leaves from the branches so that flowers and bare branch alternate, thus emphasizing the lovely arched line.

CALADIUM *Great joy and delight*
The unusual colors and patterns of these leaves remind the Japanese of rich brocades. They are ideal for modern arrangements, using only a leaf or two with a single brilliantly colored blossom.

CALENDULA *Sadness of separation, broken love, heartache*
Ideal combined with branches of any kind.

CAMELLIA *Pride*
The red camellia also symbolizes nobility of reasoning; the white variety, ideal love. Tea ceremony masters like to use single blooms, which can be arranged with great effectiveness and drama. Retain only two or three leaves, to emphasize the beauty of the blossoms and the supple branches.

CANNA *Forever, eternally*
To avoid a heavy look, substitute thin, narrow leaves of other plants, and use the canna leaves with other flowers.

CARNATIONS *Passion*
White carnations also mean "living for love"; red carnations indicate a less strong passion. Yellow carnations say "I do not believe you." Ferns or other greenery combine well with these popular flowers.

CASTOR-OIL PLANT *Destiny, fortune*
This plant is ideal for arranging in or out of bloom, for the leaves have an interesting hand shape, with red or green-and-red "fingers."

CATTAIL *Recovery from illness*
The old Japanese name meant "screen grass," because cattails were used to weave fences. When fresh, they are used for creating naturalistic waterside scenes in large, shallow containers. When dried, especially with their leaves bunched and tied into various shapes, they are used for abstract creations.

CHERRY *Nobility*
The cherry blossom is the national flower of the Japanese people. Flowering cherry branches are so glorious that it is unwise to combine other flowers with them, but they may be used in combination with non-flowering branches, as for example with evergreens.

CHESTNUT *Impartiality, fairness*
In autumn, chestnuts appear and the branches are lovely to use in arrangements. Retain only a few leaves on each branch, so that its line may be visible and the contrast between leaves and nuts is strengthened.

CHINA ASTER *Reverence, cherishing a memory*
Combine China asters with branches of any kind.

CHINESE BELLFLOWER *Sadness, despondence*
One of the Seven Grasses of Autumn. The blue and purple tones of this flower, or a white variety, may be combined interestingly with branches of red or gold autumn foliage.

CHLORANTHUS *Great value*
The old Japanese name referred to a sum of money, in gold coins, which would now be equivalent to a million dollars. One reason for this name is the coral color of the berries—coral was a highly prized rare gem. Chloranthus is widely used for ceremonial New Year's arrangements—looking toward a large fortune in the coming year. It combines well with bare branches, for it has beautiful green leaves in addition to its large, colorful berries.

CHRYSANTHEMUM *Noble simplicity*
The white chrysanthemum is symbolic of a faithful wife; the red says "I love you." Deep colors say "believe me." The yellow varieties indicate vague memories. Avoid using huge blossoms in formal ar-

rangements—they are more beautiful used singly. The leaf is often as important as the bloom, so try to incorporate as many leaves as possible into the design. Use the contrast of slightly opened, half-opened, and fully opened blooms when using the smaller sizes.

CLEMATIS *Gentle love*
The white clematis means "out of gratitude, to repay." The purple variety means "unchanged, for eternity." The Japanese name means "temple bell" or "lantern flower." Combine with any kind of branch.

CLIVIA *Nobility*
This regal flower is best arranged alone, with its own sword-shaped leaves. If it is to be arranged with branches, use it as a complement in a large-scale arrangement.

CLOVER *Honest labor*
The three-leaf clover is a symbol of hope, religion, love. The four-leaf clover means love, honor, health, wealth, and good luck in love. Blossoms bunched together and combined with leaves can be interestingly arranged in a crystal vase. Vines may be used with clover blooms for line.

COCKSCOMB *Grotesque*
Though an autumn flower, cockscomb is not effective used with autumn leaves, for the colors are too similar. Combine with evergreens.

COLEUS *Tragic love*
Coleus leaves are so unusual that it is best to use just one, with a single flower, in a modern container.

COLUMBINE *Inconstancy, fickleness*
Columbine combines ideally with palm leaves or ferns.

COSMOS *Pure love of a virgin*
The white cosmos indicates purity and elegance; the red, a warm heart. Use the twisted stems to create interesting modern designs.

CRAPE MYRTLE *Unpreparedness*
The Japanese name, meaning "the monkey slips," refers to the extreme smoothness of the branches. Only used when it is in bloom and covered with brilliant red blossoms, crape myrtle combines best with large white flowers and green leaves.

CROCUS *Joy of youth, pleasure*
The yellow crocus says "please believe me"; the blue says "I believe you, but I am still worried." The red variety says "you love me so much it worries me," and the purple says "maybe I regret my prior love for you." (The white crocus appears to be silent in Japanese flower symbolism.) These small flowers are ideal for creating miniature arrangements.

CYCLAMEN *Jealousy, distrust*
White cyclamen indicates a warmhearted person. The light-colored varieties say "I understand you." Red cyclamen's message is "I will not economize." This flower is very effective when placed in a container so that the stems do not show. Use the blossoms grouped in one corner of a modern vase for a very contemporary arrangement.

DAFFODIL *Unrequited love*
Any green leaves or branches can be used with daffodils, or they can be effectively arranged with their own leaves or with white-painted branches.

DAHLIA *Gratitude*
The white dahlia expresses gratitude to parents. The red dahlia's message is "you make me happy," while the variegated ones say "I think of you constantly." Yellow means "I am happy that you love me." When combined with branches, small or medium dahlias should be used. If large blooms are to be arranged, put just one in the corner of a modern vase and complement it with ferns or other linear material.

DAISY *Innocence, fond memories*
The Japanese name means "long-lived chrysanthemum." Daisies are especially useful for covering a kenzan that holds other flowers.

DAPHNE *Grandeur, magnificence*
Daphne is best arranged during its flowering season, in naturalistic fashion, with large, smooth-petaled flowers such as tulips.

DELPHINIUM *Sweetness, beauty*
Use as a complement in Moribana arrangements, with bushy material for the main branches, or with large green leaves in modern arrangements.

DEUTZIA *Shyness*
The Japanese name means "hollow tree," a reference to deutzia's hollow stems. They are very popular for arranging because of the clusters of fragrant white flowers and brilliant green leaves. Strip the stems partially to bring out their lines.

DIANTHUS *Love*
White dianthus denotes talent, the red means cheerfulness. The double varieties say "my love will never die." Variegated blossoms signify talent. Because of its shape and color range, the dianthus is representative of woman. Dianthus is ideally arranged in a natural style, with bushy foliage used to complement the flower.

DOGWOOD *Continuity*
The Japanese name means "water wood," because dogwood grows in damp places and requires a large amount of water. Combine branches in flower with any green material, taking care not to hide the smooth lines of the branches.

ENKIANTHUS *Nobility*
The Japanese name means "star-filled sky," because when it blooms, the whole bush is covered with small white blossoms. Ideal arranging material spring, summer, and autumn.

EUCALYPTUS *Temptation*
The shape, symmetry, and leatherlike texture of the leaves give character and interest to this material. There are several varieties, but the most commonly used is the long-stemmed, large-leafed kind. The stem is easily bent into interesting shapes, but some of the leaves should be removed to stress the line.

EUONYMUS ALATA *Pomp, splendor*
The Japanese name means "Chinese brocade tree," referring to its colorful autumn foliage. The bare stems are especially suited to arrangements in the Abstract style.

EUONYMUS JAPONICA *A long time, but not eternity*
The variegated types, rimmed in yellow or white, are especially useful in Ikebana, particularly Moribana and Nageire styles. They must be heavily stripped before use.

FLAMEFLOWER (Tritoma) *Disbelief*
The long, clean stems with their dramatic flower heads allow flameflowers to play the role of *shin* very well. Open-petaled flowers, like dahlias or daisies, with their own leaves, provide interesting contrast.

FORGET-ME-NOT *True love*
Use these flowers wired together in bunches and combined with branches.

FORSYTHIA *Submissiveness, good nature*
The old Japanese name meant "bird's wing," because of the wing-shaped blossoms. The graceful curves of the branches make forsythia an ideal material at any season. Place arrangements so that the branches can droop naturally—hanging from a shelf, for example.

FOXGLOVE (Digitalis) *Decision*
Attractive combined with large wide leaves or ferns.

FREESIA *Innocence*
Use as *nejime* with any long-stemmed leaves or flowers. Do not combine with bushes. Used alone, it is lovely for modern arrangements.

GARDENIA *Purity*
The gardenia means "I am very happy." Work with buds in arranging, for the flowers open very quickly, and the finished arrangement will actually show open flowers. Strip leaves from around the bloom to show the stem line and prevent a heavy, overly full look.

GENTIAN *Righteousness, justice*
Use with long leaves in a small Nageire arrangement, or combine with branches and daisies.

GERBERA *Sadness*
Excellent for modern arrangements, used with its own leaves or others.

GLADIOLUS *Secret*
The old Japanese name means "foreign iris." Use the leaves as you would the blossoms in arrangements.

GLOBE AMARANTH (Bachelor's Button) *Undying love*
The Japanese name means "thousand-day pink," because of its excellent keeping qualities. Interesting arrangements may be made by tying a number of blossoms in a bunch and setting them in a contemporary vase. Any type of green may be combined with these flowers.

GLOXINIA *Coquetry, flirtation*
Gloxinia blossoms have a velvety texture which makes them very effective used singly in a tall slender crystal vase, in combination with several long, slender leaves.

HAWTHORN *Waiting for success*
In Japan, the fruit of the hawthorn is added to fish as it cooks, to soften the bones and make them edible. Very beautiful in arrangements, it is necessary to strip off most of the leaves to reveal the beauty of the blossoms.

HIBISCUS *Fragile beauty*
The Japanese call hibiscus the "drunk lady flower" because it is white when it first blooms, and then turns pink. It is best arranged alone, using buds and only one or two open blossoms.

HOLLYHOCK *Simplicity, peace*
The white hollyhock also symbolizes a pure heart, and the pink variety, true love. Both flower and leaf of this plant are attractive, but the stem is large and straight, and is best augmented with intertwining vines.

HOSTA *Devotion*
Use in small-scale naturalistic arrangements, with its own leaves. These leaves are also very interesting combined with other flowers.

HYDRANGEA *Conceit*
White hydrangea also symbolizes a wanderer. Avoid using more than a few open blooms. Rather, contrast full and partly open blossoms with a few buds to prevent an overly heavy look.

IRIS ENSATA (Japanese Iris) *Elegant spirit*
One of the traditional flowers for Boys' Day in Japan. The shape of the narrow leaves is very much like that of a Japanese sword, thus symbolizing courage. The tall, straight stems stand for straightforwardness, and the purple or white flowers for nobility. Use a shallow dish and stones to re-create their natural waterside setting.

IRIS LAEVIGATA (Rabbit-Ear Iris) *Good fortune*
The traditional Japanese flower of the early summer season. Arrange like other iris.

IRIS SANGUINEA (Siberian Flag) *Messenger*
The Siberian flag is considered to be feminine, just as the Japanese iris is masculine. Though it grows in dry soil, it can be used interchangeably with other irises.

IRIS TECTORUM *Correspondence*
This plant is native to China, and there is an old Chinese superstition that if it is planted on the straw roofs of barns, the farm will be safe from typhoons. The old Japanese name means "safety for children,"

an obvious derivation from the old Chinese tale. Use the leaves as abundantly as the blooms in an arrangement.

Ivy *Friendship, marriage*
Attractively used in hanging arrangements, or entwined around a piece of weathered wood. Ivy combines beautifully with small white flowers of the chrysanthemum type.

Job's-Tears *Unity*
Combine with waterside plants in a large, shallow container to create a landscape. Or use only the stems with their clusters of seeds to create an abstract arrangement in autumn.

Kerria Japonica *Noble spirit*
Autumn, when the vine is in flower, is the ideal time to use kerria. Use a large shallow bowl filled with water, so that the reflection of the lovely arch of the vine may be enjoyed.

Kudzu Vine *Recovery from illness*
One of the Seven Grasses of Autumn. The leaves, large, smooth, and almost round, are very interesting combined with many flowers other than their own.

Laurel *Victory, honor*
Use with stock or similar flowers.

Lilac *First love, friendship*
When using lilacs in arrangements, add green leaves as complement, and perhaps a few smooth-petaled flowers such as tulips.

Lily *Purity*
The many varieties of lilies are all ideal for arranging. The blossoms usually grow facing outward rather than upward, so try to use blooms that have no tendency to droop.

Lily-of-the-Valley *Returning happiness*
Arrange the leaves in an interesting design, using a small kenzan to secure them. Only a few blossoms are needed to complete the picture, which can be very effectively presented in a crystal champagne goblet.

Loosestrife *Wishes granted*
The Japanese name means "tiger's tail," a reference to the shape of the blossoms. Arrange in natural style, using almost any kind of branches.

Lotus *Pure love*
Ceremonial arrangements for Buddhist temples very often used the lotus flower and leaf. The interesting shape of the seed pod makes it an excellent material for contemporary arrangements.

Lupine *Avarice*
The Japanese name means "upright wisteria." Combine it with vines, ferns, or any green materials.

Lycoris *Temptation*
These flaming-red flowers, shaped like a sparkling fire, are often found in graveyards. Parents warn their children not to pick them or to bring them into the house for fear it will catch fire and bring certain death to the family. Such tales prevent most children from handling these flowers, whose roots contain a very strong poison. Because of this legend, lycoris is only used in modern arrangements.

Magnolia Grandiflora *True, sincere love*
Bloom and leaves are so large that this flower is best used for large-scale arrangements. Otherwise, use only one blossom and remove most of the leaves.

Magnolia Liliflora *Love of nature*
Excellent for Nageire-style arrangements. This variety produces its blooms before its leaves, so other green leaves must be added.

Maple *Neatness*
Excellent Moribana and Nageire material, from spring through autumn. The leaves must be carefully stripped to bring out the lines of the branches. Almost any flowers go well with maple.

Marigold *Health*
The Japanese name means "thousand-happiness chrysanthemums." A most versatile plant, it can be combined with almost any material in almost any style.

Marvel-of-Peru (Four-O'Clock) *Diffidence, bashfulness*
The Japanese name for this flower means "face powder," for a fine powder may be found inside the fruit. The leaves are as lovely as the blossoms, so this flower is ideal in combination with bare branches.

Miscanthus *Sorrow*
One of the Seven Grasses of Autumn. In the summer, before the ears form, the tall, slender leaves are very handsome and useful for arrangements in any style, even the Abstract. In the autumn, bunch the ears to make modern arrangements.

MORNING GLORY *Attachment, mortal love*
The blossoms do not last very long, but cutting them early, before the dew has left them, prolongs their life. It is best to use only one or two blossoms, combined with the interesting line of their vines.

NANDINA DOMESTICA *Domestic assistance*
Known as the "sacred bamboo," although it does not belong to the same family. Nandina, which bears red or white berries, is used in arrangements for festive occasions, and traditionally a spray of leaves and a bunch of berries are laid on top of a gift of food to attest to its purity. Nandina is not arranged when it is in flower.

NARCISSUS *Self-love*
White narcissus also means "veiled in mystery"; variegated kinds indicate unrequited love. Yellow ones say "please take my love." Summer narcissus indicate satisfaction or gratification of lust. Often used in traditional flower arrangements, the beautiful leaves are sometimes more important than the blossoms. Narcissus combine wonderfully with evergreens.

NASTURTIUM *Victory*
The Japanese name means "golden water lily," because the leaves are so similar. Arrange with their own leaves in small-scale modern arrangements.

OAK *Prosperity*
Especially suitable for arrangement in autumn. Chrysanthemums, especially medium-sized white ones, are the perfect complement.

ORNAMENTAL ONION FLOWERS *Patience*
One of the recent additions to the list of Ikebana materials, onion flowers, with their smooth, irregularly curving stems and thistle-like heads, appeal to the modern arranger.

PANSY *Friendship*
The message of the pansy is "think of me." White pansies stand for elegance and gentleness, purple ones symbolize honesty and faithfulness, and yellow ones indicate a small happiness. They really need no definite arrangement to enhance their colorful beauty, but they may be tied into a bunch and set into a modern vase with none of the stems showing. Or they may be combined with branches or dried materials.

PATRINIA *Thoughtfulness*
One of Japan's Seven Grasses of Autumn. The Japanese consider patrinia to be especially feminine, because of its slender, delicate form. Combine the tall stems of this flower with slender grasses for an elegant arrangement. Or take the blooms from the stems and wire them in a bunch at the base of the stems as a focal point.

PAULOWNIA *Nobility*
The emblem of the Empress of Japan, and the informal emblem of the royal family. Use flower-bearing branches in naturalistic arrangements and seed-bearing branches, with their dramatic velvety golden berries, in more abstract ones.

PEACH *Domesticity, congeniality*
The peach blossom says "you stole my heart." This is one of the traditional flowers for Girls' Day in Japan, and is associated with femininity in the same way that plum branches are associated with masculinity. Peach branches should not be bent or manipulated—this material should be used in as natural a way as possible. It combines well with evergreens and with small-petaled flowers like stock or candytuft and their leaves.

PEONY *Shyness*
In China, peonies are considered to be the king of all flowers, and they are also very popular in Japan. The tree peony and the regular peony belong to the same family, and are so similar that they are known as the "twin sister flowers." When arranging either sort, use only one fully open blossom. Fill in with buds and half-open blooms. No other material is needed.

PETUNIA *Idealism*
Combine with branches, or with long green leaves like those of the phoenix.

PHLOX *Coquetry*
Use this charming flower to complement branches in Moribana arrangements, or mass the flower heads and rest them in the mouth of a dramatic container.

PHOENIX *Sentimental recollections*
Any feathery leaves of this type are ideal for the contemporary styles of arrangement, combined with any flower. They lend themselves to trimming and reshaping for dramatic effects in the abstract manner.

PINE *Happiness and long life, endurance*
The king of trees, pine is used in Japan on festive occasions. A traditional New Year's combination, called "The Three Friends of Winter," may consist of pine, bamboo, and flowering plum.

PITCHER PLANT (Nepenthes) *Danger*
This insectivorous plant is used only for arrangements in the Abstract style. Combine with dried materials or anthurium in striking modern containers.

PLUM *Courage, hardiness, loveliness*
Plum is associated with the masculine, and with nobility and purity. In arrangements, it is ideally combined with pine. Straight young flowering branches may be used with large-petaled flowers such as tulips.

POINSETTIA *Joy*
Combine with evergreens or with white-painted branches in any contemporary style. Use only one or two blossoms.

POMEGRANATE BLOSSOMS *Lovers*
The brilliant orange blossoms and green leaves contrast beautifully in arrangements. In autumn, when the fruit appears, interestingly shaped branches are effective. Many of the leaves should be stripped to allow the lines to contrast with the fruit. White chrysanthemums or daisies are lovely complements.

POPPY *Rest*
The white poppy indicates sleep, the pink indicates solace. Orange poppies symbolize vanity, and deep-red ones, enthusiasm. Not often used in classic styles, they are ideal for modern arrangements.

PORTULACA *Unrequited love*
The Japanese name means "pine-needle peony," because the shapes are so similar. Try wiring the blooms together to give them weight, and then sinking them into a crystal bowl, allowing the blooms to float rather than to rest against the mouth of the vase.

PRIMROSE *Hope*
The white primrose means "charming, lovely"; red indicates quest for fortune; purple indicates authenticity and reliability. These small flowers are best arranged by tying them into bunches and resting the bunches against the mouth of a vase.

PUSSY WILLOW *Recovery from illness*
Early opening of the bud may be induced by peeling back its skin. By forcing open only a few buds, a lovely contrast between the silver of the open ones and the red of the unopened ones is produced.

QUINCE *Triteness, mediocrity, the commonplace*
The only reasonable explanation for this inappropriate symbolism would seem to be that quince blooms at almost any season and in every kind of weather in Japan. But the old Japanese name meant "wood melon," because of the melonlike shape of the buds, and this name was corrupted to the word for "fool." Quince is the most perfect material for any style of Ikebana. It can be bent to any shape, the blossoms will last for two or three days even without water, and the dramatic angles of even bare branches lend themselves to arranging.

REED *Anxiety, music*
Reeds are ideally arranged in a long, shallow bowl, their height used as a background for iris or lilies cut shorter.

RHODEA *Eternal youth*
The Japanese name means "ten-thousand-year green." Often arranged in Seika style for happy occasions. Or use a few leaves, combined with one bright flower, in an unusual vase.

RHODODENDRON *Devotion, brotherly love*
The beautiful shape and color of both leaf and blossom make the rhododendron ideal for arranging. Try to use more buds than fully opened flowers, and strip off quite a few leaves to allow the interesting line of the branch to show. Several leaves from around the blooms should be removed to eliminate the formal, symmetrical look.

ROSE *Love, beauty*
The white rose symbolizes love and respect, the yellow rose, jealousy and stagnant love. Pink stands for a beautiful girl, and deep-pink ones indicate shyness. The red double rose is a symbol of harmony. Single-petaled varieties mean "simple, uncomplicated," and dead-white roses mean "promise for a whole life." White buds symbolize delicacy, red ones, innocent hope. Rose thorns mean relief that a misfortune did not turn to tragedy. The rose is beautiful arranged in any manner.

SALVIA *A lovely heart*
This brilliantly colored flower is effective when used with highly colored leaves or in a bright vase, to create a very modern small arrangement.

SEDUM *Restfulness*
The thick, waxy leaves are interesting in modern arrangements. In the fall flowering season, combine with autumn foliage.

SILK TREE *Vainglory, vanity, ostentation*
The Japanese name means "sleeping tree," because the leaves fold up at dusk. Gently curving branches lend themselves to Nageire arrangements. The leaves combine well with other flowers.

SMILAX *Memory of love*
The long thorny branches and handsome clusters of green berries make smilax an ideal material for Nageire or modern arrangements. It combines well with any flowers.

SNAPDRAGON *Haughtiness, arrogance*
The Japanese name means "golden fish flower." A very versatile material, snapdragons may be combined with any leaves or branches, but should be the only kind of flower in an arrangement.

SORBUS *Caution, prudence*
Summer, when it bears clusters of white flowers, and autumn, when it turns color, are the best seasons for arranging sorbus. Moribana, Nageire, and naturalistic modern arrangements are best.

SPIREA *Victory*
The Japanese name means "snow-covered willow." The beautiful white-flowered arcs are ideal material for arranging, especially when the branches still have a few unopened buds as well as open blossoms, and autumn, when the leaves begin to turn, is also an excellent time to use spirea.

STOCK *Beauty of eternity*
Arrange with any green material, especially phoenix, but do not combine with other flowers.

SUNFLOWER *Respect*
The Japanese name means "turning with the sun." Contemporary and Abstract styles are best. The dried seed pods are often used in Abstract creations. Do not combine sunflowers with other blossoms.

SWEET PEA *Tender memory*
Several sweet peas wired together will stand securely in a kenzan. Several such bunches may then be combined with ferns or other interesting greenery.

THISTLE *Independence, dignity, vengeance*
The leaves and stems of most thistles are unattractive. Mass the blossoms and use them with large, smooth leaves, like those of the monstera.

THOROUGHWORT *Hesitation, indecision, scruples*
One of the Seven Grasses of Autumn. Long, slender green leaves are especially effective with thoroughwort, but any branches combine well with it too.

TUBEROSE *Dangerous love*
Tuberoses may grow to a height of three feet, and are excellent for tall, slender arrangements. The stem, which is uninteresting, may be covered with the leaves of another flower.

TULIP *Charity, benevolence, kindness*
The white tulip also symbolizes lost love; yellow, hopeless love; red, a confession of love; purple, immortal love. Variegated tulips mean "beautiful eyes." Ideal for flower arrangements, the tulip may be combined effectively with many materials, and is especially lovely used in combination with branches.

WATER LILY *Purity of heart*
The blossom opens in the daytime and closes in the evening; thus the Japanese name means "sleeping flower." Water lilies are best arranged by floating several blooms in a shallow bowl, thus re-creating their natural setting. Such an arrangement is cool and summery, ideal for hot summer weather.

WEEPING WILLOW *Grace*
Weeping willow can be used to great effect at all times of the year, and combines well with almost any kind of material.

WISTERIA *Welcome*
Arrange wisteria in a tall vase, in Nageire style, with its own vines and leaves. The dried vines are attractive for abstract arrangements in the modern style.

ZINNIA *Remembrance of an old friend*
Zinnias bloom through the summer and early autumn, so the Japanese call them "hundred-day flowers." Ideal for summery arrangements, they combine well with any kind of branch.

FOLLOWING IS A LIST OF THE CREATORS OF THE ARRANGEMENTS ILLUSTRATED:

Kasen Yoshimura, President of
  the Ryūsei School
Kyōko (Mrs. Kasen) Yoshimura
Takashi Yoshimura, Vice-presi-
  dent of the Ryūsei School
Kako Akasaka
Senka Aoyama
Bikyoku Asami
Tōhō Fuji
Ryōun Fuku
Kishū Gotō
Bien Handa
Kyokusen Haruhara
Yūsui Hattori
Kayū Igarashi
Yūsen Igarashi
Bisen Ishii
Ryokuji Ishiwata
Kahō Kawabata

Kōgetsu Kikuchi
Hanae Kobuyama
Suiun Kondō
Hōshū Kubota
Hisao Kumazawa
Eiyū Kurihara
Keigetsu Maruyamano
Gyōsen Matsuda
Kōzan Matsue
Wakō Miyazaki
Kaei Mizuno
Aiko Nagakubo
Keisen Nagashima
Baichō Nakajima
Seigetsu Nakazawa
Hyakusui Nakata
Kōyō Nawa
Kōfū Fukawa
Shōfū Okōuchi

Kahō Otaki
Shōgetsu Ozawa
Shōju Ozeki
Baiun Satō
Shōzō Satō
Shunrei Satō
Seiju Sekimoto
Senko Shiozawa
Shōshū Sonoda
Seizan Sudō
Kisui Sugai
Kyōun Suzuki
Mitsuyo Takayama
Kotoko Wakabayashi
Kōfū Yamamoto
Keizan Yanaihara
Rinzan Yanagihara
Seihō Yonekura
Seiha Yui

Photographs by
Kiichi Nakamura, Eric Pollitzer, Teruhisa Yahagi, and the author

INDEX

(PAGE REFERENCES TO ILLUSTRATIONS ARE ITALICIZED)